Navajo Lifeways

CONTEMPORARY ISSUES, ANCIENT KNOWLEDGE

MAUREEN TRUDELLE SCHWARZ

FOREWORD BY LOUISE LAMPHERE

University of Oklahoma Press : Norman

Also by Maureen Trudelle Schwarz

Molded in the Image of Changing Woman: Navajo Views on the Human Body and Personhood (Tucson, 1997)

This book is published with the generous assistance of The McCasland Foundation, Duncan, Oklahoma.

Library of Congress Cataloging-in-Publication Data

Schwarz, Maureen Trudelle, 1952–
    Navajo lifeways : contemporary issues, ancient knowledge / Maureen Trudelle Schwarz ; foreword by Louise Lamphere.
        p.   cm.
    Includes bibliographical references and index.
    ISBN 0-8061-3310-4 (alk. paper)
        1. Navajo Indians—Religion.   2. Navajo Indians—Social conditions—20th century.   3. Navajo Indians—Health and hygiene.   I. Title.
    E99.N3 S358 2001
    979.1'004972—dc21

                                                            00-53276

1 2 3 4 5 6 7 8 9 10

IT HAS BEEN SAID

It was spoken there
In the beginning and before
At the sight of light
Amongst the swirling
Mists of knowledge
Her turquoise fire lit in heart
His crystal fire lit in mind
On opposite sides of crisscross
Waters flowing
Moving upward spiral
Into common blue wisdom
Understood by scaly, feathered, furred and
Sometimes metamorphosed beings

They built the trails, the paths, and the roads to
Journey
Of every thought and word possible
It was spoken there
In transit
Up reeds to this yellow place
Of enlightenment, of common understanding
Of what was, is and would be
Carried ever so carefully
Into a glittered existence
Only to be dismantled and thrown
Into a vast domain of darkness
Like in the beginning
What was ordered and careful
Became chaos and scattered
And
Comes back into place only when
The spoken words are spun into
Stories.

SUNNY DOOLEY (NAVAJO)

Contents

Foreword

This collection of six essays shows how Navajo people are using their traditional beliefs to cope with contemporary issues. Some of these are crisis issues, for example the outbreak of hantavirus in 1993. Others are chronic issues, such as how to deal with relatives who are problem drinkers or how to think about the devastating and disruptive effects of the Hopi-Navajo land dispute. Throughout these essays, the voices of Navajo consultants, particularly Harry Walters, Mae Bekis, Sunny Dooley, Sadie Billie, and Wesley Thomas, give us the Navajo perspective on each of these issues. Maureen Schwarz supplements the commentary of these and other consultants with her own careful analysis, introducing each situation and its historical context, discussing the relevant anthropological literature on the topic, and explicating Navajo concepts for the reader.

Navajo Lifeways begins with a brief introduction that summarizes the Navajo creation story. This orally transmitted history, encapsulated in a few pages by Schwarz, provides the essentials for understanding Navajo cosmology and the importance of Changing Woman and other Holy People in the creation of

Navajo life. Schwarz builds on her previous book, *Molded in the Image of Changing Woman,* which explicates Navajo views on the body and personhood. Three principles—homology, complementarity, and synecdoche—underlie the Navajo theory of the body as it is encoded in belief and religious practice. For example, the principle of synecdoche (the part stands for the whole) dictates that there is a life long connection between the person and detached parts of the body, such as skin, saliva, fingernail clippings, hair, and the umbilical cord. In chapter 2, on Navajo relocation, Schwarz tells us that the Navajo bury their cords near their homes, often in a place (such as in a sheep corral or near a loom) that will associate the person with later activities (such as being a good sheepherder or weaver). The removal of Navajos from the Hopi Partitioned Land (as a result of the settlement of the Hopi-Navajo land dispute) meant that Navajos were forced to leave the places where their cords were buried—that is, places to which they were anchored. Through her analysis, Schwarz clarifies for non-Navajo readers the wrenching experience of resettlement and the struggle of a number of families to remain on their ancestral land. Chapter 4, "Snakes in the Ladies' Room," deals with similar issues. Schwarz explains why the sighting of snakes in a bathroom of a Window Rock Administration Building caused such concern. Snakes, despite their peaceful nature, are potentially dangerous if contacted in improper circumstances; this danger extends to contact with bodily elements such as skin, urine, feces, hair, or nail clippings that may be found in a ladies' restroom. Schwarz uses this particular incident to explicate Navajo notions of personhood.

As chapter 1 outlines, in 1993 when the "mystery illness" later named the hantavirus caused the deaths of several Navajos and others in the Four Corners Region, Navajo healers met with biomedical doctors to discuss the crisis and possible solutions. The healers argued that the cause of all disease was disharmony in the Navajo world. An excess of rain and snow in the winter of 1992–93 brought an abundance of piñons and new vegetation. The excess vegetation fostered a large rodent population, leading biomedical investigators to examine the population of deer mice who, it was soon discovered, were carrying the virus. Contact with urine, saliva, feces, or dust infected with the virus led to infection in humans. The Navajos took the explanation even further, invoking their own explanations of why such a disease might have come at this particular time. Many saw it as an indication of disharmony or a breakdown in the complex web of relations fundamental to maintaining the Navajo way of life. "People have strayed from traditional beliefs and respect for nature," many said. Navajo elders spoke about the various ways in which this was happening, from a loss of respect by young people for traditional beliefs to toxic waste dumping and mining. They called for the performance of traditional ceremonies (like the Navajo Blessing Way) to restore order, bring families together, and strengthen ties and relationships.

Likewise, the Holy Visit, the subject of chapter 3, provided Navajos with another warning that they were neglecting their connections to the Diyin Dine'é (Holy People), abusing their relations with the natural world, allowing their language and culture to disintegrate, and failing to respect their relationships with "k'ei," or kin and clan relatives. In May 1996, during a period of drought, two Holy People visited the home of Sarah Begay and her mother, Irene Yazzie, leaving their footprints and a series of prophetic messages concerning the laxity of Navajos in these four crucial areas of Navajo life. Schwarz links this visit to a long history of prophesies in Navajo culture, periods in the past when the Holy People have warned the Navajo that their own behavior has created disharmony and impending disaster. Many Navajos traveled to the site of the visitation, bringing prayers and offerings. In June 1996, a Navajo day of prayer brought Navajos from all religious traditions (Christian adherents, Native American Church participants, and Navajo traditional healers and participants) to Window Rock, while thousands of other Navajos listened to live radio or television broadcasts of the events. Speaker Kelsey Begaye of the Navajo Tribal Council (now Navajo Nation president) emphasized that in addition to the drought and the anguish brought about by the Navajo-Hopi land dispute, Navajos must be concerned about the ways in which they have strayed from their spiritual strengths and values and must begin a journey back to being a strong Nation.

The final two chapters examine the ways Navajos deal with crises that have affected their own close kin. In chapter 5, Schwarz analyzes the role of weeping by Navajo women mourning the loss of kin who have died of cancer and other diseases related to their former employment in the uranium mining industry. Schwarz shows us how new forms of protest are closely connected to Navajo conceptions of personhood, the importance of kin, and patterns of mourning. Chapter 6 deals with problem drinking, an issue faced by many Navajos whose close kin have become binge drinkers. In severe cases, in which families have exhausted their repertoire of activities to help "'adláanii," or drunks, return to a life of sobriety and harmony, Navajos may finally cut off their relations with the person. This is considered a "social death," wherein the individual is transformed from a beloved family member to a "lost one."

This book speaks to two audiences. For non-Navajos, it breaks down the stereotype that the Navajo and other Native American groups are either people who have lost their cultures or isolated "exotic folk" who live apart from the rest of American culture and society. These essays show how Navajos use traditional beliefs and practices to meet the challenges they face in a complex, modern society where most Navajos drive pickup trucks, frequent fast food restaurants, and watch TV along with other Americans, and where increasing numbers of Navajo

students use computers in the classroom, graduate from high
school, and attend institutions of higher education. For Navajo
readers, these essays reassert the long history of the Navajo as
creative and adaptive people who have borrowed and utilized
aspects of other cultures and societies with which they have
interacted (the Pueblos, the Hispanos, the Americans) but who
have retained a strong sense of their own historical and religious traditions. It is this creative flexibility and resilience that
will allow future generations of Navajos to retain their language
and culture and continue to forge programs and institutions
that will help them meet the challenges of modern life.

LOUISE LAMPHERE

University of New Mexico

Preface

Three strands of thought have occupied my primary interest throughout the time that I have been conducting research on Navajo life—cross-cultural conceptions of personhood, oral traditions, and contemporary issues. This collection of essays illustrates the intersections of these strands by examining ways in which Navajo views on personhood—from its gradual development to its potential deterioration—and Navajo use of accounts from their oral history have influenced Navajo reactions to specific issues and events in the last decade.

My motivation in presenting these essays in book form is that contemporary Native American issues go largely underrepresented in the academic press (and elsewhere), and many people have told me that they are using my previously published articles on the hantavirus outbreak of 1993, the Navajo-Hopi Land dispute, a visitation by Navajo Holy People in May of 1996, and some snake sightings that occurred in 1994 in reading packets for courses in multiple disciplines. With this in mind, I have used these essays, as well as new pieces on the expression of emotion by women who lost relatives to illnesses directly related to work in the uranium mining industry and on extreme cases of problem drinkers who become socially equivalent to the dead, to build the book.

The main theme linking the various chapters is the importance of oral traditions in shaping Navajo understandings of problems and situations. This is explained in the introduction, which provides a brief overview of Navajo oral history, meant to serve as a backdrop for the later chapters. Each of the essays has been reworked to update information, eliminate redundancy, and improve the overall coherence of the manuscript.

Field research from 1991 to 1995 was supported by the Costume Society of America, the Jacobs Research Fund, the Arizona Humanities Council, the National Science Foundation, the Royalty Research Fund (University of Washington), the Institute for Ethnic Studies in the United States (University of Washington), and the Graduate School Research Fund (University of Washington). An Andrew W. Mellon Fellowship for 1998 to 1999 afforded me the time to construct this manuscript from the previously published and unpublished essays on contemporary issues in Navajoland. Special thanks go to Patricia Hill and Ann Wightman of Wesleyan University for their enthusiastic interest in this project and their consistent encouragement at all stages of its gestation. Release time from teaching at Syracuse University in the autumn of 1999 allowed me to revise and polish the manuscript on the basis of insightful suggestions from readers for the University of Oklahoma Press. Special thanks to my colleagues in the Department of Anthropology at Syracuse University for encouragement and to the Maxwell School of Citizenship and Public Policy Dean's office for the aforementioned release time and for covering the cost of the index.

Before leaving for my first season of fieldwork, I contacted the Navajo Nation Historic Preservation Department (NNHPD), obtained an ethnographic fieldwork permit, and devised con-

sultation consent forms to comply with the NNHPD requirements. Prior to starting an interview, I asked every person with
whom I consulted to complete, sign, and date one of these
consent forms. Among other things, these documents asked
each consultant to indicate whether or not he or she wanted
his or her name used in any future publications. Most of the
people with whom I consulted indicated that they wanted to be
credited for their contributions and asked that their names be
used in all future publications. In accordance with the wishes of
these people, the actual name of every consultant who chose
this option appears in the text. Those who chose not to have
their names cited are simply referred to as "anonymous elder,"
"anonymous woman," or by some similar designation.

There are two notable exceptions to this policy. First, unlike
with most of my previous research, each person with whom I
consulted about the Holy Visit, except Harry Walters of Tsaile,
Arizona, opted not to have his or her name used in this publication. So to maintain anonymity, fictitious names have been
used for all Navajo people mentioned in personal narratives in
this chapter. To affirm the veracity of what they had to share,
each of the individuals with whom I consulted framed his or
her narrative with a qualifying clause such as "This is exactly
what I was told. I did not change one word"; "By clan we were
sisters"; or "My uncle told me." The implication is that clan relatives would not distort information imparted to kin and that
the teller made a concerted effort to relay the information
verbatim. Second, due to the sensitive nature of the topic of
problem drinking, and my wish to avoid causing undue embar-
rassments, I substituted fictitious initials for the actual names
of individuals mentioned in the excerpts from my fieldnotes
that appear throughout that chapter.

While readily acknowledging themselves as situated subjects
who were in positions to "know" certain things and not to have
access to other bodies of knowledge, the Navajo people with

whom I consulted consistently referred to the "natural order"—
the Navajo philosophical system that consists of the paradigms
established by the Navajo Holy People during their construction of the Navajo universe—as a cohesive whole. Hence, all
totalizing statements found in the text, such as "the Navajo
system" or "the Navajo view," are simply meant to refer to this
philosophical system in the manner employed by the Navajo
consultants with whom I conferred.

Over the years, my research has been aided in numerous ways
by dozens of Navajo people. I cannot name each person here,
but I want to single out five of my Navajo colleagues for special
thanks: Sadie Billie and Harry Walters of Tsaile, Arizona; Mae
Bekis of Tó'tsoh, Arizona; Sunny Dooley of Vanderwagen, New
Mexico; and Wesley Thomas of Pocatello, Idaho. Sadie Billie
took a profound interest in my research and introduced me to
the extended Tso/Billie family. At various points, Mae Bekis,
Sunny Dooley, Wesley Thomas, and Harry Walters each acted as
sounding boards, patiently discussing and clarifying the ideas
presented. Special thanks go to Sunny Dooley for writing the
frontispiece poem especially for this book. It beautifully conveys
Navajo views on oral history. Thanks to Gary Witherspoon for
aiding my developing understanding of Navajo philosophy and
to Charlotte Frisbie for her insightful criticisms on various
portions of the text. Thanks go to those scholars who served as
anonymous readers for the University of Oklahoma Press. I
appreciate the painstaking attention each of you gave to the
manuscript. It was greatly strengthened through incorporation
of your numerous, detailed recommendations for corrections
and revisions. Last but not least, thanks to my husband and children for continued unconditional love and support.

•   •   •

Chapter 1 of this book appeared in a different form in "The
Explanatory and Predictive Power of History: Coping with the

Navajo Lifeways

Introduction

I think what is always really amazing to me is that Navajos are never amazed by anything that happens. Because it is like in a lot of our stories they are already there.

SUNNY DOOLEY

Because of their longstanding and deep involvement in global and national economics and politics, the Navajo are the ideal subject for a case study on the contemporary life experiences of an American Indian people. During this decade alone, Navajo people have been confronted by unusual occurrences involving illness, spirituality, land rights, uranium mining, problem drinking, and other issues that have repeatedly challenged their ability to cope. Following current events as they have unfolded on the Navajo reservation throughout this period, I have been continually impressed by how Navajo people seem able to make sense of events, no matter how diverse or unusual they initially may seem. I have come to realize that, as Sunny

Dooley of Vanderwagen, New Mexico, pointed out, the source of this assurance, this ready knowledge of the best ways to contend with circumstances as they arise, lies in the vivid accounts of origin and emergence recorded in the Navajo oral tradition.[1]

Singly and collectively, the essays in this book demonstrate how Navajo origin stories form a charter and guide for life, which holds moral force, delineates aspects of personhood, and informs an evolving Navajo identity. Navajo exegeses directly relevant to the topics at hand are foregrounded throughout this work to allow Navajo people to speak for themselves. The Navajo people with whom I or others have consulted on these matters made implicit or explicit reference to various elements and versions of this oral tradition. Consultants' allusions to origin accounts are best seen as firmly located in a contemporary context of narration and heard as efforts to conceptualize alternatives to established and traditional norms. Navajo exegeses provide a unique window into contemporary Navajo life, allowing outsiders to garner at least a partial understanding of Navajo concerns, perspectives, and values.

To put Navajo explanations and understandings of the hantavirus outbreak of 1993, forced relocation, prophetic visits by Navajo supernaturals, untoward contact with snakes, the perils of uranium mining, and problem drinking in context, this book examines Euro-American concepts of history, summarizes the various kinds of histories written about the Navajo, and then turns to the Navajo history presented in the origin stories. These narratives are the philosophical wellspring from which Navajo determine how to cope with each of the circumstances discussed herein.

WHAT IS HISTORY?

History is culturally ordered, differently so in different societies, according to meaningful schemes of things. The converse is also true: cultural schemes are historically ordered, since to a greater or lesser extent the meanings are revalued as they are practically enacted. The synthesis of these contraries unfolds in the creative action of the historic subjects, the people concerned. For on the one hand, people organize projects and give significance to their objects from the existing understandings of the cultural order. To that extent, the culture is historically reproduced in action.[2]

Neutral or pure history does not exist. As with all things cultural, histories are partial and biased, constructed by positioned subjects who know certain things and not others. Noting that "historical facts" do not exist because every event is ultimately reducible to a "multitude of individual psychic movements," Claude Lévi-Strauss points out that historians "choose, sever and carve" up the multiple individual experiences that constitute events, then use these parts to construct a history, which "is therefore never history, but history-for. It is partial in the sense of being biased even when it claims not to be, for it inevitably remains partial—that is, incomplete—and this is itself a form of partiality."[3]

All people everywhere have chosen, severed, and carved up individual experiences to devise histories that account for and validate their beginnings, explain their present, and to a greater or lesser extent, predict their future. To borrow Ward Churchill's insightful phrase, many histories are "fantasies of the master race."[4] Such fantasies often constitute dangerous weapons, such as the propaganda written by victors to validate war, conquests, and even genocide.

Having endured four centuries of war, conquest, and colonization, the Navajo today make up the largest Native nation in the contiguous United States. They number close to 220,000 individuals, most of whom occupy a 25,000-thousand-square-mile reservation that spans parts of Arizona, New Mexico, and Utah.[5] Their complex history—as internally recorded and as seen by outsiders—is marked by relations with Spaniards, Mexicans, Americans, and many Native groups. Since all history is inherently partial and constructed, no single Navajo history is "out there" waiting to be collected, transcribed, and validated by being written down. Various sources shed light on the complexities of Navajo history, including linguistic analyses, archaeological evidence, historical documents such as personal journals and military reports, as well as the Navajo oral histories. These sources, combined in complex ways, allow contemporary Navajo people to choose among many different versions of their own history.

WRITTEN HISTORY

From linguistic and archaeological clues, Euro-American scholars have constructed a story of Navajo origins, cultural adaptation, and development that fits well with master narratives documenting the migration of the first Americans across the Bering land bridge and their dispersal through North, Central, and South America. The Navajo belong to the Athapaskan language family, one of the largest linguistic groups in all of North America. At the time of European contact, Athapaskan-speaking groups inhabited what is now the western interior of Alaska through the northern interior of Canada and from the Yukon and British Columbia eastward to the western shores of Hudson Bay. Athapaskan speakers also populated the Pacific coast states of Washington, Oregon, and California, as well as the southwestern United States. The Navajo are one of the Southern Athapaskan-speaking groups.[6]

Considerably less consensus exists regarding the amount of time involved in the southerly movements, the route or routes taken by the early migrants, and whether more than one migration was involved.[7] Estimated dates of the Navajo arrival in the southwest range from 1000 A.D. to 1525 A.D. Whatever the migration route or routes may have been, the "Querechos," as the Navajo were called by the Spanish explorers, were occupying *Dinétah,* "the area the Navajo consider their ancestral homeland," when first contacted by Antonio de Espejo's expedition in 1582.[8]

At the time of European contact, the Navajo had a hunting and gathering-based subsistence system, which was supplemented by some agriculture.[9] Extended family units, centered on matrilocal residence and the strength of their clan system, lived in widely dispersed settlements across a vast region. After livestock were first introduced into the region by Spanish settlers, a herding economy based on sheep and goats developed. The Navajo population and their area of settlement gradually expanded as new crops, animals, and technological innovations continued to be added to their subsistence base during the Spanish and American periods.

Like Native people throughout the Americas, Navajo endured many hardships at the hands of European and Euro-American conquerors. For example, in the nineteenth century an extended period of war resulted in nearly nine thousand Navajo being rounded up and forced to walk three hundred miles to *Hwéeldi* (Fort Sumner, New Mexico), where they were incarcerated by the U.S. military from 1863 to 1868.[10] On 1 June 1868 a treaty was signed that established a reservation on a portion of the Navajo homeland, to which the captives were allowed to return. The treaty required Navajo people to refrain from any further military actions against Euro-Americans and to send their children to American schools.[11]

After the Navajo returned to the reservation, their economy and population gradually recovered.[12] Trading posts began to flourish on the reservation in the late 1800s, and a barter economy developed wherein male lambs and items of Navajo manufacture were traded for coffee, flour, lard, canned goods, and other food staples.[13] During the closing decades of the nineteenth century, the first biomedical physicians began servicing portions of the Navajo reservation.[14] Tracts of land were annexed to the original reservation at numerous times between 1878 and 1934, and separate tracts of land were subsequently secured for outlying Navajo groups—the Alamo (1946), Cañoncito (1949), and Ramah (1956).

The early years of the twentieth century were riddled with cultural and economic hardships caused by sustained droughts, loss of livestock due to poor forage and a series of severe winters, and an estimated 10 to 15 percent reservation-wide mortality rate sustained during the Spanish influenza pandemic in the winters of 1918 to 1919.[15] Lack of rain and overgrazing, coupled with fluctuations in livestock and wool prices, resulted in a shift toward increased dependence on wage labor and the production of woven goods and silverwork for the off-reservation market.[16] To accommodate developing resource extraction-based industries, including coal and uranium mining, a federally designed centralized government—the Navajo Nation Council—was installed on the Navajo reservation in the 1920s. Since its inception, Navajo leaders have adapted and molded this system into an effective means for controlling and dispensing necessary goods and services.[17] Federally mandated stock reductions diminished family herds in the 1930s, which increased dependence on wage labor, on and off the reservation, and helped increase acceptance of non-Navajo religious beliefs and practices such as Catholicism, Protestantism, Mormonism, and the Native American Church.[18] And, as will be discussed in chapter 3, these were also decades of intense internal prophetic activity. Increased exposure to the non-Navajo world, through military service and employment in war-related industries during World War II, led to increased use of government-run health care and educational facilities.[19] The so-called "Navajo-Hopi land dispute" over an area of Arizona that both tribes consider to be ancestral homeland has monopolized enormous amounts of time and energy since the turn of the century and, in the minds of some, remains unresolved.[20]

In the face of these various changes and challenges, Navajo language and culture have proven to be exceptionally resilient. As a leader in bilingual education and in the development of educational curricula centered on native values, the Navajo Nation has experienced high language retention, relative to other American Indian groups, and Navajo tenets of philosophy are currently taught at all grade levels, as well as in courses at Diné College, the first tribally operated college in the country.[21] Although reservation unemployment rates far exceed national norms, thousands of Navajo are employed in the fields of health care, education, government service, commercial farming, or in resource-based industries such as timber and mining. Navajo who are employed off the reservation or in towns on the reservation return to matrilineal family homes in remote areas as frequently as possible to participate in family activities. Those in need of medical attention freely combine biomedical care and treatments administered in state-of-the-art facilities across the reservation with traditional care and treatments, administered either at home or in biomedical facilities. Most Navajo who have adopted non-Navajo religious doctrines and practices still participate in traditional healing rituals held for themselves or for members of their extended families.

Despite the plethora of outside-written histories, many contemporary Navajo people rely on Navajo oral history stories, which are encoded in designs found on *ts'aa'*, or "ceremonial baskets," as their most important source of information.[22] The stories contain the ancestral knowledge that is the Navajo charter for life. No direct correlation exists between Euro-American notions of Navajo history and Navajo notions of their own history. The Euro-American histories, framed by a linear notion of time, objectify historic events as "truth," placing them firmly in the past. In contrast, the ancestral knowledge contained in the Navajo origin stories is "just one more element of present reality, not an objectified, distanced, inert position of wisdom or truth."[23] For Navajo individuals, history is "not an attribute or vehicle of an objectified representation of knowledge about reality" but "the process of what is constantly in the making."[24]

ORAL HISTORY

The Navajo believe the universe preceded human existence. Thus, in order to explicate the power of the Navajo intellectual system and to understand the structural principles of Navajo philosophical orientation that underlie "the process of what is constantly in the making," it is necessary to consider the Navajo view of the world and their place in it. Several distinct types of beings coexist in the Navajo universe: the *Diyin Dine'é,* "Holy People," the *Nihookáá Dine'é,* "Earth Surface People," and animals, plants, rains, and mountains. Humans are not separate or distinct from other beings or aspects of nature. All beings and aspects of nature are *alk'éí,* "those who should be treated with compassion, cooperation and unselfishness by the Navajo"— treated, in other words, as kin.[25]

   Navajo oral tradition describes the Navajo origin as a successive emergence upward through a series of subterranean underworlds. The Navajo consider themselves the Nihookáá Dine'é, created on the earth's surface by *Asdzáá Nádleehé,* "Changing Woman," the most highly revered of all Navajo Holy People. She directed them to live within the geographical area demarcated by the four sacred mountains.[26] The Navajo origin and creation story describes the preparation of the physical world, the creation of its inhabitants, and the delineation of the Navajo role in this world.[27] It establishes an ethnic identity for all Navajo, defining meaningful relationships among individual members of the community and between the community and the cosmos.[28]

Navajo people routinely refer to their oral history as a charter for life, and over four hundred composite accounts of the Navajo origin story have been transcribed by generations of researchers and by the Navajo tribe itself. Statements suggesting ontological status are potentially misleading, however, because even though an integral core of common elements permeates all recorded versions, the accounts vary widely in detail.

Story differences reflect personal factors such as the narrator's stage of life, clan affiliations, or level of ceremonial or other specialized knowledge acquired through occupational training. I rely largely on the versions transcribed by Stanley Fishler, Pliny Goddard, Berard Haile, Washington Matthews, Aileen O'Bryan, and Ethelou Yazzie, because they contain the most complete accounts of the events pertinent to this discussion.[29] With the exception of Yazzie's account, these versions are limited by the fact that they were each collected from male consultants, the majority of whom had specialized training. In addition, many of these accounts were heavily edited.[30] In the following summary, only the events alluded to by Navajo consultants during our discussions about the topics central to this book are presented, with the intent that they serve simply as a general backdrop.

The common elements in the Navajo oral histories combine to form a core worldview, a paradigm for ritual action and use of space, structured on homology, complementarity, and synecdoche. These histories offer a means to understand the Navajo cultural construction of the world. For the Navajo, the origin story contains the essence of all that exists or is possible, and it therefore holds significance for contemporary people and their problems. For example, these stories contain the clues

necessary to: unravel the mystery illness; understand the importance of the Holy Visit of 1996; appreciate the debilitating
effects of forced relocation or contact with snakes; recognize
and inspire activism on the part of women whose relatives have
succumbed to illnesses directly tied to uranium extraction; and
accept the loss of a loved one to the seductive power of alcohol.
When faced with such dilemmas, contemporary Navajo have
found answers in the various versions of the origin story to questions such as: How is it possible? Where did it come from? How
do we cope with it? We must go deep into the womb of the
earth, back to the beginning of the world before we can answer
these questions—and then look at the many different interpretations of the origin story.

THE ORIGIN STORY

The First World, small in size, was much like a floating island in
a sea of water mist. There were columns of colored vaporous
matter, often referred to as clouds, in each of the cardinal directions; white in the east, blue in the south, yellow in the west and
black in the north. These columns of colored clouds were
primordial; they "contained within themselves the elements of
the First World."[31] The white column and black column met in
the east, and there a male being was formed. Simultaneously,
the blue cloud and the yellow cloud met in the west, and there
a female being was created.[32]

In this world, "[m]an was not in his present form," but the
male and female beings conceived at this time were destined
to become man and woman.[33] These beings are considered by
many to be *Altsé Hastiin*, "First Man," and *Altsé Asdzáán*, "First
Woman," the Diyin Dine'é who directed generative processes
in this and subsequent worlds. The other beings dwelling in this
world were thought of as Air-Spirit or Mist Beings.[34] They had

no definite form or shape but were to change in subsequent worlds into humans, animals, birds, reptiles, and other creatures.[35]

In all versions of Navajo origin, each subterranean world is referred to by color. Most accounts have three or four underworlds with a color sequence from black to blue to yellow to white.[36] Each underworld is portrayed in some state of chaos and disorder resulting in the need for travel into the next world.

In the last underworld, the first male and female beings with humanlike form were created.[37] They lived as man and wife, as did their offspring. First Woman was concerned because these marriages dissolved easily. Recognizing that the role of marriage was to guarantee offspring and the continuation of life, she determined to develop a plan to strengthen the bond between men and women to ensure enduring marriages.[38] She created genitals and sexual desire to enable men and women to attract each other for a lifetime.

First Man, First Woman, and their progeny flourished for a time until lust led to adultery, which in turn led to a conflict between First Man and First Woman. During the separation, their libidinal desires became ever stronger. To appease their sexual passions, the women masturbated with various objects— cactus, deer tendons, or rocks—while the men tried to relieve their longing with mud or the flesh of freshly slain game animals.[39] Eventually, realizing that they could survive without the other sex but that they could never flourish, the men and women agreed to rejoin and live as one group.

Shortly after the reunion, Coyote stole a child from *Tééhootsódii*, "Water Monster," who in retaliation caused a great flood to overtake the world. Hearing of the imminent flood, First Man directed that everyone should quickly gather their personal belongings and flee to an appointed mountain. As the people climbed higher and higher, the water continued to rise. Once gathered at the summit, they sequentially planted various plant species in hopes that one would grow high enough to allow the people to climb it and escape from the approaching flood waters.[40]

> First Man planted a cedar tree, hoping to have it reach the top of the sky so that everyone could climb to safety. The tree grew quickly, but it was too short. Next, he planted a pine tree. However, it was not tall enough to reach the top of the sky, either. The third effort by First Man to find a means of escaping the water was to plant a male reed, but it also failed to reach the top of the sky. The fourth attempt was to plant a female reed. It grew to the very top of the sky.
>
> The people crowded into the great female reed and began to climb up. The water followed them as they climbed inside the giant reed.[41]

The journey upward culminated in the emergence onto the earth's surface at the *hajiinái,* "place of emergence."

> After all the people were upon the earth, Coyote remembered that he had forgotten something down the hole. He wanted to go back down the hole and find the things he had hidden there. . . . He had left down there his secret power, his witchcraft power. The rest of the gods did not trust him and some went down the hole with him. . . . Many of the gods (Supreme Sacred Wind and others) went down with Coyote to find all of his secrets. When he had found all of them, he was standing on the right side of the shaft and the other gods were on the left. They were all trying to get up the ladder first.[42]

The Diyin Dine'é who accompanied Coyote back down to the last underworld outsmarted him so that they were able to

lead the way up the reed. This boded well for future generations, for it is said that if Coyote had been the first to ascend
the reed, he would have destroyed the world with his secret
powers.[43]

Shortly thereafter, the male and female Water Monsters, who
had followed the people up the great reed in an attempt to
regain their child, stuck their heads out of the reed.

> I don't know if they [the people] had their sacred stones
> with them. Then they got an abalone basket [white (?)
> shell used as a receptacle] and abalone shells [pieces] and
> put this on the female Water Monster's head between her
> horns. For the male Water Monster, they put white shell
> [turquoise] and a white shell basket in the same way. They
> used those because white shell and turquoise represents
> the male. . . . Then they pleaded with the Water Monster
> to let them take the baby with them, so that in the future
> the people may have plenty of rain, so that the rains may
> come all of the time. "We have made offerings in packets
> to you, this also will help provide us with plenty of rain."
> After that the monsters left.[44]

This ceremonial act established the precedent for Navajo
people to accompany prayers for rain at mountain springs with
offerings of *ntł'iz*, "hard goods" (precious stones and shells).
The people "kept the baby, because taking the baby caused the
Water Monster to bring rain, but made an offering as a fee to
the Water Monster to compel it to control the force of rain-
storms."[45] Once the Water Monsters were appeased, the people
turned their attentions to establishing a life for themselves in
this new location.

At the place of emergence, First Man and First Woman built
a sweat house in which they thought and sang the world, as the
Navajo know it, into existence.[46] To strengthen the earth and

Figure 1. Navajo Cosmology

demarcate Navajo sacred geography, the Holy People put a
mountain at each of the four cardinal points. Next, they
created plants and animals with which to populate the world
and dressed each mountain with a particular precious stone
or shell and various cosmic elements. Each of the sacred
mountains, colors, qualities, holy personages, and ntł'iz, which
make up the fundamental components of Navajo cosmology,
became associated with a season of the year, a time of day, and
a phase of life (see figure 1 for placement of each in Navajo
cosmology).

Also at this time, the sun, moon, and stars were created
and placed, and day, night, and the seasons of the year were
established, as was the necessity for births and deaths.[47] The
need for the latter (births and deaths) was established by
means of Coyote's interference.[48] First Man and First Woman
intended for people to live forever. To ensure this immortality, they cast a "piece of hard, black wood" or, as in the following account, a "hide scraper," into a body of water.[49] But for
Coyote's intervention, there would be no death. As the story
goes,

> [T]he people all wanted to know what would become of
> them. So someone threw a hide scraper into the water and
> had this to say.
>
> "If it sinks we will eventually perish. But if it floats we
> shall all go on living."
>
> It floated, and everyone was glad.
>
> But then Mą'ii the Coyote stood up. And he had this to
> say:
>
> "Wait a minute here. Let me do this," he said.
>
> And before anybody could object, he picked up a stone
> and spoke this way:
>
> "If it floats, we will all live forever. But if it sinks, every-
> body will die sooner or later."
>
> Of course the stone sank, and everyone grew angry.
> They called Mą'ii names and they cursed him. Some of the
> people even threatened to throw him in the water. But he
> cried out, and this is what he said.
>
> "Wait!" he said.
>
> "Listen to me."
>
> "If we all go on living, and if the women keep having
> babies, there will be too many people. There won't be any
> room. Nobody will be able to move around. There will be
> no space to plant corn.

"Isn't it better that each one of us should live here for
just a while, until old age slows us down?
Not just until we can't hunt. Not just until we can't
plant and harvest. Not just until we can no longer speak.
"Then we ought to move on, leave everything behind
for the young. Make room for the next generation."[50]

Once these various aspects of life were established, the newly
created world was said to be in a state of "natural order," in
which all living things were in their prescribed places and in
their proper relationships with all other living things. But, this
orderliness was not to endure. The perfect order of the world
was disrupted as a result of the sexual aberrations and excesses
of the last underworld. The women who had masturbated with
quills, cactus, antlers, stones, and bones gave birth to misshapen
creatures that grew into monsters. When the women saw that
their newborns were deformed, they abandoned them. They
left them where they were born to die. At first the women did
not even tell the men about the birth of these deformed beings.
The monstrous babies, however, did not die. Instead, they flourished, grew huge, and began preying on the healthy children.
The birth of these monsters resulted in death and destruction
throughout the world.

To resolve this dilemma, the Diyin Dine'é arranged for
Changing Woman to be found on one of the central mountains of Navajo sacred geography—*Ch'óol'į́'į́* or Gobernador
Knob. One morning at dawn, a dark cloud appeared at the
summit; seeing this, First Man and First Woman sent a message to *Haashch'ééłti'í*, "Talking God," to investigate. Talking
God attempted to reach the top of Gobernador Knob from
each direction—south, west, north, and finally east. When he
approached from the east, he saw the cloud, with a rainbow
and soft falling rain. He looked again, and a baby girl was lying
under the rainbow and rain.

Talking God gave her over to First Man who took her home to First Woman. Under the direction of the Holy People, First Man and First Woman fed the baby sunray pollen, pollen from clouds, pollen from plants, and flower dew. Owing to this special care, the baby matured at an accelerated rate: in two days she walked, in four days she talked, and in twelve days she began to menstruate.

Her menstruation symbolized the restoration of healthy reproduction on the earth and was cause for great rejoicing. The first Blessing Way ceremony, the *Kinaaldá,* "puberty ceremony," was celebrated in honor of the event. Shortly after this ceremony, Changing Woman mated with the sun and gave birth to twin sons, Monster Slayer and Born-for-Water. When they reached adolescence, the twins wanted to know who their father was, so they went on a quest to find him. Along the way, they met Spider Woman who told them that their father was the sun and gave them magical tools with which to reach him. When they found their father, he made them endure several trials to prove they were his children. They persevered, and finally Sun supplied them with weapons to slay the monsters. The twins worked together to slay all the monsters except Hunger, Poverty, Lice, and Old Age.

When Monster Slayer came to slay these monsters, they gave sound reasons for their indispensability. After Hunger, Poverty, and Lice made their pleas, Old Age spoke up, reiterating the need for the "give and take" of births and deaths as rationale for sparing him:

> "In spite of all, I am going to live on, my grandchild," he said. "How surprisingly little sense you have, my grandchild!" he told him. "You have not the right thing in mind, I see," he told him. "Should you kill me, dying would cease," he said. "Then too giving birth would cease," he said, "and this present number of people would continue

in the same amount for all time to come. While if I live
on, old age will do killing and giving birth will go on in
the future. As giving birth goes on ahead, so deaths will
go on the other way," he said.[51]

Once the monsters were slain, Asdzą́ą́ Nádleehé (Changing
Woman) grew lonely for companionship.

The White Bead Woman [who is most often considered
to be one and the same as Changing Woman] wished now
to have her own people. She wished to have a people that
she could call her grandchildren. They would carry on
the lore that she would teach them. They would respect
and hold holy the prayers and chants that she would give
them.[52]

To fulfill her need, Asdzą́ą́ Nádleehé created the members of
the original four Navajo clans. After their creation, Asdzą́ą́
Nádleehé and the other Diyin Dine'é decided to turn the world
over to these Nihookáá Dine'é, entrusting them with stewardship over the geographical area demarcated by the sacred
mountains, known today as *Diné Bikéyah,* "Navajoland."

At this juncture, the teachings of the Holy People were
imparted by Asdzą́ą́ Nádleehé. She taught the Earth Surface
People critical bodies of knowledge—songs, prayers, and ceremonies—with which to sustain themselves in their special form
of life and to restore proper relations whenever disruptions
occurred. In combination, these various types of knowledge
became a charter between the Navajo and the Holy People,
guaranteeing that if the Nihookáá Dine'é carefully followed
them the natural order of the Navajo world would be preserved, and their special way of life would flourish.

To maintain good fortune and avert catastrophe, prayers and
offerings such as *tádídíín,* "pollen," or ntł'iz, "hard goods," must

be made to the Holy People at specific sites within Navajo sacred geography. These ceremonial acts serve to bring rain and to protect home, family, livestock, and the land.[53] For Navajo to leave the land would be potentially dangerous, because it would violate Navajo stewardship as well as their reciprocity with the Diyin Dine'é.[54] Once this knowledge was transferred, Changing Woman and the other Diyin Dine'é departed to take their places as inner forms residing within features of Navajo sacred geography.[55]

These stories are compressed metaphoric accounts with many different levels of abstraction that allow for great flexibility and adaptability in interpretation. They explain how Navajo culture is historically ordered and demonstrate how history is reproduced in the action of living.

The Mystery Illness of 1993

Evil Over the Land: A deadly illness plagues the Navajo Nation.

TIME,
14 June 1993

In the Navajo way, danger of this magnitude is not supposed to affect us because the Holy People protect us. What have we done wrong to deserve this?

LOLA BEGAY

In the spring of 1993, a mysterious illness characterized by flu-like symptoms and leading to fluid buildup in the lungs swept through the American Southwest, killing healthy people in a matter of hours.[1] The now famous "mystery illness" claimed its first Navajo victim on 14 May 1993.[2] Media attention was swift and relentless. Popular magazines, national television news broadcasts, syndicated shows, and newspapers lured their audiences with inflamed captions and headlines: "Four Corners

Disease: Another Deadly Virus Comes of Age";[3] "The Death
Bug";[4] "On the Trail of a Killer Virus."[5] The media attention
had wide-ranging ramifications for Native people of the Four
Corners area, including discrimination, the cancellation of
numerous conferences and events, and a major decline in
tourism.

The twenty-seven victims who succumbed to the illness during the spring and summer of 1993 were both male and female,
from all walks of life and all ethnic groups, with an average age
of thirty-four.[6] Because of the ethnicity of the first reported
victim, the media quickly dubbed this a Navajo illness. A front-
page headline in *USA Today* labeled it the "Navajo flu," and CBS
Evening News referred to it as the "Navajo disease." This labeling
stuck despite the actual demographics and resulted in widespread discrimination against American Indians. In June, twenty-
seven healthy third-graders from Chinle, Arizona, were barred
from visiting their pen pals at a private school in Los Angeles.[7]
Throughout the summer months, Navajo and other American
Indians were refused service by restaurants and merchants in
the towns bordering the reservation.[8] The discrimination was
due to fears that these individuals might be carrying the disease. By late July the death toll had reached twenty-six, and the
tourist industry in the entire Four Corners area recorded severe
declines in business.[9] Discrimination and loss of revenue compounded the effects of the mystery illness, reaching beyond the
lives of families of victims to affect the entire Navajo Nation and
all people living in the Four Corners region.

Faced with the devastating effects of an illness that killed people of all ages, including seemingly healthy young people, in
less than forty-eight hours, national health regulating agencies
and the families of Navajo victims responded very differently.
Officials of the Indian Health Service (IHS) and the Centers for
Disease Control (CDC) in Atlanta turned to the modern scientific methods of biomedicine for answers, putting hundreds of

scientists in laboratories and research facilities across the country on the case. Members of the Navajo Nation turned inward and looked to their own history for answers, because like many American Indians, they have an active relationship with their history. For contemporary Navajo individuals, the stories making up their history constitute a philosophic system that serves as a charter and a guide to life. In this case, it offered a means for coping with a devastating illness. The parallel but unrelated strands of cultural thought—western biomedical and Navajo philosophical—overlapped and converged when biomedical experts and Navajo experts collaborated at critical points in the investigation.

Both biomedical theory and practice and Navajo theory and practice eventually concluded that deer mice were the bearers of the illness. Biomedical and Navajo experts did not agree, however, on the ultimate cause of the mystery illness. The former blamed hantavirus carried by deer mice; the latter believed the disease represented monsters created by disharmony.

In the Navajo origin story, the separation of the sexes, the birth of monsters, the finding of Changing Woman, the birth of her hero sons, and the slaying of the monsters can be analyzed to account for the origins of disease and difficulty and to explain how well-being is to be restored. At different levels of abstraction, the monsters symbolize disease, immorality, or misconduct in Navajo history. Navajo people used the explanatory and predictive power of the philosophical system based on their oral history to cope with the mystery illness, one of the most traumatic experiences in recent Navajo history.

FAIRY TALES OR METAPHOR? THE TWELVE LEVELS OF KNOWLEDGE

HW: Ok, that is level one, right there. Level one.
MS: Level one? Ok.

HW: Yeah, level one, but there are twelve levels. When you get to it, it is very complicated, even for me, I know. I think I will just stay at the two levels.[10]

How can stories such as those comprising Navajo oral tradition help contemporary people cope with an illness as devastating and unpredictable as the mystery illness of 1993? Although Navajo origin accounts generally are spoken of as if they hold ontological status, the interview excerpts in this chapter and book show that the relationships between origin stories and current practices are not self-evident. The stories compress historical knowledge and human experience into vivid narratives that can illuminate and educate. As teaching tools, or parables, they are open to different levels of analysis. In the Navajo world, the stories are useful because they contain numerous messages at each of the various levels of interpretation, depending on the degree of analytic abstraction applied by the Navajo listener. As Harry Walters explains, all components of Navajo culture are based on four main levels of knowledge, each of which can be subdivided into three additional levels:

OK. I won't go into the twelve, because, uh, that is very complicated, and then, you have to know ceremonies to get into that. . . . All components of culture are based on that. If you were to categorize them [the components of Navajo culture] into philosophy, art, music, or history, things like that, it will not work. But if you put it in the four levels, it will work. And so the four main ones are *hózhǫ́ǫ́jí hane'*, and then *diné k'ehjí hane'*, and the third one is *hatááł k'ehjí hane'*, and the fourth one is *naayéé'jí hane'*.[11]

Hózhǫ́ǫ́jí hane' is the elementary level of knowledge, or philosophy, used to teach young children. Diyin k'ehjí hane' expands on the first level by incorporating information about the twelve

Diyin Dine'é, mentioned in all ceremonies and stories, who represent different principles in nature. The third main level, hatááł k'ehjí hane', includes songs and prayers associated with each episode in the origin stories. Naayéé'jí hane', the fourth level, is specifically concerned with the stories associated with *Naayéé'jí,* or Protection Way, ceremonies and is limited to people who have specialized ceremonial knowledge. Altogether, twelve distinct levels of knowledge are encoded into each episode of the origin stories. Navajo educators draw upon these levels of abstraction to illuminate ancestral teachings.

As an experienced educator, Walters knows that a learner must be able to put new information into a familiar context to grasp the lesson at hand. He turned to the Changing Woman portion of the origin narrative to illustrate for me the different levels of knowledge that can be drawn out of a single account: "Remember I told you that on level one, level one is basic elementary, you know, Changing Woman was found on the mountain, she became an adolescent after twelve days."[12] Walters was alluding to a familiar episode in the Changing Woman story where she is found and raised in a "miracle way." The following excerpt is a typical rendition of this episode, as told to me by Wilson Aronilth of Tsaile, Arizona:

A miracle thing happened, a child came into the world to save our people, and this child came into this world in the form of a little baby girl. . . . Myself, a lot of these English translations throws off a lot of our stories, but that's the way that I think they call it, Talking God, but in Navajo we say "Bił haayoolkááł Haashch'ééłti'í." When you say—if you understand the language, it's self explanatory—it's the Holy Spirit that found the child and then brought it to First Man and First Woman's home and raised it in a miracle way. She was fed with air, light, water, moisture mist, plant pollen. Moisture and mist and pollen are some of the most natural ingredients and she grew up miracally in twelve days, and on the twelfth day she reached her pubertyhood, she became a woman.[13]

Walters explained that on level two the story of how Changing Woman was found and raised is interpreted in a slightly different manner:

HW: Level two is diné k'ehjí hane'. It says, Changing Woman was found and she was dressed in white shell. She was not found as a baby, she was found as an embryo, an undeveloped egg. First Man brought her home and he said, "This is all there was. The baby that was crying. Nothing else." So when First Woman took it, it became a baby. Then she said, "this is . . ."

MS: Did she put it in her womb and carry it, or did she just—

HW: She just took it.

MS: She just took it and then it immediately became a baby?

HW: Uh-huh.

MS: OK.

HW: And she was dressed in white shell. That is why she was called White Shell Woman.[14]

The key difference between level one and level two is that on level two Changing Woman is not found as a fully formed baby. Talking God went to investigate the dark clouds seen over Gobernador Knob. At the base of the mountain, he heard a cry. He climbed to the peak and found the source of the crying. But instead of a baby girl, Talking God found an embryo, which he gave to First Man, who took it home to First Woman saying, "This is all there was. The baby that was crying. Nothing else." The embryo immediately transformed into a fully formed baby when First Man put it into First Woman's arms. Important information about the role of Navajo women and about Changing Woman's position in the Navajo cosmos is encoded in this version.

Because the embryo developed only after being placed in First Woman's arms, precedent was established for the role of women in Navajo society and human development. The primary culturally sanctioned role for women is that of nurturer. That is, Navajo women are to be mothers, whose most important responsibilities are to foster and sustain the development of children. Children will develop from embryo to fetus to infant, and on through all stages of life, only with the nurturance and guidance given by mothers. The primary relationship between mother and child is one of sustenance. On the basis of this link, the concept of mother extends to all factors in the world that contribute to the sustenance and development of human life. Therefore, as Gary Witherspoon has pointed out, the term for mother, *amá*, has a wide range of referents in the Navajo world, including "one's mother by birth, the earth, the sheep herd, the corn field and the mountain soil bundle."[15] Virtually anything that contributes to sustenance and development is a mother in the Navajo world.

Harry Walters summarized the fourth-level version of the Changing Woman story to demonstrate how subtle changes are made in story content in order to teach effectively at increasingly abstract levels of knowledge.

The fourth level, naayéé'jí hane', deals with the same [episode in the origin] story but [considers] stories that are associated with the Naayéé'jí ceremonies. Ceremonies like the Evil Way. The Crystal Gazing, Protection Way, uh, Hand Trembling, or Enemy Way. Red Ant Way, the Big Star Way, uh, or the Upward Moving Way. These are the Naayéé'jí ceremonies and then so they deal in a different [body of knowledge]. So the story would go like this, First Man heard a baby crying on the mountain, and he went up there and instead of finding a baby, he found a corn growing. It was a young corn, it must have been maybe about five or six inches high. And then underneath it was a corn beetle. And then, uh, he was surprised. And he reached down to pick up that corn beetle, and it turned into an embryo, an undeveloped embryo. And then, he took that and he brought that home to his wife, and he says, "This is all it was." And when she took that, it became a baby. And then so, she dressed her in White Shell, and she became known as White Shell Woman.[16]

At this level, the episode encodes information regarding the interconnection among all Navajo persons. In this account, it was First Man who investigated the strange phenomena seen on Gobernador Knob. As he climbed to the summit, he heard a different sound at each of the four directions: an undifferentiated cry in the east, a bird cry in the south, the cries of other birds in the west, and the sound of a corn beetle in the north. Upon reaching the top, he saw a dark cloud with a rainbow and falling rain. He looked again and saw a young corn plant; again, and saw a corn beetle, which turned into an undeveloped embryo as he picked it up. When he took the embryo home to First Woman, it developed into a baby in her arms. In this version, corn plants, corn beetles, and embryos are interchangeable. On the most abstract level of knowledge, all persons who live now or who have ever lived in the Navajo world are constructed of the same fundamental elements and structured on paradigms of directionality (sunwise movement and the trajectory of growth) and complementarity.

In both advanced versions of this episode, First Woman became the child's mother when she provided the sustenance for the embryo to develop into a baby. Once the baby was fully formed, First Woman dressed her in white shell. Thereafter, she was referred to as White Shell Girl until her puberty when she was given the name White Shell Woman or Changing Woman. White shell is the ntł'iz associated with the east, the direction also associated with dawn, spring, and, by extension, birth. Dressing the baby in this sacred material directly associates Changing Woman with the beginning of the day, the beginning of the annual cycle, and the beginning of life.

To make sure that I fully grasped the lesson, Walters moved on to the next episode in the Changing Woman story, the birth of the Twins and their slaying of the monsters. The level one version of this episode is as follows:

> In the third underworld some of the people engaged in abuses of their capacity to reproduce. These abuses included incest, adultery, masturbation and immodesty. The consequences of these abuses did not become apparent until the females started to give birth to various sorts of monsters that began to terrorize and devour the people. The capacity to properly reproduce was lost, and death and despair set in. To save the world and the people, First Man came up with a plan. . . . According to First Man's plan, Changing Woman would save the world by first restoring the power of reproduction, and secondly by giving birth to the Twins who would slay the monsters.[17]

With this version of the story in mind, I reasoned that because the "capacity to properly reproduce was lost," women had only been able to give birth to monsters after the separation of the sexes in the third underworld. Therefore, Changing Woman must have been the first well-formed entity created after the separation. I decided to ask Walters if this was so:

MS: Was she [Changing Woman] the first person that was not a monster after the separation of the sexes?

HW: No. There were babies that were born. That is what the—

MS: There were healthy babies that were born?

HW: That was what the monsters lived on.

MS: But, I thought that—

HW: All during the time that they were there. But the monsters were born right after, right after the separation. Not all of them, there were only twelve.

MS: There were only twelve monsters?

HW: Yes, not all women gave birth to monsters.

MS: I thought that the women lost their capacity for reproduction due to the sexual abuses that they engaged in during the separation of the sexes. So they weren't able to give birth to babies again, until Changing Woman was born, and she is the one that brought the capacity for reproduction back to—

HW: No!

MS: No?

HW: There were babies that were born during the time when the monsters were roaming. They would stop pregnant women, and they would ask them, "When are you due?" To make sure that they were there when they [delivered], because that is what they ate!

MS: Oh, so they were giving birth, but the monsters were eating them all, so that is why—

HW: Uh-huh.

MS: They had a capacity for reproduction but the children weren't surviving?

HW: Uh-huh. Now, see, what does that signify? See, that is the next level of teaching. Were there actually monsters?[18]

What? There were no monsters? By way of illustration, Walters was walking me through the steps of reasoning he takes as a modern Navajo scholar. He and other contemporary Navajo philosophers know the monsters are metaphors for something else. They reduce this episode to the essential problem: for some reason the children were not surviving. So, they reason, something was causing high levels of infant mortality. What was it?

> HW: Maybe they were, the women . . . they were infected with something where infant mortality was a hundred percent. That is why the population began to dwindle. See, that is another way of looking at it. That is another level. . . . Maybe because they were committing incestuous acts and all kinds of, uh, uh . . . .
> MS: Uh-huh.[19]

Perhaps the women were infected with a disease that caused the infants to die. On this level, the monsters represent the diseases or whatever was causing the high rates of infant mortality. They are metaphors for diseases and health problems. Walters continued, "Instead of monsters. So what Changing Woman did, she set laws and said, 'Now, this is the proper behavior, moral behavior. You follow these, you will have healthy babies.' See that is another level."[20]

He had moved on to the next level of abstraction, from monsters to diseases to immoral behavior. The story of the separation and subsequent reunion of men and women in the last underworld encapsulates important information about the male-female relations of all entities. It documents that neither sex can function or properly reproduce without the other. If infant deaths were caused by the incestuous acts and other sexual aberrations committed by the people at the time of the separation, then on this level the monsters represent moral dilemmas.

The reunion demonstrates that, although they are different, men and women are complementary—that is, necessary parts of a whole, with equally important roles and responsibilities. Changing Woman did not simply bring back the capacity for reproduction; she established order by demonstrating the contrasting yet complementary male and female principles that would come to be known, respectively, as *naayéé' k'ehjigo* (often shortened to *naayéé'jí*), "on the side of protection," and *hózhǫ́ǫ́jigo* (often shortened to *hózhǫ́ǫ́jí*), "on the side of peace, harmony, and order." To maintain the "natural order of the world, Changing Woman gave the Nihookáá Dine'é laws to govern "proper behavior, moral behavior." The monsters were born because of moral aberrations before and during the separation of men and women. The knowledge given to the Nihookáá Dine'é by Changing Woman and the other Holy People when this world was turned over to them was meant to guide future actions as well, so members of the Navajo world can avoid such problems. This knowledge enabled Navajo ancestors to have healthy children who would survive. To make sure I understood the lesson, Harry Walters asked me to paraphrase my new understanding:

> MS: So, it is not that she brought back the capacity for reproduction. She gave them something that was the ability to have healthy children that would survive?
>
> HW: Yes, yes.
>
> MS: And the monsters are metaphoric for something else?
>
> HW: Yes. Uh-huh, yes that is another way to look at it. See that is what I mean by different levels.
>
> MS: I know, I know, and most of the people that would talk to someone like me would give it to me at that level one.
>
> HW: Yeah, the elementary level.
>
> MS: But then,
>
> HW: That is gonna just read like a fairy tale.[21]

The gifts from the Holy People to the Nihookáá Dine'é—
the songs, prayers, ceremonies, and stories—continue to inform
the contemporary world. Across the vast Navajo reservation,
elders and teachers use the vivid narratives of Navajo oral history to teach Navajo people about their roles and responsibilities in the world. These compressed metaphoric accounts are
powerful tools that can illuminate, educate, and offer solutions
to the concerns of contemporary life. Because of the power
these narratives hold, access to the different levels of knowledge, as well as to specific bodies of knowledge, is controlled
by elders who limit individual exposure on the basis of various
factors, such as age, gender, and occupation.

MONSTERS IN THE CONTEMPORARY
WORLD: THE MYSTERY ILLNESS

My great-grandmother used to say that every disease that we
should ever encounter within this particular world was created at that time [during the separation of the sexes]. So, I
think sometimes you know like when I talk to my mother,
and father like about the AIDS epidemic, or of all these new
diseases happening, they are just saying that the prophecies
are coming true. Because you know, some of these particular things were subdued. They were laid to rest, and it was
said that they would come again when the people would
start doing the same kinds of practices. The same kind of
things that they did at the time, that is when they will reap-
pear again. And the people, if they are not keen enough to
understand their significance, it will do them in.[22]

At a press conference on 2 June 1993, Peterson Zah, then-
President of the Navajo Nation, announced that in addition to
the many "medical experts, physicians, investigators and offi-

cials" currently searching for answers regarding the mystery illness, the Navajo Nation was going to use the special services of
its own health professionals—Navajo medicine men.

> You know, Western medicine can only do so much. Western
> medicine has its limitations. And, we're going to call on
> some Navajo medicine people to help us analyze this situ-
> ation, to see if there are other avenues that are available
> to us, as a nation, so that we define what it is that's causing
> these deaths. And so we're not going to just heavily rely
> on all the statistics and data that are being gathered. Yes,
> we need those. But in certain situations, we have to rely
> on what we have lived with, traditionally, for all these
> years.[23]

As spokesperson for the Navajo Nation and the team of IHS
and CDC epidemiologists and other physicians working on the
case, Zah used this press conference to formally appeal to tribal
elders for help in solving the mystery illness.

The elders responded with characteristic candor and direct-
ness. Shortly after Zah's appeal, fifteen elderly healers met with
biomedical doctors at the Window Rock Civic Center to discuss
the crisis and possible causes and solutions. Some, such as Ben
Muneta, a Navajo trained as a biomedical epidemiologist, credited the convergence of the Navajo traditional medical system
and the biomedical system with directing the biomedical experts
to the cause of the mysterious illness. At the meeting, the Navajo
healers instructed the federal health investigators to sit and
listen. Having analyzed the situation in the context of Navajo
oral history, the elders told the investigators the cause of the
disease was disharmony in the Navajo world.

Excess of any kind is a form of disharmony. Excess rain and
snowfall in the winter of 1992 and the spring of 1993 had resulted
in an unusually wet year that brought an abundance of piñons

and new vegetation. The elders told the federal investigators that Navajo oral tradition mentions three times in this century when many Navajo people died or would die of sudden powerful diseases: 1918, 1933, and 1993. In each of these years, there was an exceptionally abundant piñon crop because of unusually wet winters and springs, and the rodent populations were also very high. Reference to the excess vegetation and rodent populations unraveled the mystery for the federal investigators.

Ben Muneta credits the traditional healers with cracking the case. Muenta recalls that at their meeting, the elders were "almost writing it on the wall for us."[24] The federal investigators constructed a theory for the cause of the illness based on abundant vegetation leading to an increase in the rodent population and an increased chance of exposure to rodents. CDC and IHS officials trapped rodents and began analysis of fecal and urine samples. In a matter of days, they had concluded that a form of hantavirus was responsible for the illness. Carried by deer mice in the Four Corners region, the virus is transmitted directly from rodents to humans either through contact with urine and saliva or through inhalation of dust infected with the virus.

Muneta sees a parallel between the theory constructed by federal investigators on the relationship of mice to humans and Navajo oral tradition. Navajo oral history dictates that humans and mice exist in two systems that must be kept totally apart: the outside/night world and the indoor/day world. The elders said that mice are considered to be "bearers of illnesses from ancient times if the two worlds mingle."[25] Mice are to be excluded from Navajo homes because illness from them can be transmitted through the air or upon contact. In the old days, Navajo families burnt clothes mice had touched. "The elders said this was because of saliva or droppings that may have gotten on the clothes."[26]

So parallels do exist between Navajo and biomedical views of deer mice as illness-bearing rodents. Although IHS and CDC officials credit the traditional healers with helping them find an answer to the disease, their explanation only fits the biomedical model for health, illness, and healing—not the Navajo model. Even though the cooperation of experts from the two systems narrowed the focus to mice, the two systems ultimately established very different causes and treatments for the illness. Experts from the biomedical world decided that hantavirus carried by deer mice was the cause, and they called for a reduction in the rodent population. Navajo experts maintained the disease represented monsters caused by disharmony, and they called for a return to the old ways.

These opposing views reflect a fundamental difference between biomedical and Navajo explanations for wellness, illness, and healing. Biomedical researchers seek a one-to-one correlation between cause—hantavirus carried by deer mice— and the symptoms of illness. Navajo experts do not deny a correlation exists, but they do not stop with such a simple one-to-one correlation between cause and symptom. Navajo theories are informed by history rather than by microbiology. As a result, many Navajo experts were not satisfied with biomedical answers. The elders searched for a deeper cause. They asked: Where did it come from? What caused the virus to come into the protected area of the Navajo world? How do we cope with it? Navajo experts turned to their history for the answers. For example, upon hearing the news that scientists had identified hantavirus as the probable cause of the illness, Navajo medicine man Earnest Becenti from Church Rock, New Mexico, stated emphatically, "There was no disease and it was no mystery. We didn't have to wait for scientists to tell us what happened. We know what it is. We brought it upon ourselves."[27]

THE PROPHECIES ARE COMING TRUE: "WE CREATED THOSE MONSTERS OURSELVES"

After the Four First Beings started for the east, First Woman turned her back and said: "When I wish to do so I will send chest colds and disease among the people; when I wish to do so I will send death, and the sign will be the coyote."[28]

The monsters that you probably have read about were created by us. They were not sicked on us by somebody from the outside. But we created those monsters ourselves, because first of all they manifested themselves within us. The monsters like selfishness, greediness, envy, hate, jealousy. All those things that we don't like about ourselves came out.[29]

We were warned by Changing Woman that the time would come when our clan system will be tampered with and then chaos would reign and giants will once again walk the earth.[30]

Elders claimed that the Navajo people had caused this crisis themselves by failing to do the things they were told to do by the Holy People in order for their way of life to continue. Lori Belone, a medicine woman from Tolani Lake, Arizona, told a reporter that she believed medical experts would never find a scientific cure for the mystery illness because the problem was caused by the Navajo people.[31] Earnest Becenti believed the cause of the mystery illness was that many of the young people were not following Navajo traditions. Nelson Dempsey, an elder from Indian Wells, Arizona, believed that the mystery illness was caused by the wrongdoings of the Navajo people. He said, "We are losing our traditional ways, youths no longer respect elders or each other, our ceremonies are being desecrated, commercialized, and the youth are involved in satanic cults."[32] In other words, the monsters, like those subdued by Changing Woman's hero sons, again walk the earth because the people are acting improperly. Becenti told reporters, "We need to get back into harmony."[33]

Elders such as Becenti called for a return to harmony because they attributed the disease to disharmony, a breakdown in the complex web of relationships fundamental to maintenance of the Navajo way of life. Illness results from disharmony or imbalance. Disharmony results from disruption of the proper relationships among all entities in the Navajo universe, as set forth in the charter given by the Holy People. Harmony must be restored for healing to occur. This involves the patient, the extended family, the clans, and ultimately, through kinship and association, the entire Navajo Nation. In the case of the mystery illness, elders saw the solution in the restoration of certain critical relationships.

The breakdown in the relationship between young Navajo and their culture and the breakdown in the proper relationship between Navajo people and Mother Earth are the problematic relationships cited most frequently by the majority of elders consulted about the mystery illness. Elders cited numerous contemporary activities exemplifying the breakdown and contributing to the crisis. These included performing summer ceremonial dances in "Song and Dance" contests throughout the year, telling portions of the origin story out of season, playing the Navajo shoe game after winter, selling artifacts and medicine bundles, and performing ceremonies in the sweat house with females present.[34]

Navajo elders told Muneta and other biomedical practitioners that the disease came because the Navajo "people have strayed from traditional beliefs and respect for nature."[35] Elders frequently note physical changes in the land that they believe reflect a breakdown in the proper relationship between Navajo and Mother Earth. The changes result from a wide range of

activities, including road and water projects, toxic waste dumping, and mining.[36] Mae Bekis of Tó'tsoh, Arizona, told me she
believed the illness had nothing to do with mice but was caused
by the uranium mining pits that have been torn into Mother
Earth for decades.[37] Each of these physical changes in the land
reflects defilement of Mother Earth and a breakdown in proper
relations. To restore proper relations, elders directed, "We must
first provide offerings to the earth, then perform the good way
ceremony. Not just one home—but all."[38] Because the entire
Navajo Nation was affected, all families had to participate in the
healing for harmonious relations to be restored. Planning and
performance of the Blessing Way ceremonies called for by the
traditional healers took cooperation and effort on the part of
dozens of people in every family.[39] As a result, the ceremonies
strengthened familial ties and relationships.

    Each of the problematic activities mentioned—"Song and
Dance" contests, telling origin stories out of season, lack of
respect for elders, and defilement of Mother Earth—represents
a breach in the contract between the Navajo and the Holy People.
Elders asked about the illness continually alluded to the charter given to the Navajo by the Holy People when the world was
turned over to the Navajo. The Navajo ancestors were told certain things that they and all future Navajo people were to abide
by, and they were warned that if they did not obey, bad things
would happen. The elders' view was that when the illness threat
finally subsided, the Navajo people would have to relearn to
respect their culture and traditional ways. "We must take it seriously, because we have nothing else."[40]

OUTCOMES

The mystery illness of 1993 was traumatic. It killed many people,
stealing their potential from the future of the Navajo Nation. It

is easy to highlight the negative aspects and the terror of this mysterious illness, as the media did, by focusing on the daily death toll and the anguish of the victims' families. By recalling and applying stories of their history, however, thousands of Navajo individuals were able to survive this trauma. They coped with it, lived through it, and tried to overcome it. Turning to their own history for viable solutions, elders and other experts used the illness as a teaching tool, placing it into the larger cultural context of Navajo history. The vivid narratives depicting the problems faced by Navajo ancestors—and the solutions they found—serve as a guide for contemporary Navajo life, teaching how to live in this world and how to cope when things go wrong.

Striking parallels exist between the mystery illness of 1993 and the monsters born to the women after the separation of the sexes in the last underworld. On an elementary level, there were monsters; on a more abstract level, there were diseases killing children, stealing the potential of youth from the Navajo as a people. Similarly, the mystery illness of 1993 killed many healthy young people, taking their potential from the Navajo Nation. On an elementary level, the Twins slew the monsters, thereby restoring the capacity for successful reproduction; on another level, the monsters as metaphors for diseases and health problems causing infant mortality were slain by cures for the diseases. On yet another abstract level, the monsters born to the women after the separation of the sexes represent immoral behavior. These monsters were slain with knowledge of rules for proper, moral behavior. Changing Woman set laws and said "Now, this is the proper behavior, moral behavior. You follow these, you will have healthy babies."[41] The correlations between the monsters born after the separation of the sexes and the mystery illness of 1993 led Navajo experts to conclude that this modern disease, a manifestation of improper, disharmonious behavior of contemporary Navajo, could be overcome only by knowledge and practice of proper, moral behavior.

When placed into the larger context of Navajo oral history, the mystery illness served as a means to account for and validate Navajo beginnings—the paradigms established in the origin stories and the charter given to the Navajo by the Holy People. Within this context, elders could use the illness to explain problems of the contemporary world—lack of interest on the part of young people in traditional ways, "Song and Dance" contests, telling origin stories out of season, lack of respect for elders, and defilement of Mother Earth—as the inevitable outcomes of the breakdown in the proper relationships prescribed by the Holy People. Elders also used the illness as an opportunity to predict the future by noting that Navajo people must relearn and respect Navajo culture and traditional ways to facilitate the restoration and maintenance of proper order and balance in the world.

Seeing the mystery illness in this light caused many Navajo to pause and rethink who they were and where they were going as a people. In some cases, interest in traditional ways was rekindled. In other cases, individuals reaffirmed personal commitment to keeping the Navajo way of life alive in the modern world. This personal reflection contributed to a restoration of proper relations in portions of the Navajo world. Yet the monsters continued to walk the earth: new cases of the mystery illness resulted in the death of three more Navajo people in the spring of 1994.[42] The challenges to life continue as life continues. Ultimately, monsters in the contemporary Navajo world can only be slain by acknowledging and applying the ancestral knowledge contained in Navajo oral history.

CHAPTER TWO

Navajo Relocation, 1974–1999

The law is really tearing us apart, tearing us away from our land.

NANCY WALTERS,
in Osawa, *In the Heart of Big Mountain*

I was born right here, and we are not going to move one inch. They'll have to jail me first. If they want to build me a home, they can build it right here. I was born and raised here, my cord is here. . . . I don't want to live any place but here.

BLANCHE WILSON,
in Kammer, *The Second Long Walk*

Poignant verbal and visual images of individuals of all ages caught in the throes of the largest forced relocation of American citizens since the internment of Japanese-Americans during World War II have captured and held the collective imagination of the American public for more than two decades. Navajo opposing enforcement of Public Law 93-531 (the Navajo-Hopi Land Settlement Act of 1974) and refusing to leave Hopi Partitioned Land (HPL) in the former Joint Use Area have offered sincere pleas and a tradition-based rationale for their position.

Cross-cultural misunderstandings abound. On the one hand, it has been difficult for many Euro-Americans, accustomed to moving for career or educational purposes, to comprehend the Navajo sense of place. Outsiders are frequently baffled by Navajo reluctance to give up a dirt floor *hooghan*, "traditional Navajo home," with no running water or electricity, for a new house with modern conveniences. It has been equally difficult for Navajo elders, who have come into contact with various non-Navajo (journalists, lawyers, volunteers) involved at one level or another in the relocation, to understand why Euro-Americans relocate *simply* to attain or augment material wealth. Noting this contrast, Katherine Smith of Big Mountain, Arizona, draws on Navajo philosophy to explain her profound connection to the land in terms of the relationship between mother and child.

> We are not like that [referring to the Euro-American propensity to move]. We just live on this, in these six sacred mountains all the time, all of our life. When you are in the pregnant, you are inside of your mother. You got your mother's breath and it's the same with the Big Mountain, that way. It is my breath. See, I was born around the Big Mountain and so that is my mother too. So, all of my life, I just will always be thinking of this place. My spirit is going to be here forever.[1]

This attachment to place—first established during the prenatal stage of life and reaffirmed at every step on the path toward full Navajo personhood—is solidified shortly after birth through burial of the umbilical cord. This act anchors an individual to a particular place, providing a lifelong spiritual and historical connection to one's home, the importance of which is implicitly understood in the Navajo world. Contemporary Navajo from all walks of life find occasion in a variety of circumstances to refer to the places where their umbilical cords are buried, and whether they are politicians seeking re-election or people facing relocation, Navajo men and women frequently refer to those places as "home."

Forced relocation from one's true home, such as that mandated by PL 93-531, can have grave results for Navajo people because, as Jerry Kammer notes, "They believe that their minds can be fully at rest only at the place where their umbilical cords are buried. They believe that if they move away, their minds will return to that place."[2] Some, such as Jack Hatathlie of Coal Mine Mesa, Arizona, believe that if this profound connection were fully explained to the proper authorities, people would be allowed to stay.

> My umbilical cord is buried here on the land near Crow Spring. It is buried in a sheep corral. It was buried in a sheep corral so that I would like and make a living with livestock. . . . We also, as parents, did that for our children. Some of their umbilical cords are buried in the sheep corral. . . . We belong here. . . . Our way of life is here. Maybe if we tell them about our way of life, maybe they'll understand us. They should try to understand Native people. All Native people have their own teachings and way of life.[3]

Despite this topic's visibility in the media and the foregrounding of Navajo narratives in several works on the subject, this rationale given by Navajo relocatees and resisters has been strangely muted.[4] Time after time, Navajo like Blanche Wilson, Nancy Walters, Katherine Smith, and Jack Hatathlie, with whom chroniclers of this ongoing crisis in federal government/American Indian relations have consulted, refer to their profound connections to their mother, the earth. Clearly, for these people attachment to the land goes beyond mere sentiment to actual physical and social connections that are components of their personhood. Consequently, forced relocation constitutes a breach of personhood—a severing of the vital connection between an individual and a place. Yet to date, these references have been given only secondary consideration by scholars, journalists, and film producers.[5] As a result, no systematic analysis of Navajo perceptions of this connection—this vital link—has been undertaken.

Careful attention to the comments of Navajo affected by PL 93-531—references to home as the place "where my umbilical cord is buried," to their senses of "connection to the earth," and to the debilitating effects resulting from breach of this association—reveals profound reasons for the strong reactions on the part of these people asked to leave their homes. Their reactions in turn shed light on some of the complex, contested points of view about the cultural construction of all persons in the Navajo world and raise new issues about forced relocation.[6] Disruption of the vital associations people have with their matrilineal homes—sometimes their places of birth, often the locations where their umbilical cords are buried—can have grave effects because all Navajo persons are constructed according to the principles established by the Navajo Holy People: homology, complementarity, and synecdoche.

These concepts structure the relationship of parts to the whole in a world constructed according to paradigms set forth in the Navajo origin story. Parts share similar structure (homology). Wholes are made up of dual integrated components (complementarity). And every part is equivalent to the whole, so that anything done to or by means of a part is held to have influence upon the whole (synecdoche). As a result, Navajo tradition dictates that the vital connection between an individual and parts of his or her body—the afterbirth, sloughed off skin

cells contained in bath and shampoo rinse waters, the umbilical cord—and his or her matrilineal home should never be severed under any circumstance. The philosophical underpinnings
that govern Navajo views on the cultural construction of the
human body, personhood, and effect provide a context from
within which information gleaned from the personal narratives
of those Navajo who have been most intimately affected by this
turn of events can be better understood.

THE NAVAJO-HOPI LAND DISPUTE

The so-called Navajo-Hopi land dispute stems from President
Chester Arthur's executive order of 1882 that granted 2.5 million acres of land around the Hopi mesas for the Hopi and
"such other Indians as the Secretary of the Interior may see fit
to settle thereon." This wording was highly problematic because
the reserved area included land where hundreds of Navajo people had been living for generations, and although the Navajo
were not specifically mentioned in this executive order, they
were not specifically excluded either.

Since 1891, numerous attempts have been made to reconcile
by legal means boundary conflicts between the Hopi and Navajo
families living in this area. In 1962, a federal court awarded
exclusive title (both surface and subsurface rights) to grazing
district 6—the area encompassing all of the Hopi villages except
Moenkopi and relatively little land on which Navajo resided—
to the Hopi. This executive order ruled that the remaining 1.8
million acres of the 1882 reservation was jointly owned by the
Navajo and Hopi tribes, including both surface and subsurface
rights. This area became known as the Joint Use Area.

This legislation did not resolve the dispute. Beginning in
1972, it resulted in mandatory Navajo livestock reductions and
a moratorium on construction of any new homes, schools, and

health care facilities, or any new infrastructure such as roads and power lines, or any new commercial development, without the consent of both tribes. Ultimately, it led to the partition of the land in 1974.

Because partition mandated the relocation of all members of either tribe living in the area granted to the other, over ten thousand Navajo and one hundred Hopi were slated for compulsory relocation. Despite the commitment of enormous amounts of time and money (totaling nearly 350 million federal dollars) toward resolution by both tribes and the federal government, this dispute remains unresolved.

The Navajo-Hopi Settlement Act was signed into law in October of 1996. It contains an Accommodations Agreement whereby Navajo families remaining on HPL were given the option either to sign up for relocation or to sign a seventy-five-year lease with the Hopi by 31 March 1997. According to Roman Bitsuie, Executive Director of the Navajo-Hopi Land Commission within the Navajo government, at the time of this writing all but approximately thirteen or fourteen of the Navajo homesites on HPL had either applied for relocation or signed a lease agreement.[7] Under the latter option, leaseholders are granted: a grazing permit; use of a three-acre homesite with a maximum of ten-acres of farmland, access to rangeland for grazing livestock (the exact amount is dependent on the available land in the area), and use of land for diverse traditional activities ranging from gathering herbs to visiting sacred sites; and permission to make repairs on existing structures or to construct new ones within the homesite. The terms of the lease agreement are of concern to some of the affected Navajo people in part because they prohibit Navajo burials on HPL, and they place leaseholders and their families under Hopi criminal and civil jurisdiction while leaving issues such as probate, domestic relations, child custody, and Navajo benefits and services under Navajo jurisdiction.[8] Ongoing discussions between those who have signed lease agreements and representatives of the Hopi tribe attempt to clarify the terms of the Accommodation Agreement in regard to access to or protection of sacred sites, as well as burial and land use issues.[9]

ANTHROPOLOGICAL PERSPECTIVES ON THE BODY AND EFFECT

Interest in the influence events can have on the health and well-being of people has a long history in anthropology. Victorian scholars, who in their attempts to understand all known human beliefs and behaviors sought to reduce complex phenomena to underlying laws and/or to dovetail them into grand evolutionary paradigms, investigated these effects under the rubrics of magic and/or religion. Three "laws of sympathetic magic" were observed in societies throughout the world—similarity, opposition, and contagion. These "laws" were believed to be windows into the human mind, representing universal principles of thought.[10]

The "law of similarity" maintains that "like produces like"— if rain is needed, pouring water out will produce it. The "law of opposition," closely tied to the law of similarity, maintains that opposites work on opposites.[11] The "law of contagion" maintains that "things that have once been in contact continue ever afterwards to act on each other."[12] The last of these is based on the principle of synecdoche—the identification of the part with the whole.

The principle of synecdoche holds that people, objects, and other entities that come into contact may influence each other through the transfer of some or all of their properties.

> Teeth, saliva, sweat, nails, hair represent a total person, in such a way that through these parts one can act directly

on the individual concerned, either to bewitch or enchant him. Separation in no way disturbs the contiguity; a whole person can even be reconstituted or resuscitated with the aid of one of these parts: *totum ex parte*.[13]

Put another way, "the personality of a being is indivisible, residing as a whole in each one of the parts."[14] Connection remains in force even after separation. Therefore, the potential for influence continues after the physical contact has ended, and it may be permanent. Moreover, this connection can extend the physical limits of the person to include "[e]verything which comes into close contact with the person—clothes, footprints, the imprint of the body on grass or in bed, the bed, the chair, everyday objects of use, toys, and other things."[15] This extension of personhood on the basis of synecdoche is crucial to the Navajo construction of the human body and the rules governing effect.[16]

Classic anthropological investigations into such influences have tended to focus narrowly on restrictions surrounding exposure to menstrual blood and the use of parts of the body, bodily fluids, and offal in witchcraft.[17] Anthropological studies of menstruation and menstrual substances have focused on limitations placed on the activities of women, to the exclusion of other explanations for menstrual restrictions and prohibitions.[18] To date, studies of witchcraft and sorcery have tended to focus on the role these practices play in social control, maintenance of social distance and economic distinctions, relief of psychological tensions, or on the reasons for the existence of such "bizarre" behaviors among millions of contemporary people.[19]

There are several problems with these classic studies. For instance, in many cases the ideologies and rituals associated with parts of the body and bodily substances have been extracted and analyzed separately from their cultural context. Focusing on menstrual blood and the parts of the body used in witchcraft and neglecting to study other bodily substances that can affect people, these studies have tended to highlight the polluting or dangerous effects of the substances and thereby have ignored their potential beneficial influences. Research on the Navajo is no exception.[20] Most prior studies did not fully explore the complex rules defining who or what can affect what or whom in particular circumstances, or what these effects might tell us about the cultural construction of the human body, self, and personhood in the societies under investigation. Such analyses have predominated because until more recently the body's centrality was either taken for granted, or, as some have argued, largely ignored.[21]

Nevertheless, for pioneers in the anthropology of the body, the human body was the symbol par excellence—a universally important means of metaphoric expression, communicating information for and from the social realm. Scholars such as Mary Douglas and Victor Turner found that bodily conditions were inextricably linked to classifications of the world, yet they took very different stances on that relationship.[22] In their analyses, the body, bodily boundaries, and bodily products conversely mirror or classify the world. In the Navajo world "symbolic statements about the supernatural-natural world provide the basic paradigm for interpreting bodily processes of health and illness."[23] The philosophical principles enshrined in oral history, which govern the construction of the Navajo universe, stand as paradigms for understanding the human body and bodily processes. Thus, Navajo understandings of the body and bodily experiences are cultural constructs—rather than natural or biological facts.

THE CULTURAL CONSTRUCTIONIST PERSPECTIVE

[T]he body has been, and still is, constructed in almost as many ways as there are individuals; it seems to be all things to all people. Thus the body is defined as good or bad; tomb or temple; machine or garden; cloak or prison; sacred or secular; friend or enemy; cosmic or mystical; one with mind and soul or separate; private or public; personal or the property of the state; clock or car; to varying degrees plastic, bionic, communal; selected from a catalogue or engineered; material or spiritual; a corpse or the self.[24]

Until relatively recently, the human body has remained "virtually invisible to the vast majority of sociocultural anthropologists,"[25] while most anthropologists specifically interested in the body, health, or illness accepted that the physical body fell "naturally" into the domain of the physical sciences—that is, outside the scope of social and cultural anthropology.[26] Theoretical insights since the 1970s, however, have disenfranchised Western science in general and biomedical constructions of the body, health, and illness specifically.[27] As Michel Foucault has demonstrated, even anatomists do not observe a universal biological body through dissection, because the clinical gaze is a cultural gaze.[28] Moreover, anatomical constructs of internal organs, such as images of female reproductive organs as inverted versions of male organs, are cultural constructs that serve to resolve ideological problems in the social and political realms.[29]

This decentering of biomedical views is rooted in the idea that the meanings attached to the body—its boundaries, substances, and essences—are constructed on the basis of cultural understandings rather than universal physiological facts. It can no longer be assumed that "dialectics exist between an infinity of cultures and a universal biology," but rather it has been realized that a multitude of dialectics exist "between cultures and local biologies."[30] Cultural constructionists accept the body as culturally shaped, constrained, and invented. Focus on bodily representation of social meanings has opened up studies of the influence of substances and events and thereby generated new insights into the cross-cultural variation in constructions of the body and bodily experience. Accounts of fluid, boundless, and elusive bodies have proliferated.[31]

The discounting of purely biomedical explanations of biology and human experience has revealed the idea of the self to be yet another cultural construct and has resulted in new understandings of the cross-cultural variation in constructions of the self and individual experience.[32] Consequently, over the last few decades, the classic anthropological opposition between the self—the awareness of oneself as a "perceptible object"—and the person as a social construct has blurred.[33]

Groundbreaking studies based on research carried out in Melanesian, Southeast Asian, and African societies have shed light on the role of effect in the development of bodies, selves, or persons cross-culturally and on how personhood can be extended to entities that might be considered "inanimate" in Euro-American worldviews. Anthropological analyses that began to appear in the 1970s, acknowledging the complex role effects from exposure to bodily substances or other events can play in the development of bodies and persons, continue to offer new insights.[34] In combination, these various accounts have resulted in a shift from a focus on the "body" or "self" per se to a focus on the whole *living* body, the "person."

NAVAJO VIEWS OF PERSONHOOD

See, everything that we see, everything that my mother sees around her, is an animate object. She can't hardly relate to the, to earth or anything else around her as an inanimate object, because everything around here is alive to her. And so, in that way she sees this, this earth as a part of her, it is alive, in a philosophical sense.[35]

In the Navajo world, where nonhuman entities—baskets, houses, and Mother Earth—have qualities of personhood, the attachment to place is inalienable from the definition of life. Harry Walters clarified this point when I asked him what defines "being alive" in the Navajo philosophy and theory of life. He told me that "for living things it is to have your foot, to have your feet, planted into the earth and your head in the sky. In your Mother Earth and Father Sky. Everything that is alive has its feet planted in the earth and its head in the sky. Birds, plants, animals, insects, people. So this is what determines what life is."[36]

On the broadest level, the Navajo sense of place is defined by the parameters for Navajo sacred space established by the Diyin Dine'é. Because the universe preceded human existence, and the space within which Navajo life is lived is structurally organized on the paradigms established in the origin stories, understanding of the principles of Navajo philosophical orientation underlying the cultural construction of the human body, personhood, and effect, can only come through consideration of this ancient knowledge.

The columns of clouds at the cardinal points of the First World contained the elements fundamental to life in the Navajo world—moisture, air, substance, and heat. These elements are finite in quantity and in a constant state of flux. They have been continually formulated and reformulated in a perpetual process of transformation since the First World.[37]

After their emergence onto the surface of this world, the Diyin Dine'é used these primordial elements in various formulations to construct entities to fill this newly demarcated world. As Walters notes in the following passage, these primary elements were and are the seeds for all past and future creation. All persons who live or have ever lived in the Navajo world—plants, baskets, humans—have been constructed of these elements.

> HW: The element, the element is, it is in everything. It is holy. When you put it together in a certain composition it is a human. And [when] it is put together in a

certain composition, it is a tree. And [in] another certain composition, it is an insect.

MS: Now, I see what you mean, OK.

HW: Yes. And then . . . when those die and go back, and
then we drink the same water, we breathe the same air,
and we eat the food from the earth. And then all of these
things, the elements come together and where they are
put together there is life again. The elements are the
seeds, the plants, so that is the cycle right there. See? It
is a cycle.[38]

Moisture, air, substance, and heat are not all that is needed
for life to exist. Every life form constructed through reformulation of the primary elements is permeated by vibration in the
form of sound (language) or movement. This fifth element—
vibration—is also necessary for life.

Individual persons such as looms, humans, and houses are
constructed from a variety of manifestations of these basic elements, depending on the specific entity under construction.
Regardless of the particular form these elements may take, one
thing remains constant: some type of moisture, air, substance,
heat, and vibration must be included in the formulation for life
to exist. When constructing the first Nihookáá Dine'é, Changing
Woman followed the paradigms established by the Holy People
in the construction of the world at the place of emergence. The
human body is, therefore, a homologue of the Navajo universe,
composed of the same primordial elements as all other Navajo
persons and sharing structure including sunwise direction and
complementarity.

THE FIRST NIHOOKÁÁ DINE'É

From the beginning of the basket, when the earth was created, when the universe was created, when the sun was

created, when Changing Woman came into being, turquoise basket existed, white shell basket existed. They were
used then. Obsidian basket and crystal basket were used.
The Holy People used these baskets to create us. We were
created as the first Earth Surface People. . . . Changing
Woman and the Holy People did it; created us.[39]

Changing Woman is mother to all Nihookáá Dine'é on several
levels. Beyond continuing to nurture and sustain them today as
the inner form of the very earth from which their ancestors
emerged, she constructed them here on the earth's surface
from her own flesh, corn, and the precious stones and shells
associated with each of the cardinal points in Navajo cosmology. Oral historians recount several different processes of generation that brought the primordial Navajo into existence,
including transformation of figurines or corn, asexual creation
from Changing Woman's flesh and a mixture of other materials, and eventually heterosexual reproduction, the means by
which Nihookáá Dine'é continue to multiply. In most versions
of this portion of Navajo oral history, the substance used in the
creation of humans was Changing Woman's own flesh, rubbed
from the surface of her breast, back, shoulders, sides, and arms.
She molded this substance, alone or in combination with ground
corn or ntł'iz, into soft cylindrical or round forms. The first
humans were animated by the air and vibration of Changing
Woman's voice, by the combined song of Changing Woman
and other Diyin Dine'é, or by holy winds.[40] These winds slipped
between the buckskins, blankets, or sheets of moisture covering the modeled Nihookáá Dine'é and entered their bodies.

On the most abstract of the twelve levels of knowledge inherent to Navajo philosophy, all humans are constructed of the
same fundamental elements, linked by tropological structures
including homology and complementarity, permeated by vibration in the form of sound or movement, and possessed of the

same senses and anatomical components as all other persons in the Navajo world.[41] The complete Navajo person is made up of numerous integrating parts: the physical outer form, the inner form, the body surface, body prints, the "anchoring cord," the power of movement, garments, hair, and the "feather of life." The physical outer form is animated by the inner form, which is made up of intertwined winds. Navajo people are connected to Mother Earth by the impressions left in the ground by their hands, their feet, and their reclining bodies, as well as their "anchoring cords," and to Father Sky by the "feather of life" at the top of their heads.[42] Made in the image of the first Nihookáá Dine'é who were constructed here on the earth's surface out of the primordial elements used to construct all life in this world— moisture, air, substance, heat, and vibration—contemporary Navajo people are homologues of the Navajo universe. Yet, every newly formed Nihookáá Dine'é must be guided at each step on the path to Navajo personhood, including the steps taken to affirm personal association with the matrilineal home.

DEVELOPING AN ATTACHMENT TO PLACE

I was told, you know, wherever you were born, wherever your little cord was cut, you know, always remember that, with a smoke there and pray for yourself. I do that every now and then. I know the spot where I first hit the earth. In spirit, you know, in my mind and down deep in my heart, I am from Big Mountain and I will probably die thinking that way.[43]

In addition to the initial establishing of the connection, during the prenatal stage of life, between an individual and a particular place, the vital connection to one's matrilineal home is reaffirmed throughout life. The principle of synecdoche dictates that a lifelong bond exists between detached parts of the body—skin cells, fingernail clippings, saliva, hair—and the person from whom they originated. Consequently, people must demonstrate personal responsibility over parts of their own bodies, and adults must exercise responsibility over those of children. The Navajo cultural system dictates that particular parts of the body—afterbirth, blood, and umbilical cords—hold the most potential to influence the body or cause an effect upon it and that the human body is more open to influence at critical times in the life cycle—in utero, at birth, at puberty, and during pregnancy. Navajo people use their understandings of the Navajo philosophical system to make choices on a day-to-day basis to maximize positive, nurturing effects and minimize debilitating influences on themselves, their loved ones, and their world. Family members foster an attachment to place in developing Navajo persons through manipulations and treatments at the critical points in the life cycle. Thus, at every step from birth to death the connection between individual and place is reaffirmed in the action and process of contemporary living.

Regardless of their stage in life, Navajo in need of ceremonies return to their matrilineal homes to have rites performed under the sponsorship of concerned relatives. This allows waters used in ceremonial shampoos and baths to be poured out near a person's true home. In addition, various manipulations of the detached parts of the bodies of children are completed by concerned adults after birth and at puberty to solidify and reaffirm the individual's attachment to place. Four days after the close of the Kinaaldá (the puberty ceremony), a young woman's hair must be ritually washed at dawn. The female relative assisting her in this process is directed to save the rinse water and pour it out next to the young woman's home so that "she will always be drawn back home."[44] Moreover, detached parts of a newborn's body are usually buried near its mother's matrilineal home shortly after birth.

Staff at reservation hospitals are sensitive to family concerns over the care and disposal of parts of an infant's body.[45] Particular concern focuses on the placenta, the water used in the child's first bath, and the umbilical cord. Placentas are taken home from the hospital to be buried so they can "become one with Mother Earth again."[46] Placentas are most frequently buried in a deep hole in the ash pile north of the family hooghan or in a badger hole.[47] The placenta may also be placed in a live bush, buried beneath a juniper or pinyon tree, where it is "put away" with a cornmeal blessing, or placed in another location of special significance to the family.[48] If the child remains in the hospital for an extended period due to complications in childbirth, prematurity, birth defects, or illness, hospital staff will save the umbilical cord when it detaches from the child and give it to the mother to take home.[49]

UMBILICAL CORDS

When the umbilical cord has dried so that it can be taken from the infant, it must not be thrown out where an animal might get it, as it is considered part of the child and has symbolic control over its destiny.[50]

Placement of a child's umbilical cord has a profound effect on the child's future occupation and personal proclivities. It also establishes a child's relationship to his or her physical landscape, anchoring the individual to Mother Earth and to a specific place. The Navajo system governing the cultural construction of personhood dictates that the umbilical cord be placed in a location considered by the parents and grandparents to be most beneficial to the child's future.

When a family wants a boy to be good with livestock, the parents or grandparents bury his cord in a corral, tie it to the tail or mane of a horse, or tie it to a sheep.[51] A boy's cord is buried in the family fields when they want him to be concerned with farming.[52] A girl's cord is buried underneath the place where the loom is erected in the family hooghan if they want her to become an expert weaver.[53] A family in need of a shepherd will bury a girl's cord in the sheep corral to insure that her thoughts are with the livestock.[54] They bury a girl's cord inside a hooghan, or outside under the ground near the home if the family does not live in a hooghan, when they want the girl to become a good homemaker.[55]

Regardless of the particular place selected by the family, it is of the utmost importance that a child's dried and detached umbilical cord be anchored to something of substance—a horse, a loom, or Mother Earth—and not lost or left somewhere inside the home. Such anchoring is paramount because loss or misplacement of a cord can result in lifelong disorientation or antisocial behavior. Flora Bailey was told by a consultant that if a boy's cord was lost, "the boy runs around and is no good."[56] Dorothea Leighton and Clyde Kluckhohn were told that if the cord is kept in a sack in the hooghan, the child will steal.[57] To avoid such problems, parents and grandparents take great care in the placement of umbilical cords. The majority of people I consulted stated that in their families the cords of new members were buried in auspicious places. I was told that umbilical cords were intended to be buried because this "anchors the baby to the earth."[58]

Burial of the cord in the earth anchors the child to the "belly button" of Mother Earth and establishes a lifelong connection between the person and a place, just as the cord anchors a child to its mother when it is in her womb and establishes a lifelong connection between mother and child. The presence of this anchoring effect is evidenced by the spirals on the human body, which represent a continuous connection from Mother Earth to the person. This connection traverses the body, beginning at the navel and continuing to the spirals at the back of the top of the head, from which it extends out of the top of the head.[59] The spirals at the navel and the top of the back of the head demonstrate the path of this connecting cord, which is most frequently anchored to Mother Earth. As Sunny Dooley points out, a direct correlation exists between the spirals found on the human body and the spirals found at the center of ts'aa' (ceremonial baskets), which represent the "belly button" of the earth (see figure 2).

> SD: This particular crevice at the bottom right here [pointing to the spiral at the center of a ceremonial basket], they will say it is the "belly button" of the earth. And, the umm, I don't know what you call it, but on the top of your head? Up here.
>
> MS: The spiral, the whorl that is on the top of your head?
>
> SD: This, the whorl, that is where that particular thing concludes. So it is sort of like a beginning and the ending for that. . . . It just represents that you are blessed with life, because this is like a basket of life. And you are living within the belly button of your mother, the earth. So, it is sort of like a bottom and a top. It is not really considered a bottom or a top, but it is just an entity, that, you know, like when you think of a screw? Maybe, like you are screwed into the earth? Do you know what I mean?
>
> MS: I see, OK, so the spiral represents your being screwed into the earth. I like that.[60]

The act of burying a child's cord securely "screws" or anchors that person to a particular locale. In the modern world, where economics compel most Navajo adults to work away from home, people feel a profound sense of belonging to the locations where their cords are buried, and they return as often as

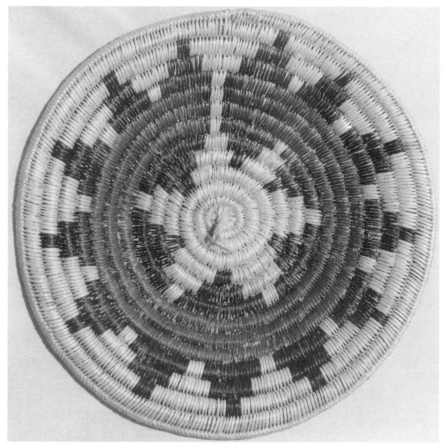

Figure 2. Navajo Basket

possible during weekends and vacations. Many feel it is contrary to the "natural order" for the connection between individual and place to be severed under any circumstance. For example, in a letter to the editor published in the *Navajo Times* on 12 May 1994, Mervyn Tilden, a resident of the Fort Wingate Indian Village in Church Rock, New Mexico, protested his impending eviction on the grounds that he had an inalienable connection to this location because this was where his children's umbilical cords were buried. In the following excerpt, he points out that like the monsters born because of moral aberrations that took place before, during, and after the separation of the sexes in the last underworld, monstrous giants currently walk the earth because the laws for proper behavior established by Changing Woman to maintain the natural order of the Navajo world are not being observed.

> My reasons here are many. Spiritually and historically, my children's umbilical cords are buried near my home according to our Diné [Navajo] traditional beliefs and this has always been "home." As we wait on the Chapter's eviction notice, we see a giant before us with chaos following close behind. Relocation is not the Navajo way and is in contradiction to Changing Woman's Law and Hózhǫ́ǫ́jí, the "Beauty Way," for it is physical, spiritual, and cultural genocide.[61]

Subsequently, in a response to a 10 April 1995 request from the Church Rock Chapter Planning Committee for all occupants of his condemned apartment complex to vacate the premises, Tilden correlated the rise in gangs, drugs, and violence among reservation youth and the abandonment or destruction of umbilical cord sites resulting from development, forced relocation, or, as in his case, eviction.

There is still no answer to another question I've been asking for years which is: "who will take responsibility for the destruction of my children's umbilical sites and what is the justification?" I absolutely refuse to abandon their sites by my home. With their aggression in this matter is it any wonder why we are losing our youth to gangs, drugs, violence, etc.? Such Navajo career politicos who are responsible for these acts of cultural genocide only contribute to the demise of our God-given rights and heritage as Diné (Navajo) people.[62]

Tilden's statements clearly demonstrate how the connection between an individual and a place is solidified through the act of burying a person's umbilical cord at that location and how, as was documented a half century ago, loss, misplacement, or mishandling of a cord can result in the kind of disorientation or antisocial behavior experienced by many of the Navajo who have been relocated off HPL.

ILLNESS, PROBLEM DRINKING, AND DESPAIR

I ain't leaving this place alive. My roots are way down in the land and my feeling for living is in it too.[63]

Washington [the federal government] says, "Go away. Go some place else. Go walk among people and places you don't know." We're not hard enough to survive in places that we are not familiar with. If we leave here, we will grieve *for* our homeland and it will kill us.[64]

We are undergoing all sorts of pressure day and night. When you are under such pressure, men and women are dying off. We are suffering all kinds of losses—human losses.[65]

The personal narratives of those slated for relocation are replete with anguish. Summarizing the sentiment of those facing disconnection from their homes, Ruth Benally of Big Mountain, Arizona, said, "Are you trying to kill us? Moving away from here would be dying a slow death."[66] Such "slow death" results from being cut off from the personal renewal attained from communion with one's special area within Navajo sacred space. As Deezbaa' June of Big Mountain, Arizona, pointed out, visits to one's matrilineal home offer opportunities for personal rejuvenation.

> You consider any job site as an artificial setting. When we do come back over here [to Big Mountain], you know, we sense that permanence. And it gives us a sense of rejuvenation, new hope, a new horizon. And sometimes we have a Blessingway ceremony, ceremonies with my mother. She might light a pipe. And so there is a real sense of rejuvenating life itself in many ways. This is our place, our place of birth—we're bound to this land here.[67]

Relocatees who are denied access to their matrilineal homes are deprived of the nurturing effects of this experience, and the lives of Navajo remaining on HPL are riddled with anxiety over the impending loss of this access. The physical, social, and mental costs of such prolonged stress are staggering. The mental health division of the Indian Health Service on the Navajo reservation reports that Navajo facing relocation request psychological counseling at much higher rates than Navajo people living on Navajo Partitioned Land (NPL).[68] In addition, studies show that within the first five years after the passage of PL 93-531, 25 percent of Navajo relocatees lost their homes after using them as collateral for loans. Relocatees frequently "experience family instability, health problems, depression, and suicide attempts."[69]

Personal narratives poignantly capture the pain and grief endured by people after leaving their homes. Descriptions of the disorientation, illness, and social problems put a face on the experiences of relocatees: "Sometimes I sit up late at night and smoke my pipe and think about it, because it hurts all over."[70] "I think of home a lot. . . . I think and dream about that place where I once had my sheep. . . . I also think about my ancestor that walked that land. This worries me, this troubles me."[71] "Worrying about relocation made my blood [pressure] go up."[72] By Navajo accounts, the disorientation resulting from forced relocation has driven many to seek comfort through the "numbness of alcohol."[73] As Mae Tso of Dinnebito, Arizona, explained,

> This is the way it has become for us. I worry about it, and I can't sleep because of it. I have become sick. Some have lost hope completely. There is such cause for depression. Only when I think firmly that I will remain here am I well in my mind. If I was beaten unconscious or put to sleep, then maybe I would be taken to the place where we are supposed to move to. But it would not be of my own will, and as soon as I was awake I would get up and come back to this place.[74]

Furthermore, Navajo narratives suggest that the long-range debilitating effects resulting from forced relocation will extend far beyond the lives of relocatees. For example, while discussing problems experienced by herself and her husband since relocating off HPL, Mabel Begay from Coal Mine Mesa, Arizona, told Kammer, "My husband and I are worried *about the land* from where we moved. We are not eating well, nor are we sleeping. We are very depressed. We realize what we have done to ourselves."[75] Mabel Begay's reference to her worry *about* the land, like the plea of the unidentified woman in *Broken Rainbow* that if forced to relocate "we will grieve *for* our homeland," reveals that in the view of some Navajo people, forced relocation threatens the health and longevity of Mother Earth and the Navajo relocatees.[76] Navajo testify that the requisite ceremonies—prayers and offerings of ntł'iz or tádídíín—routinely conducted at sacred sites, as well as the ceremonies routinely conducted at matrilineal homes, serve to rejuvenate these locations. As a part of Mother Earth, each customary use area is dependent on the nurturing of members of the Navajo family given stewardship over it, people who are intimately connected with that place through incorporation of detached parts of their bodies—umbilical cords, afterbirths, skin cells—into various sites surrounding their matrilineal homes.

FINDINGS

All I can see in my mind is, I see the land and I see the people. I see, ahh, the homes that are there, you know, a lot of things that are familiar, you know, the livestock, landmarks. When you think about relocation, I just think about who's dying. Our religion revolves around the land. Our prayers are in with, are tied to the earth *here*. In a sense the government is pointing the gun at their heads and saying, well, "You leave," you know. So they're saying that your prayers are not important, "Move from this land." So if they go to another place, there is yes, the earth there, but it is not the same thing because Big Mountain is, it is a sacred mountain and there is a Navajo shrine up there. And, um, once you separate them, they will die.[77]

Consideration of the various methods used to influence children—prenatally and throughout childhood—as well as the
actions taken by Navajo adults on behalf of themselves, shows
that the vital connection between every Navajo and her or his
matrilineal home is established through burial of the afterbirth
and the umbilical cord, and through careful disposal of the
waters saved from a child's first bath whenever possible. This
connection is reaffirmed throughout life by disposal of bath
and shampoo rinse waters during or following ceremonies and
by ceremonies conducted during visits to this special location.
Thus, Nancy Walters's claim that PL 93-531 is "tearing us apart"
affirms that forced relocation constitutes a breach of personhood—a denial of the vital physical and social connections
between an individual and his or her true home, which are
components of every Navajo.

The principle of synecdoche dictates that separation of Navajo
from these places does not disturb the contiguity between an
individual and his or her umbilical cord or other detached parts
of his or her body. But, as pointed out by Mervyn Tilden, abandoned umbilical cord burial sites lack the proper care—the nurturing prayers and tobacco smoke described by Nancy Walters—
necessary for their continued health. When such sites are not
given proper care, harm can come to the person with whom
they are most intimately connected. Such neglect may result in
a rise in social problems—gangs, drug abuse, problem drinking, violence—or health-related problems—disorientation,
depression—like those currently being experienced by Navajo
relocatees.

Moreover, denying Navajo people access to their matrilineal
homes cuts the land off from the nurturing care of those especially connected to it. This explains why Navajo relocatees often
express concern for the land they have been forced to leave
behind. The dependency between Navajo and the earth is reciprocal: The health and well-being of Mother Earth is dependent

on the care of those people who have been given stewardship over particular locales, just as Navajo people are dependent on the continuing nurturance of their mother, the earth.

Despite the hopes of Navajo people such as Jack Hatathlie, the explication of Navajo reasons for protesting relocation off HPL will not bring a halt to the forced relocation of the remaining Navajo—the monstrous gears of governmental bureaucracy are, after all, set in motion. But, coupled with the numerous other analyses of the effects of compulsory relocation on Navajo people, it might serve to highlight the need for cross-cultural understandings.[78] Such understandings, which can only be gained through careful consideration of Native exegeses, might prevent similar policies from being instituted elsewhere in the world and thereby circumvent the subjection of other Native peoples to pain and suffering such as the Navajo relocatees and resisters have experienced.

CHAPTER THREE

The Holy Visit of 1996

*The next thing I knew there was a loud boom overhead
and then a whistle. It sounded like someone was talking
outside so I went out to see what was going on and saw two
white-haired, older Navajo men. . . . I got scared and
started to go back into the house when one of them said:
"Don't be afraid, we are here to help you. You already
know what we're here for."*

SARAH BEGAY

*These Holy Ones told her they had come to ask where all
the people had gone, for no one was leaving offerings of
corn pollen and stones [ntł'iz] at the sacred places anymore.*

HIGH COUNTRY NEWS,
5 August 1996

*Part of the warning concerned the four sacred moun-
tains, and implied that the absence of traditional offerings*

being made there by Navajos was causing the current
drought.

HOPI TUTUVENI,
24 May 1996

[The visitors asked] why the deities no longer are receiving
prayers from the people. They warned that if the Navajos
continue to forsake tribal traditions, they face grave danger
in the future, and Navajo deities would not be able to help.

ARIZONA REPUBLIC,
28 May 1996

On 3 May 1996, amidst the worst drought of the century in the four corners region, an event considered by many Navajo people to be of profound significance to the entire Navajo Nation occurred at Rocky Ridge, an isolated area near Hard Rock, Arizona, on HPL in the former Navajo-Hopi Joint Use Area. Two members of the Diyin Dine'é visited the home of Sarah Begay and her 96-year-old mother, Irene Yazzie, with a series of prophetic messages concerning four areas of laxity on the part of Navajo people.[1] In the view of these Diyin Dine'é, Navajo people have been negligent in their responsibilities regarding prayers and offerings; *k'éí,* "relatives and others with whom one has peaceful, friendly relations"; language and culture; and nature.[2] After delivering stern warnings, the Holy People disappeared, leaving only four moccasin prints encircled by a finely ground substance at the location where they had stood.

Mrs. Begay recalled being flustered by the incident: "I seemed to have been running in circles at the house, not knowing what to do afterwards."[3] She decided to drive to the home of her closest neighbors, a ceremonial practitioner and his wife, to seek their assistance. Upon learning of the visitation,

The couple rushed off to her home. . . . The medicine man attempted to find in which direction the visitors went or might have left. The couple looked around the house and around the place where the visitors were standing. No tracks of movement were found. No tracks were found to indicate which direction the two beings went.

Knowing that there was a meeting at the community house, the lady [Sarah Begay] instructed the medicine man to, "Go to the meeting and inform the community of the visitation here." He drove off to relay the incident. Soon afterward, he returned. Shortly after, a trail of vehicles descended on her house. "In a very short time, a lot of people were here," she added.

The footprints of the two visitors were found at the place where they stood. The footprints were of moccasins. An outline of white cornmeal encircled the footprints. Some people said it was white clay and others said it was white cornmeal. After a close examination by several of the people, it was noted that the white powder was finely ground white cornmeal.

A young male person stated, "Do not leave the incident at that. We need to find out from them why they visited. Ask through hand-trembling.[4] One of you knows how to find information through using your hands. A few of you are sitting here among us," he stated. A person volunteered to conduct the ceremony. Through the ceremony, it was stated, "The visitors were of the Holy People." Different hand-tremblers were used on site and they all agreed with the same results, that the visitors were members of the Holy People.[5]

The *ndilniihii*, "traditional diagnosticians expert at the hand-trembling method," who were consulted verified that the visit was real and, on the basis of Mrs. Begay's description, identified the visitors as Haashch'ééłti'í (Talking God) and *Haashch'éé'ooghaan*, "House Talking God."

Owing to their visit, Mrs. Begay's role in life altered; she became a *bił'áhoot'įįd*, "visionary." The significance of this shift lies in the fact that one of the culturally sanctioned means by which ceremonial innovation can occur is through the actions of a Navajo visionary. Prophetic visions are not considered aberrant in the Navajo world; in fact, some people maintain that the holes at the top of the backboards of traditional cradles are actually a means to inculcate in the children who use them the ability to have prophetic visions.[6] The experiences of visionaries such as Sarah Begay hold an important place in Navajo history because they have established paradigms for how individual Navajo can become vested with the power to perform new ceremonies and to educate apprentices in their performance.[7]

Throughout the month of May, news of the Holy Visit at Rocky Ridge quickly disseminated across the vast area of Navajo country.[8] As word of the prophetic incident spread, the status of the location at which it occurred shifted from an isolated homesite to a shrine, with the "footprints" serving as the requisite center for a pilgrimage space.[9] Vehicles of all shapes and sizes began making their way from every corner of the reservation to the Begay-Yazzie home, and thousands of members of the Navajo Nation (some from as far away as Canada) started on pilgrimages to the remote location. By mid-May, six thousand people reportedly had made the trek down treacherous dirt roads to visit the site and make offerings, and Albert Hale, then-President of the Navajo Nation, had requested that it be designated as a permanent Navajo shrine.[10] On Monday 20 May 1996, Ferrell Secakuku, then-chairman of the Hopi Tribal Council, visited the site and heard the story of the visit directly from members of the Begay family.[11]

Though significant and noteworthy, this visitation was not an isolated occurrence. Visitations by supernaturals, prophetic

messages, and the transformative movements frequently origi-
nating from them have a long history in Native America in general and in the Navajo world specifically, as they do globally.
Such phenomena have held a prominent place in the realm of
academic interest since James Mooney's seminal study of the
Ghost Dance religion launched a century of scholarly investigations in societies throughout Native America and elsewhere.[12]
The time-depth of this interest in such phenomena notwithstanding, American Indian prophets and prophecies have had
a contested history in academic discourse. By some accounts,
scholars have all but ignored the powerful role played by prophets in American Indian communities and in the course of
American Indian history, focusing instead, almost exclusively,
on the transformative social movements associated with the
prophets and their prophecies.[13]

Researchers have studied transformative movements within
social groups worldwide under the rubrics of the following
categories: "revitalistic movements," which emphasize the institution of customs, values, and even attitudes toward nature prac-
ticed by previous generations; "cargo cults," which emphasize
the importation of foreign values, practices, and goods; "millenarian movements," which emphasize an apocalyptic transformation engineered by the supernatural; or "nativistic movements,"
which attempt either to revive extinct or moribund elements
of culture or to perpetuate current elements in the culture. Nativistic movements are characterized by strong emphasis on the
elimination of alien persons, customs, values, and/or materials.
Any given transformative movement, such as the incipient movement resulting from the Holy Visit of 1996 on the Navajo reservation, may simultaneously manifest nativistic, cargo, millenarian,
or revitalistic elements.

These various phenomena have been collectively subsumed
under the label "revitalization movements." In his now classic
study of such movements, Anthony F. C. Wallace established a

model for what he considered to be their universal characteristics.[14] Accordingly, revitalization movements consistently are
seen to involve conscious change, to proceed through certain
stages—the steady state, stress, cultural distortion, revitalization,
and finally a new steady state—and to be linked to "relative deprivation" or "oppression."[15]

Historically, the research focus of most historians and anthropologists interested in the occurrence of such phenomena within
American Indian societies has centered primarily on whether
individual prophetic movements are indigenous or a response
to the pressures of European colonialism.[16] Experience shows,
however, that deprivation or oppression alone (relative, colonial,
or otherwise) does not guarantee adoption of a transformative
movement.[17]

More recently, research focus has shifted from examination
of such factors to elucidation of internal cultural logics. Scholars have realized that it is essential to consider the systems and
practices that give such religious phenomena coherence in the
Native societies under investigation within broader contexts,
such as the oppression of colonialism or various sources of deprivation.[18] Native exegeses shed light on ways Navajo people use
oral traditions to make connections between the past and the
present as well as establish outlines for the future, elucidate the
various systems of belief and practice that give the Holy Visit of
1996 resonance in Navajo society, and highlight some of the
complex and contested points of view about this prophetic incident and the events that have transpired in direct response to
it, explicating why it simultaneously "makes sense" to some Navajo
people and "does not make sense" to others.

Using evidence of prophecy in the Navajo world from the
early twentieth century to the present,[19] incidents such as the
Holy Visit of 1996 may be contextualized historically to: document how ceremonial innovations may originate from the dreams
or visions of contemporary people; demonstrate that prophecy

and the movements resulting from it at various times during
the period under consideration have been powerful intellectual
responses to multiple stresses including droughts, epidemics,
and social change; and illustrate how this recent incident fits
with or diverges from previous visitations that have occurred
during this century. The personal narratives in this chapter directly link this prophetic incident to the various multidimensional stresses—severe drought conditions, prolonged social
and spiritual upheaval resulting from the Navajo-Hopi land dispute, and the "pervasive feeling that people do not behave as
they should, or as they once did"—that are currently being
experienced by Navajo people.[20]

PROPHECY IN NAVAJO ORAL HISTORY

> We were told long ago that the gods would return when
> we began fighting amongst ourselves, stopped talking to
> one another and bad things were happening. . . . We've
> done this to ourselves. Most of us are too lazy to have corn-
> fields. The only thing that has been happening is wind
> and dust blowing in our face every day.[21]

Before the Diyin Dine'é departed to take their places as inner
forms residing within each feature of Navajo sacred geography,
Changing Woman imparted to the Earth Surface People all the
knowledge—songs, prayer, ceremonies, and stories—they
would need for life to continue. It was established that during
times of crisis, prophetic insights and omens from the Holy People would be conveyed to the Earth Surface People in dreams
or by means of various go-betweens, such as coyotes, owls, or
snakes.[22] But, as they began to depart from the earth, Talking
God and the other Holy People said:

"If anyone sees us it will also be a sign that an enemy is coming into the country. If he hears us call, that same person will be killed by an enemy before the day is over." And so saying they all returned to their homes and all their power went with them. They were never seen again. (Now if anyone thinks he sees one of the Holy Beings it will not be for the good of the people. It is considered a bad omen).[23]

This warning elucidates the profound significance afforded by many Navajo people to the Holy Visit of 1996.

"THIS IS NOT AN ISOLATED INCIDENT"

MS: What is going on with this Holy Visit?

HW: I am kind of skeptical about it. It really does not fall within Navajo cultural tradition, because when the Holy People left, they said they would not be seen again. They said, "If anyone says that they see us, it will not be a good thing."

MS: Well Harry, people seem to be indicating that it is not a good thing, that it is an omen that something terrible will happen.

HW: Not a good thing, meaning it will not be true. I have seen several such incidents on the reservation during my lifetime, but this one has caught the fancy of the media.[24]

MS: Have you ever heard of incidents like this in the past?

AW: Yeah but it was really never publicized, you know, it would just be like in that community.

MS: Right.

AW: And they would keep it to themselves. Maybe like
two major ones through my whole lifetime. And this
is the third one, but this was pretty well heard all over
the reservation, outside the reservation and stuff like
that.

MS: Oh, absolutely.

AW: But like before, . . . it was really kept in the community or just the relatives and they did things for them.
. . . I guess, you know, our parents heard about it and
they were aware of it because my mom tells us of one
that she had heard, you know, when she was in her
teens [placing it in the 1940s or early 1950s], and then
she said that, like I said, they weren't publicized or anything. They [those visited] just were directed to do
something like a Blessing Way or do their offerings
and stuff. And that is what happened [how such visitations were dealt with], I guess, at that time.[25]

The opening decades of this century were marked for the
Navajo by cultural and economic hardships caused by repeated
droughts, loss of livestock, and loss of kin to Spanish influenza.[26]
Early in the summer of 1920, amidst these multidimensional
stresses, a ceremonial practitioner from the northeastern region
of the Navajo reservation had a prophetic vision in which a great
flood was predicted.[27]

A strange scare seized these Indians a few days ago. In
some way the whole tribe got the idea that there was to
be a flood which would cover the lowlands and drown
nearly all the white people, and that the Navajos were to
go to the mountains and be saved. When the flood was
over if there were any white people left the Navajos
could kill them easily and thus be rid of the white man
and his ways forever. The flood was to be caused by the

"ocean running over," and some of the medicine men
and prophets have been able/by faith/to see the waters
coming.[28]

This prophetic message purportedly came to the visionary during a four-day period of unconsciousness resulting from his having been struck by lightning.[29] He prophesied that on Saturday,
3 July 1920, two suns would rise at dawn, and shortly thereafter
a flood would rage through the Navajo homeland, destroying
everything in its path except those Navajo who had sought
refuge on higher ground.

At the request of the visionary, runners carried his message to
Navajo people across a wide area.[30] Word of the imminent event
reached as far east as Chaco Canyon in New Mexico, as far west
as Winslow, Arizona, and as far south as Ramah, New Mexico.[31]
Some Navajo remained skeptical of the account, but as the superintendent at Shiprock Agency reported,

> To the vast majority of the Indians the scare is real and
> nothing short of an army could stop them from their
> march to the mountains with their flocks. They have
> already sustained heavy losses of young lambs, and have
> left fields and gardens to be ravaged by horses and other
> stock left behind. . . . A few of our Indians have not been
> stampeded, but they are very few.[32]

Fleeing to high ground made perfect sense to Navajo people
hearing of the imminent flood because a worldwide flood followed by a mass exodus to another world was an effective prob-
lem-solving technique established in Navajo oral tradition.[33]

Most sought refuge in the higher elevations of the Santa Fe
National Forest, the Carrizo, the Lukachukai, the Black, the
Chuska, or the Jemez Mountains, depending on the locations
of family homesites.[34] Writing in 1936, Edgar Hewett noted,

Only sixteen years ago we witnessed a pell-mell exodus, not permanent, however, of Navaho. Warned by an old medicine man, that on the third of July, 1920, a great deluge would destroy all the white people and all Indians who remained on the desert, they packed up, bag and baggage, and broke for the western mountains. Horses and sheep were driven headlong, many cattle were left behind, crops abandoned at considerable loss. As the great catastrophe did not come off according to schedule we witnessed them drifting back, rather sheepishly, for some weeks.[35]

Reports in regional newspapers highlighted the purported nativistic aspects of the prophecy by claiming that those fleeing deliberately attempted to conceal what was happening from local non-Natives.[36] Coupled with unexplained movements of large numbers of Navajo toward high ground, such reports caused fear of a Navajo uprising amongst non-Native people in the region.[37]

To date, few details have been documented about the actual events that transpired amongst members of the various Navajo groups while they awaited the flood on high ground. The single published account notes only that when the flood did not manifest itself on the predicted date, the ceremonial practitioners coping with this dilemma determined that those gathered could avert the imminent disaster altogether through "collective prayer."[38] No new ceremony is known to have been generated by this vision, but those who credited the visionary with efficacy reportedly carried out traditional ceremonies such as Hózhǫ́ǫ́jí, "Blessing Way," with unusual frequency.[39]

An elder from the northeastern quadrant of the reservation with whom I consulted on these matters readily volunteered the story of how local people coped with the flood prophecy in 1920 and offered details about the specific actions taken by Navajo individuals to avert catastrophe.

MS: I have been doing some research on this and I found several references to visitations and other relevant events that occurred earlier in this century. Like in 1920, there was a prophecy that there would be a flood. Did you ever hear anything about that?

AE: Yes that, I heard about it and then they put some, in these where the springs are? They put some ah, the special stones, you know, ntł'iz? The precious stones?

MS: Right.

AE: And I guess they told their Holy People that they would not want to see the water and so a lot of people said, "Nobody knew what they were doing and that is the reason why we don't have no rain anymore!" But, they said, "There is no one that knows how to get the water back. . . ."

MS: Well I heard that there were a lot of Navajo people at the time who sought high ground—that they left their homes and went to high ground. Did you know about anyone that did that?

AE: My, my mother did but my father didn't because one of his uncles said, "No," it would not happen. [He said] that, "We won't see a flood." And he said, "These poor people are moving up to the mountains for nothing!" you know? . . . But my mom did go up there, to her herd up there, but my dad stayed behind because he was tending to his, ahh, they were cutting alfalfa around that time. And so I guess my dad never left the place here, but my mom did take the sheep up to the mountain. . . . And my husband heard about it and he moved up to the mountain with his mother.

MS: Well did you ever hear what was done while they were up on the mountain? What kinds of ceremonies were done up there?

AE: It is just that there were a lot of people that did the
offerings of precious stones to, for the sacred mountain sites, you know, where they usually do those? The
offering places?
MS: Uh-huh, so they went to the sacred sites on the mountains that they were seeking refuge on?
AE: Uh-huh.[40]

Droughts continued to plague the area in 1930, 1933, and
1935.[41] These unfavorable weather conditions, coupled with
government views about endangerment to Navajo rangeland
from overgrazing, led to federally mandated stock reduction
programs that greatly diminished family herds. As a consequence, dependence on wage labor on and off the reservation
increased as did acceptance of non-Navajo religious beliefs and
practices such as Catholicism, Protestantism, Mormonism, and
the Native American Church.[42] These multiple sources of social
and economic strain also resulted in internally generated ceremonial innovations.

In 1936, a young woman from near Huerfano Mesa—one of
the central mountains of Navajo sacred geography closely associated with Changing Woman—was visited by White Shell Woman
(who is most often considered to be one and the same as Changing Woman).[43] White Shell Woman directed her in the performance of special Hózhǫ́ǫ́jí ceremonies, which were distinguished
by specific additional procedures. These special rites were widely
learned and carried out in the northeastern portion of the
Navajo area.[44]

In late 1936 or early 1937, a woman in the Farmington, New
Mexico, region was visited by *Hadahoniye' 'Ashkii,* "Banded Rock
or Mirage Stone Boy," a holy person associated with mineral
deposits in the area.[45] One morning, Hadahoniye' 'Ashkii quietly
entered the woman's hooghan as she sat with her back to the

door preoccupied with a household task. After a moment of silence, "someone tapped her on top of the head."

Turning around she beheld a little man. He was not over three feet tall and was very, very old. All of his clothing was of a rich, wine color. The woman saw that the skin of his chest, where his jacket hung open was vari-colored; banded like rocks that she had seen near her home.

After watching her for a moment the little man began to talk. "You listen to what I am going to say," he admonished her. "Things are not good in the country. Times are bad; the people arc bad. The rain does not come and the sheep do not increase. We do not live the right way anymore. The whole world is the same. People have forgotten the right way to live and everyone thinks the wrong thoughts. It is not good. The people should hold ceremonies. They must pray for things to be good again."[46]

Before departing, Hadahoniye' 'Ashkii gave her specific instructions regarding requisite ceremonial rites.[47] He told her that in order for rain to come, Hózhǫ́ǫ́jí needed to be held wherein the one sung over must be a woman of the *Tódích'íi'nii*, "Bitter Water Clan." Navajo seeking blessings for their families must make offerings of ntł'iz.[48] These special Hózhǫ́ǫ́jí were meant to benefit the entire world, not just the Navajo who participated in them.[49]

The first such ceremony was held at the home of the visionary who was a member of the requisite clan—Tódích'íi'nii. Others were held "near the Hogback," at locations east and north of Shiprock, New Mexico, at Red Rock, New Mexico, and elsewhere.[50] After these numerous ceremonies, Hadahoniye' 'Ashkii reappeared to the woman in a dream.[51] He commended the Navajo for performing the proper ceremonies and, as a gift, left a "double handful" of corn that subsequently multiplied tenfold. Upon request, the visionary distributed four kernels of this special corn per person and directed recipients to use it as seed to grow corn for their ceremonial needs. In contrast to the anti-white sentiment associated with the flood prophecy of 1920, this visitor predicted that good would eventually come to Navajo people from the various programs instituted by the federal government.[52]

The experiences of numerous other visionaries have been reported since Hadahoniye' 'Ashkii's visit. A Navajo named Mose Blackgoat tried to popularize an innovative ceremonial that was purportedly taught to him in a dream while he slept in a cave, but his untimely death ended his crusade.[53] Sometime between 1936 and 1941, a woman from the Shiprock area was visited by a person she believed to be Jesus Christ while she was out herding.[54] The visitor reportedly told her, "I will lead you out of these terrible troubles that the whites are making for you."[55] Sometime in the 1940s, I was told, Jesus Christ visited a Navajo family in the central portion of the reservation near Wheatfields Lake.

> AE: There was one that I heard about over in Wheatfields [Arizona], this guy, . . . I guess when he was younger, and he was riding home on his horse, and he saw someone in white, you know?
>
> MS: Uh-huh.
>
> AE: And it followed him all the way home. And then it stayed. They invited him [to stay with them], but [the person to whom the visitor appeared] said, "This, whoever it was wasn't talking at all." And so in the morning, after they prepared the food and whoever it was, they said this, he [the person visited] is my uncle too, and he said he thinks it was Jesus, you know?
>
> MS: Uh-huh.

AE: It was all in white. And then so, he said when they were
preparing a meal, and he [the visitor] went out and they
never saw him again or never did see the footprint
[referring to those left at Rocky Ridge] or nothing.

MS: Uh-huh, did he give any kind of a message?

AE: He didn't. He didn't say anything at all to them! But
ahh, you know, they were kind of disturbed.

MS: Well sure.

AE: But they said, "Well it must be something. . . . It must
be a good, a good fortune or something." So, and then
another lady from there saw the same person the next
day around noon, but they said it never stayed around,
it just went on again. Those are the two things that I
heard from C. C. from Wheatfields. And he said this
happened a long time ago, when he was just a boy, he
was about, maybe around fourteen.[56]

In 1941, in the Largo or Blanco Canyon area, a woman saw
a vision of a field filled with the skulls of white men. She reported
that the Japanese were actually Changing Woman's warrior
sons, Born-for-Water and Monster Slayer, "who were coming to
kill the white men."[57]

A woman with whom I am acquainted from the southwestern
quadrant of the reservation told me of some visitations during
her lifetime.

MS: When have you heard about visitations like this in
the past? Do you remember, like how old you were or
anything?

AW: It was just something that you heard, like they came
to the home and you know it could, like this one time
a lady dressed up, was in a *biil* [handwoven two-piece
dress] and all that, and the *kénitsaai* [moccasins with
deerskin leggings] and you know like that?

MS: Uh-huh [acknowledging that I understand that the
woman was wearing traditional attire].
AW: They said that she came to this one place and she
warned them of something that was going to happen!
But never anything as such with the like, um, footprints
and all of that [referring to the incident at Rocky
Ridge]. . . .
MS: Was the lady that came in the biil a god?
AW: That is what, according to that person, yeah.
MS: Uh-huh. Did they know which one it was, or who she
was?
AW: No, um, well this particular one that happened this
past spring, she [Sarah Begay] identified who she
thought these gods were. The previous ones, you know,
they just said you know, it was a person dressed up like
this, but they know like they weren't human beings
because, well I mean, they knew that they were gods
because of the way they moved and the way, the things
that they had to say.[58]

It is not uncommon for the exact identities of holy visitors to
remain ambiguous. For example, a visit by an unidentified holy
person was reported in the Checkerboard district in 1992 or
1993. In this case, the message conveyed was simply "to pray
more."[59] But, other factors such as the time of year when individual visitations or prophecies occur offer important insights.

Although the time of year of these various holy visitations has
not always been recorded, it is known that the flood prophecy
occurred just prior to July of 1920, and Hadahoniye' 'Ashkii visited the woman on the cusp of winter and spring. Like the Holy
Visit at Rocky Ridge, these incidents each occurred during the
window of opportunity for materials—pollen, ntł'iz, cornmeal—
to be offered at sacred sites, for seasonal restrictions delimit
when offerings can and cannot be made.

> AE: And then, in the wintertime that is the only time that you don't do offerings.
>
> MS: You don't?
>
> AE: Because of the frozen ground.
>
> MS: Oh! So that is one of the activities that you can't do in the winter?
>
> AE: Yes, uh-huh, only in the summertime. And then, after the hibernation of the "Mountain People" [bears, chipmunks, squirrels] and the "Ground People," too. I mean snakes and all these others. . . . You know, you are not supposed to do offerings when the ground is frozen.[60]

The season during which a visitation occurs directly associates it with various components of Navajo cosmology (see figure 1). The timing of visitations, therefore, connects them with particular phases of the Navajo cycle of life. At the close of the annual cycle, the world is cleansed by winter. At the start of the next annual cycle, the world is new, so a springtime visit such as that at Rocky Ridge is associated with cleansing and new beginnings. This is the appropriate time to plant, to begin construction on a new dwelling, to affirm new relationships through marriage, and for new life to begin. Thus, the message brought by the Holy People to Rocky Ridge is inherently imbued with hope for cultural and cosmic renewal.

REACTIONS TO THE HOLY VISIT AT ROCKY RIDGE

> About two weeks ago, two humanoid figures appeared briefly before 61-year-old Sarah Begay of Big Mountain and imparted a message of warning to the Navajo people. Since then, hordes of people have flocked to the area to pray, see and hear Sarah's story for themselves.[61]

News of Navajo deities' visit draws thousands to site.[62]

The drought has brought a religious resurgence. . . .
Navajos are holding family ceremonies all across the reservation and many politicians have since embraced prayer
as a way to fight the drought.[63]

Immediately following the Holy Visit at Rocky Ridge, Alfred
Yazzie of Fort Defiance, Arizona, was called upon to perform a
Hózhǫ́ǫ́jí for the benefit of Sarah Begay, her mother Irene
Yazzie and other members of their family.[64]

> She told us of this event at her home when we visited. "A
> Blessing Way was conducted for me," she added. "A rela-
> tive conducted the ceremony over me. I was washed at the
> place where the beings stood and an all night sing was
> done."
>   Many medicine men and elders had come to visit her.
> As instructed by others, she made four loaves of kneel-
> down bread. The loaves of kneel-down bread were made
> as an offering to the medicine man to conduct the
> Blessing Way. The medicine man himself requested the
> four loaves of kneel-down bread as a payment to him,
> too. Nothing was to be offered. No fabric or material
> cloths were to be placed on the ground where the med-
> icine man's "tools" generally are placed. The medicine
> man only offered a sprinkle of corn pollen in place of
> it, and then he placed his tools on top. The loaves of
> kneel-down bread, offered to the medicine man as pay-
> ment, were eaten by the attendees on the final night of
> the Blessing Way. The water used to soften the kneel-
> down bread was even consumed at the Blessing Way,
> too. . . . That was all explained to us, while we were
> there.[65]

Ceremonial practitioners also came to the site to perform the "Four Pebble ceremony, which is done when there are no rains."[66] In addition, then-President Hale visited the site on horseback. On 16 May 1996 he issued a memorandum urging all five thousand tribal government employees to visit the site in order to make prayers and offerings. To facilitate these pilgrimages, Hale granted each employee a four-hour leave to make the journey.[67]

In response to news of the incident and Hale's memorandum, familial groups began visiting the site of the Holy Visit. A woman with whom I am acquainted, who made the pilgrimage with family members shortly after the incident occurred, gave the following account of her visit.

> AW: We went. . . . And we witnessed very little, very little evidence, I mean, you know they said, "That is where they stood," and you could just see like the ah, the footprints. It is not really a footprint. It is like when you go into the ground, ground level with like [a pair of] socks on. It was hardly visible because it was just so windy. And not too many people had shown up at that time yet. But there was like maybe twenty people ahead of us when we were in line to do our, we did our offerings over there.
>
> MS: OK, so what type of offerings do you make to a site like that?
>
> AW: Well, we used our corn pollen. And then we used some of the white, ground white corn. That is what my mom wanted us to do, to use. That is what we did and we just prayed. And that is when John's mom was pretty bad and he prayed for her too. . . . But, like two weeks after it happened, I understand that the line was like almost a mile long. People were waiting to do their offerings and stuff. But when we got there, you know,

we didn't have to wait too long. And we spoke to the
lady that, you know, actually witnessed what happened?
MS: Sarah Begay?
AW: Uh-huh. And she um, she told us very little. She said
she's been, you know, been telling people over and
over what has taken place. There were people bringing
food and money, and they were doing that as a dona-
tion. And she had already had a Blessing Way done.
And that day, she was telling us, you know, she was
going to wash up that Sunday [meaning Sunday would
be the fourth day after the Blessing Way]. . . . And so
she said, she just had a Blessing Way done and she was
just waiting to wash up and um, she kind of like told us
in a group, you know, she didn't tell us one-by-one. But,
you know, we had like, a little bit, a little conversation
with her because by clan she is our sister, on our dad's
side. I guess our dad was her brother. . . . This thing
kind of got into the public [arena] and then they wanted
to take cameras out and stuff. And there was a lot of
controversy about that and then people were saying,
you know it has been heard, like you said through up
there [Seattle, Washington, from which I was calling]
and even to Phoenix and different areas. And I guess
they wanted tourists to come through and people
wanted to, I guess there was a lot of controversy and
then they kind of just banned everybody out except for
the Navajo.[68]

Indeed, a sign posted at the end of the road leading to the
Begay home stated that the site was closed to all non-Navajo.[69]
Additional signs were posted around the Begay home that listed
specific rules for proper behavior and etiquette.[70] At the request
of the family, cameras and video recorders were not allowed at
the site.[71]

Testimonials from visitors to the site clearly document rules delimiting the visits that are typical of nativistic movements. For example, one pilgrim to the site claimed that visitors in non-traditional attire were denied access.

> Next my wife's auntie takes her family to the place of the "Visit." Again there is a very large line to make offerings and prayers. My wife's auntie is dressed in traditional attire and is allowed to make her offerings and prayers. Its [*sic*] her daughter [*sic*] turn to make a offering, and [she] is turned back, she is told that no one will be allowed [who is] not dressed in traditional attire to make offerings and prayers. The daughter returns to the van[,] dresses in traditional skirt and blouse[,] and is allowed back in line to pray and make offerings.[72]

Although initial reports of the message brought by the holy visitors focused specifically on the drought being caused by a lack of offerings to the Holy People, subsequent tellings shifted to the loss of traditions on the part of Navajo people. This explains the exclusionary practices encountered by pilgrims to the site.

> MS: What did the holy visitors say? What was the message?
> AE: Well the people down there [at Rocky Ridge] were saying that it was just pertaining to water. You know, "You're not doing the offerings to us," and [the Holy People who visited] said, "You are supposed to do a lot of offerings to us so that you can have a rain, rain back and all," that is what the question was that they, I guess they brought.
> MS: So it was having to do with the drought?
> AE: Yes, it was with the drought. That's, that's the only thing it was. That is what they came for, they said.

MS: Huh? Well, because I have heard other people say that
it is because Navajo people have lost their traditions.

AE: Well that, a little bit of that too. But, like I said, at first,
I guess, it was just pertaining to water, and then later on,
the next day it was added that, "We don't dress properly,
like we are supposed to dress," or "We cut our hair. We
are supposed to wear buns," and all of this came up later
on.[73]

Speculative claims and exclusionary admonishments seem
to have gone both ways in this case, for word spread amongst
traditional people on the reservation to avoid the site because
the Begay-Yazzie family members were suspected of partici-
pating in the Native American Church. One elder told me,

AE: Well, I heard about it some and my uncle said that,
"These people they are eating peyote!"

MS: Really? . . .

AE: So he said, "Don't go over there!" Because, you know,
I don't belong to that! And my uncle doesn't belong to
that either! And we are just old, old tradition. That is
what we are holding. When I go places, you know, I
know the signs that they have in their homes. That is
how I can tell. And so, they usually have some kind of
ahh, you know, something that is on the wall or something? And then from there we know that they're, they
belong to those [are members of the Native American
Church] and then so my uncle had warned me when I
was learning he said, "Don't mix it! They don't mix!."[74]

This accusation is particularly interesting in light of another
report. A Navajo man apparently approached the site carrying
a "peyote box and gourd" (Native American Church parapher-

nalia); he was stopped and told that the "tool box and gourd" would not be allowed. Although displeased by this intervention, he returned to the site without them and was allowed to make his offerings and prayers.[75]

As the weeks passed, the number of visitors to the site steadily increased until, "At any one time, there were over a hundred people lined up to pray and give offerings of turquoise and white shell at the footprint site."[76] For some, especially those traveling with young children, the wait was just too much.

> My sister-in-law, Joe's wife went out there and wanted to do the offerings, and they said, you know they were in line for like four hours and they got hungry and the kids got restless and, I mean, they said the line was not moving fast enough so they just left. That is how bad it was. It was so publicized that people all over the reservation came around and then too like I think toward the end where there were too many people, they had to have some police escorts. You know, to kind of like keep people in line and, you know, from all that, and warn them to bring their own food or whatever.[77]

In addition to the line of people waiting their turns to make offerings, there was a second long line of people, extended to the doorway of the family hooghan, waiting to hear Mrs. Begay tell her story. "Inside with her were several medicine men and a couple of people taking notes, and the audience who sat on the floor to hear the story. In front of Sara [Begay] was a foot high stack of dollar bills and a basket with tokens, fetishes and medicine bundles."[78] Some of those who were patient enough to endure the long wait, like the woman from near Crownpoint, New Mexico, whose account of her visit to Rocky Ridge follows, were rewarded by hearing the story of the visit directly from Mrs. Begay.

The event of the Holy Visit was explained to us by the woman who encountered the incident. . . . She said, "It took place fourteen days ago. . . . I was the only one home with my mother. My mother is old," she said. "She is very old." In the morning, the older lady said "Two people will be coming to visit us." "'Who is coming to us, mother,' I repeated to her," was the response of the daughter. "I asked again, 'Who is visiting us?' to my mother," stated the daughter. "How far are they now?" the older woman would ask. "They are coming," she adds.

The daughter was making a dress for her mother for Mother's Day. While she was sewing, she heard something outside the house where they lived. The sound seemed to have come through the window. The daughter mentioned to us that she readily dismissed the noise. Shortly after the first strange noise, a second one sounded. The noise was of "blowing through a ceremonial bone whistle [ts'its'ǫ́ǫ́s]." The daughter got up and mentioned to her mother, "Someone has come to us with a bone whistle." When the daughter heard the noise again, she rushed to the door to find out what or who was making the bone whistling sound.

With the door open, fabric still in hand, the daughter looked outside to see what was going on. Nothing out of the ordinary was happening. While she was still scanning the horizon attempting to find out where the noise was coming from, the bone whistle sounded again. From the frame house where they resided, a small oak tree is standing in the front of the house. The oak tree is located on the north side of the house. The sounds seemed to have come from the top of the oak tree, in that general area. The daughter looked around and there was nothing around. When she looked back toward the north, after looking to the south, the beings were standing there.

There were two beings, standing side by side. One being was white and the other was blue. "Their hair was white. They both had pure white hair. Really white. Their hair was white and shining-like, sort of reflective," she stated. The lady was unable to see their faces, because a fog-like cloud seemed to have drifted in front of their faces.

They were standing and facing her as she stood in the front of her house. One spoke, stating "We are here to bring a message." "We are here visiting to bring a message," they repeated. "We are missing the offerings and the corn pollen," they said. "We are here for them," one stated. The lady did not say any words to the two beings. . . . The two beings stated "We will be visiting other places, too. We are here to bring a message." I do not know where else they will be visiting. . . ."[79] "Hurry in making your offerings and placing of corn pollen," the two beings told the lady. . . . As stated by the lady who spoke to us. Those were the words they brought to us. I guess somewhere people have done that. Offerings have been made in some areas. "Navajo are not living the right way now," they added. Those were the words the lady heard from the visitors.

She tried to move, wanting to walk, but could not move. She wanted to look to the side, but her neck could not move. The only movement she was able to do was moving backward. She was only able to move in that direction, so she stepped back. Taking a couple of steps back, she was able to reach the front door of her house. She opened the door and rushed back inside. "Mother something came to visit us!" the lady stated to her mother. The lady ran to her mother and embraced her. The old lady ran her hands on her daughter's body. The old lady is blind. . . . She is hard of hearing, too. The old lady was running her hands on the body of her daughter, moving her hands from top to bottom in a motion which seemed like she was brushing away something or attempting to find something. The daughter added, "It helped me calm down." After she calmed down, she went back to the front door. She poked her head outside; there was nothing out there. No one was outside. Apparently the visitors had left. . . . That is all I know and heard, that was how it was explained to me when we went to the site of the Holy Visit. I did not add a word nor did I delete a word. I have repeated the words, I heard.[80]

Others were disappointed when they were only able to hear "what the medicine men had to say about it."[81] For, the *hataałii*, "singers or medicine men and women," surrounding Sarah Begay took over the telling of the incident when she succumbed to exhaustion and her voice failed. As Irene Atcitty of Shiprock, New Mexico, explained, "We were told that Sarah [Begay] has told the story of the visits so many times that she lost her voice."[82] Despite these disappointments, pilgrims continued to arrive at the Begay-Yazzie home.

By the third week of May, the number of people making pilgrimages to the site resulted in visitors having to park more than a mile away and caused numerous hardships for Begay-Yazzie family members. Water for livestock and household use became scarce and it was difficult to find the funds to continue to host visitors.[83] Owing to these circumstances, Kelsey Begaye, then-Speaker of the Navajo Nation Council, recommended that "out of courtesy and respect [for the Begay-Yazzie family] we should slow down on the visitation[s] to the site."[84] It is hard to imagine exactly how many Navajo might have visited the location of the Holy Visit during the summer of 1996 if then-Speaker Begaye had not made this plea, but by the middle of July, over twenty thousand people had made the pilgrimage.[85] In addition to these pilgrimages and the

offerings, Navajo families across the reservation held ceremonies and many politicians embraced prayer as a means of
counteracting the drought.

In fact, then-Speaker Begaye called for an official day of
prayer to unite Navajo people of all faiths. The twentieth of June
1996 was declared the first official Navajo Nation Unity Day of
Prayer with the intention that it would become an annual event,
and tribal employees were given the afternoon off to participate.[86] The day of prayer was declared "in the hopes that Navajos would spend part of the day in traditional prayer for solutions to various problems affecting the Navajo Nation."[87]

Navajo of all faiths joined together at the Navajo Nation Civic
Center in Window Rock, Arizona, to participate in this spiritual
event that included elements of the traditional Navajo religion,
the Native American Church, and the various Christian faiths.[88]
Several hundred Navajo people crowded into the civic center
bleachers. Thousands of other Navajo living in remote areas of
the reservation who could not make the trip to Window Rock
participated by listening to or watching live radio or television
broadcasts of the event.[89] Reportedly,

> Some people could be seen pulling their cars off the road
> to pray in the afternoon. . . . Families were seen stepping
> out of their doorways to offer corn pollen. Early in the
> morning, some people offered gemstones and prayed. A
> group also went to Blanca Peak, the sacred mountain in
> the east. Christian churches in Window Rock and Tuba
> City gathered to listen to the prayer day event and fol-
> lowed with their own ceremonies.[90]

Many Navajo felt that their prayers were answered when
the first substantial rain in nearly nine months fell on Navajo
country the very next day. Although they were not enough
to break the drought, the sporadic rain showers that came in

the days and weeks following the Navajo Nation Unity Day of
Prayer were seen as a "sign of hope."[91] Yet, in his account of
the event, then-Speaker Begaye emphasized social and cultural changes that have resulted in the loss of Navajo language
and traditions over concerns about the Navajo-Hopi land dispute or the drought.

> We all live in a time of great challenges. We live in a time
> of uncertainty and there are constant changes taking
> place among us. The majority of our children are not
> speaking their Navajo language; they are not being taught
> their cultural and traditional values; the foundation of
> family values are not being emphasized to them; and we
> are straying away from our spiritual strengths and values.
> We must begin our journey back to being a strong Nation,
> we must start now. . . . In light of these conditions among
> our people, we had reports of a visitation from our Deities
> at Rocky Ridge. A special message was delivered to us. . . .
> I was asked by the Navajo people to organize a day of
> prayer where we could pause and unite in prayer. . . .
> Prayers were offered for the Navajo Nation by a traditional
> Navajo Medicineman, a Native American Church Road-
> man, and [a] Christian Pastor. . . . I believe that by the
> prayers that were offered by different religious means, we
> showed the United States that the Navajo people are the
> Diné, and no matter what differences we may have, we are
> tied by being Navajo first, and secondly by our unique
> clans system.[92]

Many Navajo felt unified as they actively participated in these
various events, but not everyone who learned of the Holy Visit
participated or even lent credence to it. In the months following the incident at Rocky Ridge, resistance to it took many different forms.

RESISTANCE

Sarah Begay is known to Hopi Tribal officials as a relocation resister, and the Hopi Tribal government is not taking this claim lightly, because it has been the practice of
resistors [sic] to use what they can to remain on Hopi
lands.[93]

Then again there is the other side that has been like saying . . . "If it was really the Holy People, you know, then
we would have had rain for the summer!" And, you know,
stuff like that.[94]

Hopis joked it was no more than a UFO sighting or pos-
sibly yet another ploy on the part of Navajos resisting relocation to reclaim the land awarded to Hopis by Congress
some 17 years ago.[95]

AE: My uncle said, "If that holy person or the two Holy
    People had really come," he said, "She [Sarah Begay]
    wouldn't be talking!"
MS: What now?
AE: He said that, "There is no way," he said, "The end of
    the world would have been already past!". . .
MS: So are you saying that he told you that if the visitors
    were real Holy People, then the person to whom they
    came wouldn't have had time to tell the story because
    the world would have come to an end?
  AE: Yeah, uh-huh![96]

Resistance to the accounts of prophets and the events resulting
from them are commonplace. In the case of the Holy Visit of
1996, it came in the forms of counter narratives about the visit
or the messages brought by the Holy People and claims that

certain practices contradict the teachings of the Holy People. Some non-Navajo people resisted lending credence to Navajo spirituality by putting the events of 1996 into a familiar and therefore easily understood context—UFOs or Euro-American notions of "magic."[97] Navajo resistance to the events that occurred after the visitation focus narrowly on the appropriateness of specific practices. Most closely scrutinized are the location of offerings, potential financial benefits for the Begay-Yazzie family, and the altering nature of Mrs. Begay's account. Considering the location of the visitation, it is not surprising that many of the counter narratives regarding this incident are attributable to Hopi people.

Although initial Navajo accounts of the Rocky Ridge events did not directly connect the visitation to the Navajo-Hopi land dispute, the very location of the visit made this ongoing conflict a subtext. Some Hopi accounts implied that the location of the visit was of special significance and that reports of the incident were simply a publicity stunt contrived by Navajo resisting relocation off HPL to draw attention to their cause.[98]

Leigh Jenkins, Director of the Hopi Cultural Preservation Office reportedly said, "No one can blame the Hopis for being skeptical about this occurrence, because everything under the sun has been used (by the relocation resisters) to hold onto the land."[99] Jenkins went on to add that "Hopis have always tried to be respectful of religion and might not doubt the authenticity of this occurrence if it were not for the fact that Navajos in the Big Mountain area are making the claim."[100]

In February of 1997, while testifying at a special session of the Navajo Nation Council focused on the plight of Navajo residents of HPL, Mrs. Begay affirmed that a direct connection existed between the visitation and the then continuing struggle of several hundred Navajo families to remain on HPL. Mrs. Begay stated,

I have seen the Holy People and they have said, "You were put on this land and this is your land." They stood there and they touched me and they talked to me.

The accommodation agreement does not means [sic] anything to me. This is Dine' [sic] peoples [sic] land. There were human beings here before us, they carved on the rocks some of our ceremonies. They created the arrowheads for us and some of our sandpaintings. For these reasons, we, Dine' people, are here at the present time. This is our land.

We were reminded of these things by the Holy People. For the ceremonial reasons, I am not negotiating. My prayers and my songs are connected with the mountains and the rainbows and the environment around here. Also, many Dine' people came and offered and prayed and sang to the Holy People at my home site. Their offerings are still here. The Holy People are still here with these blessings.

I will not allow these prayers and these blessings, my religion, to be tampered with or bought by the Hopis. Into the future, I am going to keep this place holy for all Dine' people and make sure that the prayers and blessings continue on here. . . . I will not let the Hopis have control of this Holy Place. They do not know how to keep it holy. The Hopi people have their own gods. I do not know the way that they pray and offer and sing to these gods. I could not keep their sites holy, the same that they cannot keep this one holy.[101]

The implication of Mrs. Begay's statement is that the Holy People are not receiving prayers and offerings at the sacred sites in Navajo customary use areas on HPL because the Navajo families who were given stewardship over these areas have been relocated off the land. One elder with whom I consulted maintains that Navajo people have been negligent in the making of these offerings elsewhere due to a general loss of cultural knowledge.[102] Lack of cultural knowledge also may have led to what many Navajo deemed to be aberrant practices that occurred in response to the Holy Visit at Rocky Ridge.

Pilgrimages to and offerings at the site of a visitation are not established practices in the Navajo world. There is no evidence that any of the visitations which occurred earlier in this century resulted in mass pilgrimages to the locations of the visits or in offerings at those locations.[103] So the issue of why such pilgrimages and offerings were made to or at Rocky Ridge at all remains to be considered.

I was told that Navajo elders who were consulted, such as the anonymous man quoted in the following account, pointed out that in previous years Navajo people would have known to arrange for offerings to be made at the sacred sites in their customary use areas rather than "flocking" to the site of the Holy Visit.

> AE: "People in their areas, they should go to where the offerings are done. They know where it is. There is one over here by Big Smooth Rock, that they do, [where] they used to do the offerings. And there is several places up at the mountain that they used to do offerings," he said. "These are the places to go to! Not down there," he said.
>
> MS: Yeah, so in other words, he was saying that people shouldn't go to Rocky Ridge to make the offerings?
>
> AE: Yes, he said, "They shouldn't go down there!" . . . Well I guess she's [Sarah Begay] told different stories, you know, she told people that, "In your areas," you know, "You are supposed to do this because the Holy People are missing all the sacred stones [ntł'iz]," and all of this and, "You should be doing this," and all of that. And

then here instead people just start going over there to
see what, what had happened over there.

MS: Uh-huh.

AE: And so A. J. was saying, he said, "It is the people that
are living out here, they are supposed to do it in their
own places, you know, their sacred places. And even the
Hopis, you know, Hopis, a lot of Hopis didn't go down
there [to the Begay-Yazzie home]. They did their offerings at their offering places. You know, so that is all that
I know about it.[104]

The sheer volume of the pilgrimages demonstrates a tremen-
dous need on the part of Navajo people. In personal testimonials, individual Navajo gave diverse reasons for why they felt
compelled to make the pilgrimage. For some a visit to the site
renewed familial connections, "opened the eyes of teenagers
and awakened them" to the richness of their Navajo heritage.[105]
Others, such as the woman cited below, sought intercession on
the part of the holy visitors for an ill relative. As she explained,

AW: Well, we didn't hear it from the radio. We heard it
from my brother George. . . . He visited us here and he
told us about everything, and I guess they had already
passed the word on within his community. I guess his
in-laws went out close by that family [Begay-Yazzie] to
do some type of a chore for a family and that is how the
word got around. We were kind of like one of the first
ones to hear by another person. And so at the time,
John's mom was ill and then John said, "Well this could
be the time we do offer her a prayer," you know?

MS: Exactly.

AW: "These Holy People can help us, you know, give her
strength back and then to be able to have her health
back." So I said OK, and then we just kind of like got up

one day and said, "We are going to do it." And I took
my, the mountain dirt [mountain earth bundle], the
one my dad had?

MS: Uh-huh [acknowledging that I understand she is referring to the family's mountain earth bundle, which contains several small pouches of soil from the sacred
mountains, over which she has been given stewardship].

AW: We took those and we took our white corn [meal]
and our corn pollen and we just headed out that way.
And then we picked up my mom, we told her about it
and my sister Nancy and then we just went up there and
did it, you know, with hopes that things would work
out.[106]

Whatever their individual reasons, people went to great
lengths to reach the location where the holy visitors stood
because it had become a shrine. This site is simultaneously a
shrine to Navajo identity—a place where contemporary Navajo
people can reaffirm their connections to their heritage and
where exclusionary practices delineate "Navajoness" from non-
Navajoness—and a shrine to the Holy People—a sacred place
where reciprocal connections can be made to their powers
through offerings. Although thousands of Navajo placed ntł'iz,
cornmeal, pollen, or other offerings on top of the footprints
left by the holy visitors, others felt that it was totally inappropriate for such offerings to be made at the site of the Holy Visit.

AE: We heard about the one over at the Ridge, but we
never went there because there are a lot of people, you
know, they've made different stories!

MS: Sure. What stories did you hear?

AE: Well, they said the offering was done right outside
their door. And my uncle said, "You can't do that!" He
said, "You have to do offerings away from the house,

because you don't want people walking over it." . . . And
then they were asking for money too, the people that
live there that saw these two Holy People, or whatever
it was. . . . And they had feasts there and they had offerings there, and right outside the door. And they said
they saw footprints, and some of them said, "No, there
was no footprint." And then so, they had all kinds of
different stories.[107]

Others believe that at the very least, the offerings being
made at the footprint site should have been suspended once
the white corn, turquoise, white shell, and other substances
began to build up, for such excess can lead to disharmony in
the Navajo world.

> AW: There are a lot of other things that we heard later, so
> I really don't know, you know, everyone had their things
> to say about it. How it should have been handled, or
> what else should have been done, and all of that, so.
> MS: Uh-huh. Well what types of things did you hear about
> it?
> AW: Well they said that, "They shouldn't make offerings
> there," you know, I mean that is where the incident hap-
> pened, they said, "You should just have had more Bless-
> ing Way ceremonies all over the reservation and then
> they should do some offerings in the mountains." . . .
> So, I understood that about a month later, a month
> from the day that happened?
> MS: Uh-huh?
> AW: They said that that pile of white corn was like maybe
> two feet high! At that one place! And they didn't think
> it was appropriate, you know? And they said, "Once that
> thing was piling up, they should have taken, you know,
> they shouldn't have done their offerings."[108]

Elders with whom I consulted commended the ceremonial practitioners' offerings, made at the four sacred mountains, and explained that Navajo people hearing of the Holy Visit should have arranged for *ntł'iz ni'nił* ceremonies to be performed, in which offerings would be made at the sacred sites in their customary use areas. They confirmed that people should not have traveled to the site of the Holy Visit.

> MS: What is the Navajo name for the ceremony where you make those offerings?
>
> AE: Well, we call if ntł'iz ni'nił. . . . And he said, "There is supposed to be, umm, a site set for it," you know?
>
> MS: Uh-huh.
>
> AE: "They are supposed to make a hooghan, and they are supposed to get a, the people that are related to water, you know, like Tó'aheedlíinii ["The Water Flow Together Clan"].
>
> MS: Uh-huh and how about "Bitter Water"?
>
> AE: Yes, or "Bitter Water," and then umm, what was it he told me? So, not anything that has a red. Like "Red Running to Water," who is Táchii'nii ["Red Running into the Water People Clan"], he said, "No, not that because red is not a good sign, you know, red is bad." And, what was it? Tó'aheedlíinii and Tábąąhá ["Water's Edge Clan"]. "Near the Water People." He said, "Those, that, a lady and a," well he said, "A young girl, a young boy," that haven't been, you know? That are pure still, you know. That haven't been touched or anything like that?
>
> MS: Right.
>
> AE: He said, "They are supposed to get those two and then they are the ones that are supposed to be, they have the prayer at night, and then in the morning, it is open to all people that they come and do their offerings, you

know, they put their, their sacred stones down and then
ahh, and then these two [the young girl and boy], they
are the ones that are taken up to, to the mountain or
where there is a spring. And, they're the ones that do
the offering toward that place, not in the water, just by
the water. You don't put those precious stones in the
water, you just put it by the water." And, and [he] said,
"Other people, they kind of stay home, just three or
four go up there and they do their offerings up there.
And then they come back and then they have a sing all
night on these two."

MS: Hmm, so the ceremony that is done for the boy and
the girl from the Near the Water or the Bitter Water
clans?

AE: Uh-huh?

MS: Is that a Blessing Way?

AE: That is a Blessing Way, uh-huh. . . . My uncle said it
was supposed to have been done in homes, you know,
like in our own homes with our families.[109]

The issues raised by various Navajo over the appropriateness
of pilgrimages to Rocky Ridge or offerings at the footprint site
highlight the changing nature of Navajo beliefs and practices.
Previous visitations did not result in mass pilgrimages to the
sites; people simply made the requisite offerings at sacred sites
in their customary use areas or on the sacred mountains and
then "went about their business." Presently, the language and
traditions are not being taught in numerous Navajo homes. As
a result, many contemporary Navajo simply do not know the
exact locations of the sacred sites in their customary use areas,
what types of ceremonies should be performed at them, when
these ceremonies may be performed, or by whom. Hence, many
of those who were unclear about exactly what should be done
in response to an incident such as the Holy Visit went to the site

of the visit to seek guidance. The mass pilgrimages to the site
and the offerings made while there demonstrate how Navajo
beliefs and practices are altering to accommodate a new generation of Navajo people who lack firm foundations in traditional teachings. These are precisely the individuals to whom
the message of the holy visitors was especially directed. Those
who have lost touch with time-honored traditions are called
upon to "return to the old ways" so that the natural order of
the Navajo cosmos may be restored.

THE MESSAGE OF 1996

> I think the message is, we are losing our language, and we
> are not wearing our hair as it should be. The Holy People
> left us ceremonies, everything that we need to know, the
> political, the economic knowledge. They said, "Use these
> and you will be all right. Lose these and it will be the end!"
> In Navajo we call these *yeesétką'*, "food you prepare for a
> journey." You estimate how much water, food, you will
> need. They [the Holy People] said, "Here is your yeesétką'."
> Somewhere along the line the United States Government
> gave us another yeesétką', and now he is trying to hold
> that back. I think maybe what they [the Holy People] are
> saying is "Go back to the old ways and you will be OK."[110]

In response to the Holy Visit of 1996, families across the reservation engaged hataałii to perform ceremonies in the process
of which offerings were made at sacred sites; in addition, thousands of Navajo made the pilgrimage to Rocky Ridge. Pilgrimages to the site of the Holy Visit and the making of offerings
there did not "make sense" to Navajo holding on to "old, old tradition," but such responses made perfect sense to Navajo seeking
a special connection with the powers of the Holy People, a reaf-

firmation of Navajo identity, or guidance regarding traditional teachings. In essence, these people went to Rocky Ridge because they were seeking a new sensibility in the challenging context of the altering Navajo world.

Those who stood in line for hours to hear Sarah Begay tell the story of her visitation were convinced of the authenticity of her account because it harks back to the warnings of the Diyin Dine'é, documented in the Navajo oral histories. The messages brought by the holy visitors to Rocky Ridge in May of 1996 concern the final warning—not to forget all that she had taught them—given by Changing Woman to the Nihookáá Diné'é as she prepared to take her place as the inner form of the earth. The apocalyptic nature of the message is clear: If Navajo people continue on the path they seem to have chosen, abandonment of the traditions given to them by Changing Woman and the other Diyin Dine'é and violation of the responsibilities established in the charter between the Nihookáá Dine'é and the Diyin Dine'é, the world as they know it will cease to exist. The sense of urgency evident in the message delivered by the holy visitors implied that no Navajo was exempt from making offerings that would stabilize the relationship between the Diyin Dine'é and the Nihookáá Dine'é.

Unlike the numerous cases documented by previous researchers, this incipient movement amongst the Navajo may hold the likelihood of being sustained because it has been officially sanctioned by representatives of a centralized authority—the Navajo government.[111] Then-Speaker Begaye and then-President Albert Hale engineered the national reaction—four-hour leaves were granted to all Navajo government employees to enable thousands of them to make pilgrimages to the site, the Navajo Nation Unity Day of Prayer was inaugurated on 20 June 1996, and events were broadcast over radio and television to enable thousands of individuals in remote locations to participate. This implies that perpetuation of this transformative movement might be fundamentally linked to an evolving Navajo nationalism.[112] But then-President Hale and then-Speaker Begaye are politicians with various political motivations for what they do and say in their official capacities.[113] Moreover, because their influence in regard to these matters is limited in large measure to their respective terms in office, it remains to be seen whether Navajo governmental support will continue into the future. In any case, it is too soon to know for sure whether this movement will be sustained.

This is only a preliminary assessment. If the incipient movement resulting from this visit proves efficacious for Navajo people who are facing serious, multidimensional social stresses such as alcohol abuse, youth gangs, domestic violence, forced relocation, and loss of culture and traditions, as well as the environmental stresses of sustained drought, it will endure; if not, it will cease to exist. Only time will tell as events continue to unfold. Brought to Rocky Ridge by the Holy People in the springtime, the message conveyed in May of 1996 is inherently one of hope, which holds forth the promise of cultural renewal. Perhaps for some Navajo, the pilgrimage to Rocky Ridge marked the first step on the journey back to the teachings of the Holy People.

CHAPTER FOUR

Snakes in the Ladies' Room

Snakes Alive! Serpents Make Workers Squirm.

SALT LAKE TRIBUNE,
6 August 1994

I believe snakes are one of the most serious omens that one receives and it shouldn't be ignored at all.

HERMAN SHORTY

We felt it was an invasion of our bodies.

DEBBIE YAZZA

In August of 1994 news quietly broke in regional newspapers of an unusual incident on the Navajo reservation. Snakes were sighted in a ladies restroom on the first floor of Administration Building No. 2 in Window Rock, Arizona. A client of the tribal health and social services division was surprised on 25 July by a snake in a bathroom stall. The snake "slithered back into the walls" after the encounter.[1] The incident was first reported to tribal facilities maintenance staff on 26 July when another sighting occurred. Investigators discovered large holes under one of the commodes and in the adjoining wall. Snakes again appeared in the restroom on the 28th despite efforts made by maintenance workers to plug these holes. Media reports, such as the following, described eyewitnesses as "hysterical."

> Tribal Environmental Health Director Herman Shorty said the first snake sighting was made by a client of the tribal health and social services divisions on July 25. Shorty described the clients as "hysterical," after they observed the snake in one of the restroom stalls. The women's bathroom on the first floor of the two-story health, social services and community development building is presently taped up and a July 27 memorandum from Shorty that also is taped to the door states that it is closed "due to snake sightings."[2]

The signs posted by tribal officials had little or no effect due to communication problems. Employees in the building, such as Debbie Yazza, a tribal social services accountant who expresses her personal views in the following account, remained concerned for the welfare of vulnerable clients—children and monolingual Navajo speakers—of the many tribal offices housed in the building who continued to use the facilities.

> What really upsets me is that even last week, elders were still using the bathroom where the snakes were sighted. There were signs posted on the door but many of them can't read English. We're supposed to be here to help clients and instead we're hurting them in a different way. The child care program is housed in this building and children and parents come in here, too.[3]

No snakebites were reported. In fact, the snakes, which were identified as members of two non-poisonous species (garter snakes and bullsnakes), had no direct contact with the women. Taking this into consideration, non-Navajo learning of these incidents might well wonder why the snakes caused such alarm. The manner in which non-Native newspapers, such as the *Gallup Independent* and *Salt Lake Tribune,* presented this story implied that the hysteria of the women who first sighted the snakes in the ladies room stemmed from the type of snake phobia frequently experienced by Euro-Americans.[4] In contrast, personal accounts by eyewitnesses about the incident reveal that this could not be further from the truth. Despite statements to the contrary in early accounts of Navajo life, Navajo experts told me that Navajo people do not fear snakes, nor are they repulsed by their physical appearance or attributes.[5] Snakes are treated with respect because they are recognized as powerful persons.

Popular accounts document numerous warnings against contact between snakes and humans, but such warnings in the Navajo world extend far beyond contacts with snakes.[6] The extensive ethnographic accounts of Navajo culture and society repeatedly mention the effects of certain events (other than contact with snakes) on the health and well-being of persons, their loved ones, and their unborn children. These events may include observing the construction of a drypainting, hearing certain songs, being massaged at birth or at puberty, coming into contact with Anasazi ruins or menstrual blood, witnessing a fatal accident, washing other people's laundry, or drinking breast milk.[7] Individually and in combination, these diverse examples reveal that Navajo views on the cultural construction of the human body and personhood are in part based on the premise that parts of the body—such as hair and fingernails—and bodily secretions—such as saliva, blood, skin oil, or urine—retain lifelong effect and can thereby influence the well-being of the person from whom they originated long past detachment or expulsion.

Statements made by Navajo at the time of the snake sightings give profound reasons for the strong reactions on the part
of the women who encountered the snakes, and these reactions in turn shed light on Navajo ideas about the cultural construction of all persons in their world. Contact between snakes
and humans is potentially dangerous because snakes and
humans are persons constructed according to the principles
of homology, complementarity, and synecdoche established
by the Holy People. These concepts structure the complex
relationship of parts to the whole in a world constructed
according to paradigms set forth in the Navajo origin story.[8]
Such tropological constructs acquire significance in the Navajo
world in the process of human action, that is, as aspects of com-
plexes within which human activity takes place.[9] Formalized
notions of the human body, personhood, and effect are not
purely descriptive of a static, preordained social world. They
are tools used by real people to construct and reconstruct a
world in which values and goals inherited from the past are
adjusted to contemporary problems and goals. On the basis of
shared structure and substance, snakes and humans are
homologues. As such, they have dual facets to their personhood; the left-hand side of every Navajo person embodies the
"warrior" aspects of the individual, and the right-hand side
embodies complementary "peaceful" aspects. In addition, the
principle of synecdoche extends the boundaries of all Navajo
persons. This extension results in a conflation of the constructs of "self" and "person" in Navajo understanding.[10]

Navajo reactions to the snake visitations reflect Navajo views
of the human body and personhood. Ultimately, analysis of the
Navajo philosophical concepts of association and effect offers
insights into more general anthropological questions concerning the cultural construction of the human body, the self, and
the person, rather than into snake phobia.

NAVAJO REACTIONS TO THE SNAKE VISITATIONS

Shortly after the snake sightings were reported to tribal officials, advice was sought from several Navajo medicine men. Herman Shorty, director of the Navajo Office of Environmental Health, told reporters, "We are approaching this not only from a health standpoint but a cultural one, too. . . . We have sought the counsel of several tribal medicine men because this is a very sensitive issue that warrants their advice. . . . It has become an issue of mental health and general well-being."[11] The medicine men who were consulted informed the interested parties that the visits by the snakes must be addressed at both the social and the personal level; the snakes were omens to all coming into contact with the building as well as threats to the well-being of the women using the facilities.

Tribal cultural specialist Raymond Jim told reporters that Navajo people are taught from an early age "to leave snakes alone."[12] Adults routinely warn children not to harm or kill snakes, or to associate with them. According to Navajo oral history, animals, reptiles, and humans once lived in harmony in the underworlds. At this time, "all the people were similar in that they had no definite form."[13]

> Our elders have told us that they [animals and reptiles] separated themselves from us. . . . They told the people that they will only be part of our protection songs, prayers, and sandpaintings. They went their own way and we excluded ourselves from them. . . . There's usually a spiritual and cultural reason why they have been seen inside the building. That's what the prayers and ceremonies are for, to discern the message the snakes bring. . . . Their contact with us should not be ignored.[14]

The separation of humans and snakes in the underworlds did not result in a complete breakdown of relations between the two species. Rather, as Jim noted, snake people descended from Big Snake, one of the four guardians (i.e., Bear, Big Snake, Thunder, and Wind) of the Sun's house, and took on the role of protectors.[15] As such, they are included in the songs, prayers, drypaintings, and body paintings integral to several distinct protective ceremonies. Moreover, along with coyotes and owls, they often serve as messengers to humans. The messages they bring can be negative or positive in nature; in either case, they are recognized as extremely powerful forces that must be reckoned with. Harry Walters offered the following advice when we discussed the snake sighting incidents.

HW: That is something that is out of the ordinary.

MS: For the snakes to get in there?

HW: Yes. And then something that is out of the ordinary, you know, like many years ago we had a severe drought. It began in the early spring. Some of the flowers, you know, it didn't let them bloom. Later on, about August, we had a lot of rain. And then the yucca plant bloomed. And so that is not in keeping with the "natural order." And then so, it is telling us something. You know, because we have a direct relationship with the natural world. . . . We are doing something to upset that. So the snakes would be like that. You know, snakes are usually afraid of people. They don't go, uhh, very seldom would they go to where there are people walking, or animals. Very seldom. And to go into something like that, you know, a restroom, in a building, this is not the usual habits of snakes. And then so, it is telling us something, that is what it is. And then, if it goes into the, you know, the urine and things like that. This is even, and maybe it

is telling the people that used that, you know, which
would be the women.

MS: Unhuuhn?

HW: You know, something. Now, we have a tendency to
panic, you know, for something like that. Every time a
coyote crosses our path. We run to a medicine man.
And actually these are signs, these are signs, like a coyote crossing your path or seeing an owl around your
house, the things like that. What they are saying is, "Stop
and smell the rose. Smell the flowers. You have been set
on this earth. You have not acknowledged the Holy
People that are responsible for it. Think of yourself.
Thank your creator. And acknowledge your existence
and be thankful for it." This is what it is saying and you
do that through ceremony.[16]

Following the recommendations of the medicine men, prayers
and ceremonies were conducted inside the building and herbs
were placed around the outside of the building to determine
the message brought by the snakes and to counteract the influence the snakes might exert on the people using the building.
Precautions were taken because, as Shorty told reporters, "snakes
are tied to the urinary and reproductive organs of humans and
men and women relationships. Women are the most suscep-
tible."[17] Ms. Yazza expressed profound concern for the numerous pregnant women who worked in the building and noted
that the menstrual cycles of several female employees became
abnormal following the sightings.[18] She recalled being told that
according to Navajo oral tradition, if a snake urinates where a
woman urinates, the snake considers the woman its wife. And
she cautioned, "That is not a good position to be in."[19]

This belief stems from an episode recorded in Navajo oral
history in which two old men—the Bear and the Big Snake—
transformed themselves into handsome young men in order to

seduce two lovely sisters promised to whichever young men could demonstrate the greatest skills.[20] Bear and Big Snake were denied the maidens even after successfully completing all challenges—shooting an arrow into a far off hole in a cliff wall, and slaying and scalping a great warrior in battle. After the battle, the sisters were directed to attend the Great Scalp Dance that followed and, while there, to "choose whichever young men you would like to be your husbands."[21] Bear and Big Snake, who had camped nearby, rolled and smoked herbal cigarettes, blowing the sweet smelling smoke toward the dancers. The fragrant smoke lured the young sisters to the camp, where they were drawn to two handsome young men; the elder girl went to the disguised Bear and the younger to the disguised Snake. The elder sister discovered the deception when she awoke to find "her arm around the Bear's neck, and his arm was around the girl. He was still asleep and his ugly teeth showed. She awakened her sister. A great Snake was coiled around the body of the young girl; their heads were together, and her hand was on the Snake."[22] The sisters immediately set off in frantic flight in different directions. Ever since, Snake has been searching for his human wife relentlessly, calling, "Oh, my wife!"[23]

Despite their peaceable nature, the snakes were considered a dangerous invasion of the bodies of the women who used the restroom because, as staff working in the building were told by the traditional experts who were consulted, "snakes especially affect humans through their body secretions."[24] This information particularly troubled the women because the snakes were sighted where their bodily secretions were deposited. The snakes represented a threat to the health and well-being of women who used the restroom because they might have come into direct contact with the bodily substances—urine, feces, menstrual blood, hair, nail clippings, skin cells—left there by the women.

CONTEMPORARY NIHOOKÁÁ DINE'É

After their creation on the earth's surface, the first Nihookáá Dine'é learned that they were not made to live as individuals; rather, they were immediately matched and paired to found the Navajo social order.[25] Once paired, these men and women were directed to go forth to Dinétah and increase their numbers through heterosexual reproduction. Recognizing that danger lay ahead, Changing Woman gave each clan a magical cane made of a precious stone and provided it with a pair of guardians— the male and female bear, the male and female thunderbird, the male and female wind, or the male and female big snake— to protect its members from evil and harm.[26] It is said that "[t]he people created from the left hand of White Bead Woman [Changing Woman] became the Near-the-Water-Clan, having a pet male and female big snake and carrying a cane made out of dark oyster shell."[27] During this clan's migration to Dinétah, male big snake took on an important protective role for all future Nihookáá Dine'é.[28]

In the Navajo world, where non-human entities—baskets, birds, houses, snakes—have qualities of personhood, membership in the community of life is based on shared substance and structure. Thus, all Nihookáá Dine'é are homologues of Navajo homes, cradles, and other beings, such as snakes and birds, who share directional orientation and structure, including binary form. The binary structural division shared by all persons in the Navajo world reflects duality, a fundamental principle of Navajo philosophy and cosmology.[29] Complementarity delineates and informs all aspects of Navajo life, including human relationships and the human body. As Walters explains, "Everything is in terms of male and female in the Navajo. This is the duality. There is a male part and then the female counterpart in everything, you know, even us. I am a man, but my left side is my male side, my right side is my female."[30] Pairings such as life and death, night and day, and male and female exist on all levels of the web of interconnection, which is formed by the relationships of persons to each other and to the universe. As noted by Walters, this complementary pairing establishes a base paradigm found throughout Navajo cosmology, in which male and female are paired in myriad homologues. On the cosmic plane, the universe consists of Mother Earth and Father Sky. Since the last underworld, men and women have been considered necessary counterparts. Being complete, a couple represents a stronger entity than does a single person. Therefore, on the social level, no man or woman is considered to be whole without a counterpart of the complementary gender.[31] On an individual level, every person is regarded as a whole, possessing both male and female aspects or qualities; this is a pairing that is demonstrated in the actual composition of the human body.

Wilson Aronilth says, "We are divided right in half from the tip of our head down to our feet."[32] The left-hand side of the body is considered male, while the right-hand side of the body is female.[33] As Ursula Knoki-Wilson of Ganado, Arizona, points out in the following excerpt, these contrasting sides and qualities are regarded as aspects of personhood rather than as purely physical attributes:

> What I learned is they say that your right side is your female side and the left side is your male side. And so they teach you that, you know, you're always balanced in that way psychically. That you are, you know, you respect both, the male and the femaleness within you. . . . It is more like psychic energies that they are referring to rather than, you know, the actual physical dimensions.[34]

The left-hand side of every individual is naayéé' k'ehjigo, "on the side of protection," the "warrior" side of the person, and the right-hand side is hózhǫ́ǫjigo, "on the side of peace, harmony, and order," the "peaceful" side of the person.[35] This division is not unique to humans; every living entity in the Navajo world has had naayéé'jí and hózhǫ́ǫjí components since the first underworld.[36]

These contrasting sides are not viewed as separate. Time and again, Navajo people with whom I consulted stated that they do not consider one side of the person, or one facet of any particular characteristic, to be more significant than the other; both sides and facets are necessary for harmony, balance, and health to exist. I was told that the distinction between sides is readily acknowledged on a philosophical level. Navajo people are conditioned from early childhood to perform certain activities with a specific hand, and certain activities are done to a specific side of the body in ceremony. But Navajo people do not routinely make a conscious differentiation between the experiences associated with the right or left sides of their bodies.[37] In combination, the naayéé'jigo and hózhǫ́ǫjigo aspects of the individual contribute to the development and maintenance of a physically, emotionally, mentally, and spiritually harmonious person. To be whole and remain harmonious, all Navajo must respect both the maleness and the femaleness within themselves.[38] When illness occurs, a new stage of life is broached, or an unusual incident such as the snake sightings occurs, the naayéé'jigo and hózhǫ́ǫjigo aspects of the individual play important roles.

Situations involving bath water, hair, saliva, body oils, and blood illustrate how the Navajo system governing the cultural construction of the human body and personhood simultaneously informs choices and is reproduced in practice. These situations also demonstrate the impact of practice on the system and clearly demonstrate the complex interweaving of the cosmological, social, and bodily realms that contemporary Navajo people negotiate to control and harness the power embodied in various effects as they respond to the problems and demands of the modern world.

SYNECDOCHE: BATH WATER, HAIR, SALIVA, AND BLOOD

MS: Are there any special rules regarding the disposal of a baby's first bath water?

UKW: Yeah, they are not supposed to just, you know, splatter it all over the place. They are supposed to pour it real gently to the earth. In a safe [place], you know, like maybe underneath a healthy bush or tree, something like that. But, they are not supposed to splatter it anywhere.

MS: Oh? I guess what I was thinking about was the fact that at birth the child is usually covered with some blood.

UKW: Unhuuhn?

MS: And so that would be in the bath water.

UKW: Yeah.

MS: Is there any danger associated with the blood involved in childbirth?

UKW: Well blood is not supposed to be burned. Because they say if you burn blood then it invokes fever, because it is sort of like living tissue and you burn your living tissue, so to speak. . . . So if you splatter it then the living tissue would get bruised, so to speak, then your body would, the baby's body would suffer, you know, sort of like trauma from that. So they are supposed to gently pour it.

MS: So the blood from the birth, which is no longer actually attached to the body, is still considered to have an influence over the body?

UKW: Yeah.[39]

Because synecdoche and the rules governing effect demand that all parts of the body belong to someone, this lifelong connection is linguistically encoded. In the Navajo language, it is impossible to say simply "leg" or "hair" because parts of the body must be possessed at all times; the term for every part is inalienable from a pronominal prefix. For example, the stem for hair, -*tsii*', cannot occur in speech without a prefix, such as *shi*-, "my," or *ni*-, "your," to designate possession. Such identification is critical, because parts of the body, bodily fluids, and offal offer the potential for positive or negative influence throughout life. As a result, people must demonstrate personal responsibility over parts of their own bodies and bodily fluids, and as Mrs. Knoki-Wilson noted above, adults must demonstrate responsibility over those of children. Mae Bekis of Tó'tsoh, Arizona, explained the process to me:

> MS: I have noticed when I am visiting in homes and they are trimming hair, like a little child's hair or one woman trimming another woman's hair, that they sweep up the hair and put it in a little bag. And the same with nail clippings. How is one supposed to dispose of those things?
>
> MB: I was always told that when you trim your hair you are supposed to burn it. . . . You can't throw it away because if you threw it away outside it would be blown around by the wind and then, who knows? it can be picked up by the rats, mice, the snakes and they will make a nest, and then you will have a headache, and nobody will know why you have a headache. Or the birds pick it up for their nest somewhere up on the tree or ahh, up into the highest pine tree, or way up into the rocks, you know. And you wouldn't know where your hair is and they say, they say it can give you headaches.
>
> MS: Will it affect your thinking?
>
> MB: Yeah. That is why they say, "Be careful with your hair. Always burn it."
>
> MS: Unhuuhn. How about nail clippings? Like when you trim your nails?
>
> MB: Nail clippings, always burn it too.[40]

Hair, which is composed of male rain, female rain, and the moisture of clouds, must be carefully cared for and disposed of throughout life because it is a physical embodiment of thought and lifelong knowledge.[41] Given its importance, the Holy People instructed the Nihookáá Dine'é in strict rules regarding the manipulation of hair.[42] The Holy People directed all Nihookáá Dine'é to wear their hair bound securely in a bun at the nape of the neck. When I asked women about the relationship between thinking and the hair bun, they told me the bun helps to contain and control one's accumulated knowledge so that one can think effectively and not have one's thoughts "scattered."[43]

Or worse, as Ruth Roessel of Round Rock, Arizona, pointed out, leaving your hair unsecured risks having your thoughts literally "blow away."[44] Wearing your hair in the traditional bun demonstrates that you are "thinking in the proper way," that the "mind is all set," that your "thinking is controlled," and that you are "strong and the mind is good."[45] When thinking becomes uncontrolled, illness is likely to ensue. A Navajo woman from Cortez, Colorado, noted that uncontrolled or disturbed thinking might also result from improper disposal of hair. She told me, "There is a fear of mice getting a hold of a person's hair and making its nest and home with it. That is because the individual will not think as well as he or she could."[46]

Not even the most conscientious Navajo can contain or control every bit of the body sloughed off or eliminated in the process of daily life. This is evident when the complex relationship between artists and their artistic products is considered. A lifelong connection exists between artifact and maker because, in several ways, every artistic product is literally a part of its maker. Artifacts are imbued with life through the entrance of the maker's Wind, and the designs in artifacts are extensions of the artist because they are physical embodiments of the maker's thoughts. The situation for weavers and other artists producing for the off-reservation market is further complicated by the fact that actual parts of the body of the maker are incorporated into the art in the process of manufacture. For example, as Mrs. Bekis explained, oil from a weaver's hands, her or his saliva, and hair all inevitably become integrated into yarn as it is carded and spun, and into the textile as it is woven.

> This man that is doing it [referring to a ceremony being performed in the local community] down here, he can do a sing, a Weaving Way singing too. Because you are thinking, a lot of your designs, you are thinking away. And that will affect you later on, too. Just the memory. . . . There are some ladies that can get affected by that. And they said it is just thinking away. And then you sell your mind away, your thinking. . . . By selling the rugs. And then you never know how they keep it and how they take care of it, and all that. . . . And, you know, you may think, "My hand is clean," but you have the body oils on your loom, on your [rubs her fingers together as if rolling yarn between them], when you're, and even sometimes you get to [motions running thread or yarn through her fingers and mouth], you know, fiddle with it, the yarn. . . . And you get your saliva on it, and it is sold with your saliva and it has all the body oil, and everything, and your thinking. Your hair, you know, gets in the way, gets caught in it. It is in it. And nobody knows where they take it and all that, so. That is why it affects them.[47]

As a result of the lifelong connections amongst weavers, parts of their bodies, and the thoughts contained in their designs, ceremonies are frequently needed to rectify problems that develop after their weavings have been sold.

In contrast to the unintended ill effect that may result from mistreatment of textiles, with various parts of a weaver's body inadvertently incorporated into those products during manufacture, weavers may also consciously manipulate the cultural system to attain beneficial effect. A weaver consigned to construct a biil (two-piece woven dress) for a young female relative to wear in her Kinaaldá (puberty ceremony) is confidant that the hair, saliva, and skin oil that are incorporated into the garment in the process of manufacture will transfer the weaver's best qualities—industriousness, good health, ambition, and knowledge of traditional ways—to the wearer. Moreover, she understands that the blessings invoked by the ceremony will be simultaneously transferred to her through the parts of her body and bodily substances incorporated in the garment. In addition, weavers may intentionally incorporate materials such as "fragments of animal bone, sinew, tufts of hair, stems of plants, bits of non-wool fiber, and even shreds of paper currency" into weavings for family members.[48] The rationale for such additions is the principle of synecdoche; the items are added with the clear intent of transferring desirable qualities from one person to another through the textile. Toward this end, a weaver constructing a saddle blanket for a close relative may incorporate a sliver of sinew saved from the carcass of the family's strongest horse so that the horse's "speed and strength would now be transmitted through the saddle blanket to any other mount."[49]

Beliefs resulting from incorporation of various parts of a person's body into handwoven products are not unique in the Navajo world. Rather, they are simply a few of the numerous examples demonstrating that the boundaries of the Navajo person—the social construct based on culturally sanctioned rules, prerogatives, and agency—are extended beyond the boundaries of the skin in the principle of synecdoche. Care must also be taken in the placement or disposal of bodily substances such as urine or menstrual blood, which are discharged from the body on a routine basis, for undesirable consequences can result from contact between such substances from one's own body and other powerful persons in the Navajo world.

SNAKES

Killing a snake was believed to bring aches and pains in the backbone. This could be cured only by offering a carved stick representing a snake or the sandpainting of a snake.[50]

Rattlesnake said, "In the future if earth surface people get diseases which make their ankles, knee-cap, joints, or stomachs swell, I will be the cause of it."[51]

Killing or mishandling of a snake, contact with a snake while hunting, dreaming about snakes, or violating prohibitions against the eating of snake meat may result in a variety of health problems.[52] Snakes are considered to be directly associated with numerous parts of the human body. They are tied to the urinary and reproductive organs of both sexes.[53] In addition, an explicit correlation is made between snakes and the male sex organ.[54] The phallus is considered by some to be like Big Snake searching for his wife. Snakes are also connected to the intestines and, as Mrs. Bekis illustrates in the following account of one woman's unfortunate encounter with a snake, the backbone.[55]

> MB: There is this one lady, . . . she used to live down here a ways, and she said that when she was a young woman, when ahh, she, well I guess they didn't have a bathroom or something and she went and put her, when, her napkin thing?
> MS: [Nods].
> MB: Rolled it up and put it in somewhere, you know, where she usually keeps it until she is done and then she would take it out and burn it. . . . And with some herbs and then she burns it and that is the way, I guess, her grandma or somebody told her to do. And she had been doing that, you know, putting it [demonstrates

the rolling up of a napkin]. And at her heaviest, you
know, her heaviest flow, she said she went and put
some napkins over there and then here during noon
she went out again, you know, put another one there
and here she found there was a snake right there!
And it had sucked all the blood out! And ahh, she
went and told her husband what the snake had done,
you know, that she had found it over where she was
putting these napkins. And then, he went and got a
medicine man. And the medicine man tried to get
that blood out somehow. Out of the snake. It was a
bullsnake. He said, "Bullsnake is not dangerous." But
I guess it just, they said you could see it way down at
the tip of its tail, you know, the blood was there. It
sucked so much out. And, they killed it but she still
had problems, she had back problems. And it killed
her too. But, they said they couldn't do anything
because the snake, they killed the snake, they could-
n't get that blood out of it, you know, and everybody
was afraid to dissect it and all that. And they are not
supposed to do that, and all that, you know. And she
said, it killed her. . . . She wasn't young, she was up in
the seventies or eighties when she died, but she said
she always had a back problem. . . .

MS: Now, I was told by some people that blood is never to
be burnt.

MB: Oh, well, they said it can be because you use herbs to
do it. To burn it with.[56]

Snakes, arrows, lightning, and by extension storms and other
sky phenomena, are conjoined in Navajo tradition by similarities
in form. As a result, those ceremonies that engage the power of
lightning, wind, flint, and stars in protection and curing are
found to be most efficacious in counteracting the influence of

contact with snakes. *Béeshee*, "Flint Way," *Diné binííłch'ijí*, "Small Wind Way," *Na'at'oyee*, "Shooting or Lightning Way Chant," *Níích'ihjí*, "Wind Way," and *Sǫ́'tsohjí*, "Star Chant," are recognized as ceremonies effective against the power of snakes.[57] Flint chant, indicated for illnesses that include discharge from the mouth, differs with the kind of discharge. "Phlegm is attributed to Thunder, blood to Bear or Snake."[58] "The Shooting Chant is armor against diseases caused by snakes, lightning, and arrows, but the Wind Chant features snakes as extensively; it protects against their power and the harm of storms."[59] Great snakes of the colors associated with the four cardinal directions black, blue, yellow, white are the first of several beings called upon to protect patients in the Star Chant.[60] For protection, snakes may also be painted on shields, on the soles and up the sides of ritually prepared hunting moccasins, or directly onto a hunter's body.[61]

A patient's body can also be painted with snake images. A variety of materials may be ceremonially applied to patients; these include herbal mixtures, ashes, sheep fat, pigments, pollen, cedar smoke, and an assortment of other items such as sashes, moccasins, handwoven textiles, shoulder straps, paunches, or braided wristbands and anklebands made of yucca. Every substance or artifact with which a patient is ceremonially ornamented provides a layer of lifelong protection to the surface of the body. Persons acquire an additional layer of beneficial protection each time such items are ceremonially applied to them, and these layers of protection accumulate over the years. Each protective layer, beneficial to the person to whom it is applied, can cause grave harm to an uninitiated individual. Snakes are painted on the feet and big toes of the patient as a means of protection during Na'at'oyee, Diné binííłch'ijí, and Nííłch'ihjí.[62] As Mrs. Bekis explains below, harm can result from the simple act of wearing the footwear of a person who has been painted in this manner.

Even the shoes like if ahh, somebody was initiated with
some singing, you know, like Lightning Way and ahh,
when they do the painting on their patients, like Lightning
Way and they have a, you know, they use a snake as a painting, for their patients. Right here [points to the place on
her own body]. . . . On the [outside of the] calf. And then
on your big toe, under here [pointing to a sketch she is
making of the body painting]. From the nail down is the
head of a snake that is coming down and then the tip is
the tongue here. The forked tongue? And then they said,
it does an imprint in your shoes. And you are not supposed
to wear [the moccasins or other footwear of] anybody that
is initiated like through Lightning Way, Wind Way, the
Small Wind Way, and all of this. You are not supposed to
wear somebody's shoes like that because the imprint, it
puts an imprint forever on the shoes. It just, you know, the
black paint that they use? It makes an imprint inside of
your shoes and it imprints deep into your skin. . . . And
they said the black paint that they use, it is a, it is just a clay.
The black clay, but it imprints on your body in your flesh
and they said it stays a long time in there. Even on [places
her hand on her chest]. They put it on you, on your chest
too. And then they said, that imprint stays within you as
long as you live because you are initiated.[63]

ANALYSIS

The snake sightings incidents were of serious concern to Navajo
people because they entailed the intersection of two tropes integral to Navajo cultural constructions of personhood—complementarity and synecdoche. Just as the well-being of weavers may
be affected by the mistreatment of their woven products, or a

horse's performance may be improved by incorporation of a piece of sinew from a noteworthy mount into a saddle blanket, certain properties—including the naayéé'jí and hózhǫ́ǫ́jí powers of the snakes seen in Administration Building No. 2—could be transferred to women using the restroom through contact between the snakes (or their bodily substances) and the women (or their bodily substances). Mapping of the limits of effect in each case establishes the extension of personhood outside the physical limits of the skin. The women who used the facilities visited by the snakes were at risk because the visiting snakes had direct contact with their menstrual blood, hair, skin oil, skin cells, urine, and feces that were deposited in the restroom.

Contact between snakes and humans is potentially dangerous because snakes and humans, as Navajo persons constructed according to the principles established by the Holy People at the rim of the place of emergence, are homologues sharing substance and structure—including complementarity. The hózhǫ́ǫ́jí powers embodied in the peaceful side of snakes allow them to carry omens to Nihookáá Dine'é; thus, the visitors were considered harbingers of imminent positive or negative events. The naayéé'jí powers embodied in the warrior side of snakes allow them to act fiercely when serving as protectors. When these powers are jointly harnessed and directed in a controlled setting—the songs, prayers, body paintings or drypaintings of a Béeshee, Diné biníłch'iji, Na'at'oyee, Níłch'ihjí, or Sǫ́'tsohjí ceremony—they can provide benefit. When contact with snakes occurs in uncontrolled settings, however, as when an uninitiated person wears an initiated individual's shoes or snakes and humans meet in a restroom—grave harm can result from misdirection of these same powers. This is why the snakes sighted in the ladies' restroom of Administration Building No. 2 in July of 1994 posed a threat to the women using the facilities.

The awareness Navajo people have of themselves as perceptible subjects and their understanding of the social constructs embodied in the corporeal body are informed by the principle of synecdoche, which dictates that the boundaries of individuals extend to the full area in which parts of their bodies and thoughts exist. The Navajo people I have consulted are clearly aware of themselves as agents with volition, yet they tend to highlight relations with other people and entities over personal autonomy. The Navajo case, therefore, supports those studies that challenge the assumption that an interdependent or relational sense of self is most frequently associated with non-Western societies and that an independent or autonomous sense of self is most frequently found in Western societies. And it supports those studies that demonstrate how both forms of identification are experienced by Western and non-Western people in various contexts.[64] Furthermore, it contributes to the "critical anthropology of selfhood" current in disciplinary discourse by raising the question of whether the privileging of an interdependent or relational sense of self by Navajo people is directly related to the principle of synecdoche.[65] The evidence for such a conclusion is persuasive. Without doubt, an awareness of the potential consequences of handling or disposing of detached parts of the body and bodily secretions influences Navajo perceptions of themselves as individuals with volition. In important ways, this understanding is contextualized within a relational framework that defines, codifies, and delineates who or what can affect what or whom in specific circumstances. This contextualization shifts emphasis from the part (the individual) to the sense of the whole (the social world) and bridges the gap between Navajo senses of self and Navajo senses of person. The complex network of influence inherent in the Navajo world makes the human individual part of and dependent on the kinship group and the community of life, including plants, animals, and aspects of the cosmos, and it conflates the "self" with the "person."[66]

These findings intimate that a reexamination of information available from societies worldwide (Western and non-Western alike) that are known for magic, witchcraft, sorcery, or other methods intended to affect people through manipulation of detached parts of the body and bodily substances may shed light on cross-cultural notions of selfhood and personhood. Systematic comparison of societies worldwide should be directed at discovering what correlation may exist between the principle of synecdoche and notions of self and person, as well as at determining whether beliefs about the extension of the boundaries of the body and personhood in these societies parallel those held by Navajo people. Further investigations along these lines would demonstrate that the principle of synecdoche bridges the gap between "self" and "person" in many societies, as it does in the Navajo world.

CHAPTER FIVE

Activism through Emotional Expression

To this day, the uranium is spreading its disease amongst us. The companies left piles of uranium ore beside the roads and did not clean them away. . . . They thought of us as nothing, us Navajos. It really hurts my heart and mind, sometimes I just cry [begins to weep]. I feel like they killed our husbands and with them went our spirits. . . . I think many people know about the effects of the uranium mining because so many miners have died. As a result, children have no fathers, and many women have become widows. It really hurts. We have suffered a great deal. So many of us are in pain and I often cry about it [continues to weep]. Each time you see someone suffering [crying], or hear about their sadness, it is so traumatic. I have been so devastated by it all. Even though we were compensated, I still say it is not enough. I believe that the human spirit is invaluable. . . . There is no justice for us from the compensation. We have children we need to think about. Many of them were still infants when their fathers passed away [wiping her tears].

ANNA ALOYSIOUS,
in Brugge, et al., *URANIUM: The Navajo Nuclear Legacy*

Sitting in darkened classrooms, my students and I often have been moved by images of weeping Navajo women who are spokepersons for tribal members facing a variety of challenges. In the past two decades, the surge of public concern over issues such as the injustices experienced by American Indian uranium mine workers and their families or the plight of Navajo slated for relocation off land partitioned to the Hopi in 1974 catapulted Navajo people into the limelight of global media attention. As a result, unassuming individuals from remote communities on the Navajo reservation have agreed to testify before policymakers and government officials or to consult with sympathetic outsiders including anthropologists and documen tary filmmakers.

Some of the women struggle to inform the public of the atrocities of uranium mining and the need for the eligibility requirements for compensation, under the Radiation Exposure Compensation Act (RECA), to be made more culturally sensitive. Others continue to resist relocation off HPL. Testimonials, such as that of Mrs. Aloysious, frequently are framed by images of weeping women or punctuated by bouts of crying. As a result, tears play a prominent role in the expression of the profound emotions shared with readers, viewers, or listeners.

Images of crying women come to mind when listeners hear the mournful refrain of Vincent Craig's ballad "Someone Drew a Line," which challenges "Mr. President" to "look at the old ones there as they cry because someone drew a line, someone drew a line, someone drew a line," demarcating NPL from HPL.[1] Viewers of the documentary film *Broken Rainbow* are riveted as the camera pans weeping women sitting along the barbed-wire fence dividing NPL from HPL.[2] An unidentified Navajo woman tells viewers, "Washingdoon [the federal government] seems to be very immature. They believe in lies. They have no pity and cannot see us. We go around wiping our tears because of what they do."[3] Jane Biakeddy, with tears streaming down her cheeks, says, "Because we don't count, our plans and thoughts for walking forward into a good future have been taken away from us. It seems as though our future has been beaten out of us with a stick. What is there to make us whole again? There is nothing."[4] Images of weeping women have also been captured in newspaper accounts of related events.[5]

Without exception, the weeping of women makes these testimonials compelling to hear about, to read about, or to watch. Seeing their tears or having specters of crying women drawn through another's prose, I have been moved; I have empathized with their causes.[6] These images are especially intriguing for me, however, because they bring to mind occasions during my time spent on the Navajo reservation when I shed tears and had lessons taught to me by Navajo people about rules governing the sharing of tears with family members, friends, or fictive kin. Knowing what I know about Navajo views on exposure to bodily substances such as tears, my interest has been piqued as to why individuals *choose* to share their teardrops with strangers.

Watching women cry openly in *Broken Rainbow* or *URANIUM: The Navajo Nuclear Legacy*, I found myself asking, why didn't they shield their faces, turn away, or walk away? Ultimately I wondered, did they intentionally share tears as a means of eliciting empathy? The tears were not disingenuous; the sincerity of the women involved is readily apparent to viewers. But given Navajo cultural display rules, which dictate how, when, and where personal emotions are to be social experiences, one must wonder why these women were willing to shed tears in these situations.

The full import of women sharing tears only becomes evident when this act is placed within the context of anthropological and Navajo perspectives on the body and the social significance of emotional expression. Navajo beliefs about personhood and effect dictate that emotional states of being can be conveyed via detached body parts and substances. This renders emotional expressions on the part of Navajo individuals simultaneously deeply personal and profoundly social. Navajo women who shed tears in front of government officials, documentary filmmakers, news reporters, or other outsiders know that their tears have the ability to engender understanding and compassion for their causes, thus their actions can be considered social acts with intentional consequences.

THE HUMAN COSTS OF URANIUM MINING

> Doing prayers we just cry! The children did not see their grandfather. I am the mother and father of my children. I am concerned about the land. If it was not mined all this would not have happened! Our hearts are not calm. We keep remembering. My husband died in the month of May—from that day on I've been ill in my thinking and general health. Relief comes only from placing flowers on his grave. This is how we live! Wiping tears, thinking of our loved one! Never lose the memory.[7]

Despite uncontroversial evidence that working with uranium and radium could cause lung disease, cancer, and other debilitating or fatal health problems, companies operating mines on the Navajo reservation, to produce ore for the nuclear weapons program during the Cold War era (1947–1971), refused to warn their employees or to take even the most elementary safety measures until 1971, and the federal government failed to intervene.[8] Starting in 1943, Navajo workers alternately entered the confined spaces of "dog holes," small mines lacking proper ventilation, lighting, and water supplies, to dig uranium ore with shovel and pick; blasted rocks with dynamite, thereby breathing radon gas and silica-laden dust; or extracted uranium in mills.[9] Between 1943 and 1973, an estimated 3,750 to 5,000 Navajo men labored as miners while thousands more toiled as millers in the uranium mining industry on the Colorado Plateau.[10]

Unaware of the potential danger exposure to radiation or dust-filled mines posed to their health, miners worked without protective gear, ate their lunches in the mines, and quenched the thirst generated by a hard day's labor by drinking from "hot" puddles on the mine floors formed from water that seeped from mine walls.[11]

The grief expressed by Navajo women in the venues currently under consideration stems from the loss of life resulting from involvement in the uranium mining industry. The lives of many of the men who labored in this industry have been, and continue to be, cut short due to contraction of various forms of cancer, or debilitating respiratory (pulmonary emphysema, chronic bronchitis) or nonrespiratory (fibrosis or silicosis) diseases at alarming rates.[12] The tragedy is compounded because miners and millers are not the only casualties. In case after case, widows with young children are left without any significant means of support.[13] Moreover, many family and community members were exposed to high levels of dust and radiation by direct and indirect means.

Because shower facilities were not provided for their use, Navajo miners and millers brought dust particles home from work on their hair, hands, shoes, and clothes, the latter of which were usually washed with the laundry of other family members.[14] Children obliviously played on uranium tailings. People and animals were poisoned after contaminated mining by-products were negligently dumped into local water supplies used by Navajo families for themselves and their livestock.[15] Furthermore, homes were built from the radioactive materials left behind by mining companies.[16] As a result of these types of exposure, thousands of Navajo, including women and children, have suffered serious health problems without ever having worked a day in a uranium mine.

Public Law 101-426, the Radiation Exposure Compensation Act of 1990 (RECA), was designed to compensate those suffering health problems caused by exposure to excess radiation or illness-causing levels of dust particles while living downwind from aboveground nuclear test sites or while working in underground uranium mines.[17] Notwithstanding the good intentions of lawmakers, millers were not included in this legislation and requirements for proof of eligibility are cumbersome and culturally insensitive, making it exceedingly difficult for many deserving people to qualify for much-needed compensation under RECA.[18]

ANTHROPOLOGICAL PERSPECTIVES ON EMOTION

And she [her grandmother Lydia Watchman] had this one particular tree that she used to pray to and um, she tried to tell this to the people that were reseeding, that were using bulldozers, you know, to cut down all of the trees [on a portion of HPL]. And this one day, they went and buried her, her ah, sacred spring and they went, they went over this tree that she treasured so much. She cried for mercy! Every time I start talking about relocation, every time I start to translate for anybody or having to talk on relocation issues, I just get choked up with tears. And I try to be strong but, you know, every time I talk about the relocation issue, you know, what is going on at Big Mountain, you know, it is really hard.[19]

Historically, anthropological studies of emotion have involved a complex set of arguments demonstrating tension between universalistic (positivist) and relativistic (interpretativist) approaches.[20] Prior to the last quarter century or so, emotions were generally relegated to "the sidelines of culture theory" because they were believed to occupy the more "natural and biological provinces

of human experience" and thus were seen as "relatively uni-
form, uninteresting, and inaccessible to the methods of cultural
analysis."[21] This approach is dominated by a materialistic paradigm wherein emotions are "constituted biologically as facial
muscle movements, raised blood pressure, hormonal and neu-
rochemical processes, and as 'hard-wired' instincts making up
a generic human psyche."[22] In marked contrast, cross-cultural
analysis reveals that in some social worlds "[f]eelings are not
substances to be discovered in our blood but social practices"
structured by culturally specific understandings.[23]

A breakthrough in the anthropological research of emotions
came with the realization that although our own society tends
to locate emotions firmly within the individual—as "matters of
internal psychobiology and biography" or "messages from a private place within the individual," if you will—other cultural systems frequently locate emotions in social relations or in the relationship between persons and events.[24] Comparative research
demonstrates that because they are prone to arise in contexts
involving interpersonal relations, people in many societies consider emotions to play pivotal roles in the mediation of social
activities. In these contexts, emotional comprehensions are not
perceived as "abstract, symbolic formulations" so much as perceptions that are directly connected to particular social situations and culturally valued objectives.[25]

On the heels of these realizations, emotion theory took on
new importance for sociocultural theory proper as it moved
beyond its original psychobiological framework to include concern with the relational, communicative, and cultural aspects
of emotional experience.[26] For scholars inclined to define emotions as culturally constructed, "the social situations in which
emotions variously arise or are displayed, and the social relations experienced by and partly defining the self, become critical for emotional understanding."[27] Thus, current research
tends to consider emotion as a relational construct—locating

emotion in the relationships between persons or between persons and events rather than only within the individual.[28] While such studies alert us to the "discursive, performative, and social" aspects of emotion, they do not exclude the possibility that emotion can also be bodily, expressive, or personal.[29]

Due in part to one of the fundamental teachings of the Holy People, enshrined in Navajo oral tradition and governing Navajo personhood, emotions are both internally and externally experienced in the Navajo world. Because the principle of synecdoche holds that every part stands for the whole and that contiguity is retained even after detachment or expulsion of bodily parts or substances, emotional states of being can be conveyed via detached body parts and substances. As a result, Navajo emotional experience is both bodily and socially constructed, as well as constructing. The latter is true because expression of emotion is a social act with consequences, for a Navajo individual can deliberately convey her emotions to another person simply by shedding tears in his or her presence.

LAUGHTER AND TEARS

They talk about the emotion. How it develops is, uh, you probably heard about the Navajo they honor this, when a little infant, a child is born and later, their First Laugh? [I nod my head] . . . The child will laugh and then cry. That is where that emotional development starts, they say. So it has something to do with crying and then laughing, that is what it is, they say. So in Navajo they say that is the beginning, that is where it initiates, the emotional being, or the emotional aspects of the humanity, that is where it initiates. When the baby first laughs and then cries, and then that is when they do a ceremony for them.[30]

The acknowledgement of a child-of-a-few-month's first expression of emotion occurs shortly after its first laugh, when a small celebration is held that establishes the child in relationship to her or his social landscape.[31] The purpose of this rite is to encourage generosity and to guarantee that the child will not grow up to be "stingy."[32] Infants may spend weeks merrily gurgling and chuckling to themselves before the first expression of emotion is acknowledged. Such behavior is not formally recognized because Navajo definitions of emotion are based on evidence of "some type of expression where you sort of like empathize with someone."[33] Thus, the official "first laugh" is perceived to be the moment when a child-of-a-few-months first responds with a chuckle or a laugh to direct stimulation from another person—cuddling, bouncing, or cooing. Therefore, at its core, Navajo emotional expression is simultaneously relational and reciprocal.

Accordingly, family members commemorate the child's preliminary step on the path to emotional development by firmly anchoring the child within the complex system of reciprocity and communication vital to Navajo social life, demonstrating to the Diyin Dine'é that the child will be a "good relative."[34] During this ceremony, reciprocal relations are initiated with a small gift of natural salt from the child to each member of his or her extended family in attendance.

At all subsequent stages of life, the developing Navajo person will continue to express empathy for others through laughter or tears because these are acknowledged as culturally appropriate forms of communication in the Navajo world. Although expressions of laughter are not generally circumscribed except in ceremonial contexts, Navajo people are cautioned against crying in any context without a purpose, for as a bodily substance, tears have the power to affect those present during their expulsion.[35] Sharing of tears is an established element of Navajo family life because expressions of emotion and tears are mechanisms for simultaneously defining and reinforcing the kinship system and personal attachments. This is evident at reunions and ceremonial gatherings as well as at departures.

Up until the 1960s, wailing often occurred when female relatives were reunited, even after a separation of brief duration.[36] For women, such crying episodes and the resultant sharing of bodily substance in the form of tears served to rekindle their kinship relations.

I personally learned about the significance of sharing tears during my second summer of fieldwork, at the close of my daughter's Kinaaldá (puberty ceremony). Having been raised in a family in which the sharing of tears in public was seen as a sign of weakness and thus was frowned upon, I was embarrassed when I broke into tears while trying to thank members of the Tso/Billie extended family for sponsoring the ceremony. Knowing that we were all in a "blessed state" because we had participated in the ceremony and that my tears were those of joy, family members did not find my weeping problematic. Instead, they commented that my tears demonstrated sincerity and made me "truly a relative."

When the time came for me to depart for home at the end of the summer of 1992, I learned that there was another side to tears. As we drove out to her mother's home so that I could say my goodbyes, Sadie Billie cautioned me, "No tears. Crying will make all of us sick!" She explained that tears expressed at a departure affect everyone present and make them pine for the departed.[37]

In spite of this known consequence, family members tend to cry openly when a relative prepares to leave home for an extended period of time. Some weeping is generally allowed on such occasions, for the shedding of tears at a departure has a purpose. It demonstrates how hard it is for family members to stretch their ties across physical separation. While it is accepted that every separation involves strong emotions, established limits are enforced to avoid complications. Such limitations are no-where more evident than in the context of the permanent sep-aration brought about by a death in the family.

MOURNING

> But just when everything on the earth was good and beautiful the people saw the first death. . . . Now there came two beings called Alke'na ashi, Made Again, who looked like Yei. They were sent to the East to look for the dead body. They returned and said that they had not seen it. They were sent to the South and they brought back the same report. They were sent to the West and the North without success. They were asked to look into the Yellow World where they had come from. As they were about to start they felt the flesh around their knees pinched; but they went on. They had a strange feeling of sound, like a rale, in their throats. They felt rather than heard this sound, but they went on. Then there was a sen-sation in their noses, like an odor, but they went on to the place of emergence, and they looked down. Way below them there was someone combing his hair.[38] He looked up and gave a little whistle, and they both experienced a strange feeling.
>
> When Alke'na ashi returned from the lower world they said that they had seen the spirit of the one who had died. They told just what they had felt and seen.
>
> They warned the others saying that they must not try to return to the Country of the Past for it was not well to experience such sensations nor to see such things.[39]

In direct response to the warnings of these Holy People, con-ventional Navajo mortuary practices include "strict avoidance of contact with the dead in order to prevent illness or unnatural death, and strict burial procedures and rules;"[40] moreover, cultural display rules govern when and where Navajo people may demonstrate their loss after a death.

Although burial customs are changing across the vast Navajo Reservation in response to various influences, traditional Navajo burials did not involve public ceremonies.[41] In such cases, interment was a private or family matter, and only those few people who were needed to perform the requisite procedures and were willing to expose themselves to the potentially dangerous effects of death were involved in the process.[42] Strict regulations governed the verbal and nonverbal behavior of participants as well as their attire and sustenance. Accordingly, all members of the burial party stripped to breechcloth or skirt, untied their hair and left it flowing so that not even a hair-tie was unnecessarily exposed, washed and dressed the deceased in his or her finest clothing and jewelry, and selected the items that would accompany him or her as grave goods.[43]

Once a site for interment was selected, the burial party transported the corpse and grave goods to that location. On the way, they were forbidden to spit or indulge in unnecessary conversation, and unsuspecting travelers were motioned away from their path.[44] After carefully arranging and burying the body and grave goods in the chosen place, breaking or otherwise mutilating shovels and other burial implements, and often after killing the deceased's favorite horse, the members of the burial party erased their tracks and returned home, in a "skip and hop fashion," via an alternate route.[45] After purifying themselves by various means, members of the burial party rejoined the family of the deceased, who then ended the fast begun at the time of the death.[46] All involved abstained from travel, labor, and unnecessary conversation during the four-day mourning period.[47]

Within the confines of this system of practices, keening and weeping are allowed only within the presence of relatives and

close friends. The bodily aspects of emotional expression deriving from the principle of synecdoche partially explain mourning rules that serve to limit the contact people have with grieving
individuals. People avoid such contact because they know that
the tears of mourners will convey their emotional state and cause
all present during their expulsion to experience the emotions
felt by them.

At funerals and during mourning, family members cry
openly up until the time the body is buried.[48] On the fourth day
after the interment, the close kin are advised to stop crying altogether;[49] otherwise, they will be anticipating another purpose—
that is, another death. The four-day period of mourning closes
with a ritual purification of all involved, a brief period of wailing, and a communal meal, which marks the reincorporation of
the bereaved into social life.[50] At this point, "the elders of the
family give counsel to forget the dead and turn toward life and
the living."[51] In some parts of the reservation, the Navajo system
governing mourning also requires that family members refrain
from mentioning the given name of the deceased, in Navajo or
in English, for a year or longer after death.[52]

Culturally defined mourning rules are adjusted or broken
by widows and children of miners who succumbed to illnesses
resulting from exposure to radiation or dust particles in the
mines. Prohibitions against dwelling on the deceased and past
events are ignored by widows and other relatives who also frequently make direct reference to their deceased loved ones
through usage of kinship terminology. Consider for example
the following interview excerpt in which Helen Johnson recalls
her family's experience during the period when her father
worked in the uranium mine industry and expresses her views
on the companies that benefited from such labor. She said,

> I was very young when my father died so I never discussed
> things such as his employment at the uranium mines.

Anyway, my mother told me about my father's employment with the uranium mines. She recalls my father coming home from the mines with wet stained clothes, unaware of the danger, and how he told her of the bad conditions during and after blasting. . . .

Question: What do you think about the companies that operated these mines, like Kerr-McGee and John Good and Trimax and so forth?

Well, um, they got what they wanted (uranium), of course. They were plain greedy and not honest people. For them, they had to hire workers to extract uranium from underground. The real sad thing about it was that they were never straight about what the hell this radiation was or would do to the health of these innocent people. White men (U.S. government and mining companies) are not honest people. . . . (Crying) I believe that's the white man's way of becoming wealthy.[53]

A less circumspect account comes from Jessie Harrison who, while fighting off sobs and with tears streaming down her cheeks, tells viewers of *Broken Rainbow*,

I went to Washington, two times. We need help to, somehow, so we need, ahh really help financial way . . . Kerr-McGee did not even tell us too, how dangerous this thing, [pause]. So all of my people and my husband, they killed them just like combat soldiers. They should think about, more about safety this time.[54]

As heart-wrenching as such pleas for help and compassion are to watch, they also convey important information, offering insight into Navajo experience and, insofar as these actions can be seen as deliberate, insight into Navajo female activism.

SUMMATION

I was unsure how to deal with crying (should I stop photo-graphing?). But when I asked the daughters and widows who cried (it was only those who had lost a loved one who cried), they told me repeatedly that it was part of what they wanted to share. And some noted that it was good to have some people to talk to about their grief (it seemed like they saw it as therapeutic).[55]

These case studies demonstrate the complex ways in which Navajo people use oral history as a guide to contemporary life. Because they frequently ignore mourning practices, breach public display rules limiting expression of emotion, or disre-gard prohibitions against using the given name of a deceased relative, it might seem at first glance that the women who are reeling from or battling against relocation off their homelands or coping with the loss of a loved one who has succumbed to a disease are *not* using the lessons encoded in Navajo oral his-tory. Yet, on a more subtle level, their actions reveal that they *are* following the teachings of the Holy People insofar as they are intentionally manipulating one of the fundamental beliefs governing understandings of personhood and effect in the Navajo world—the principle of synecdoche—towards their own ends.

This principle dictates that as a bodily substance, tears have the power to form a connection, or bond, between persons who are attendant during their expulsion. Essentially, all present when tears are expressed will feel the emotion being experi-enced by the person from whom the tears originate. So, if tears of joy are shared, such as mine after my daughter's Kinaaldá, all present feel joy; if tears are shared at a departure, all present will long for the departed during his or her absence or experi-ence the emotions of bereavement. Doug Brugge's commentary clearly reveals that Navajo women who have shared their tears with outsiders, such as those who conducted interviews for the Navajo Uranium Miners Oral History and Photography Project (NUMOHPP), made conscious decisions to do so.[56] Women grappling with relocation or widows and female children of deceased miners willing to discuss the circumstances leading to their distress or to the deaths of their loved ones and to shed tears in the presence of strangers participate in a conscious form of activism.

The presumed intentionality of such sharing is reinforced in the following interview excerpt from the NUMOHP project. Kathlene Tsosie-Blackie candidly acknowledges that her decision to discuss her loss with researchers was a breach of cultural proscriptions against dwelling on the past. This prohibition exists because in the Navajo view, human thought always must go forward in a clockwise spiral, never backward.[57] As Tsosie-Blackie explains,

> And like for me, it was really hard to do this interview because you go back in time and then, you know, our elders always say "go ahead" and that's how I was brought up by my grandparents, my father, my uncles; they always encouraged me to "go ahead." And as I speak I always say now, as I speak, I am my grandfather, my grandparents, my father, my uncles, my aunts, and my mother, as I speak, I am them. . . . I say my relatives have gone on to the spirit world, they come in the wind, the rain, the four seasons and I will always say that in my prayer and they guide us in the right direction.[58]

This breach was apparently outweighed by the perceived benefits to herself and others. In fact, gratitude for a sympathetic ear and a means through which to convey the concerns voiced by families of deceased or ill miners or others affected by the uranium mining industry in a public venue is readily apparent in the following statement.

> And the only thing we have is our prayers [crying] and as a relative and person that is concerned about this, you know, I really appreciate the people that are willing to help and their concerns, because they don't know how much we hurt and yet people think it's, you know, the people that did this, they think, "hey, deal with it, it's done and it's gone." It's not, it's not done and it's still there and that's why I say we really need a lot of counseling in our areas even though it's a remote area, no matter where you go there has to be some type of counseling support group [crying]. Thank you.[59]

It is not surprising that these women found the expression of tears therapeutic, for it is an acknowledged fact that "Navajo women store up worry, as part of their role as mothers," and tears are recognized as a means of cleansing the body of concerns over issues such as loss of access to one's matrilineal home or loss of relatives due to their involvement in the uranium mining industry.[60]

As the testimonies of these female spokespersons for tribal members who are facing the challenges of relocation or the untoward effects of the uranium mining industry reveal, the Navajo case provides a finely drawn example of the inextricable link between body and emotion in many cultures. Due in part to the principle of synecdoche, which dictates that emotional states of being can be conveyed via detached body parts and substances, in the Navajo world emotions are both internally and externally experienced; they are simultaneously deeply personal and profoundly social. It is safe to assume that these women clearly understood the consequences of their actions—

that their tears would convey their emotional state to all present at the time of their expulsion. The sharing of tears is therefore a social act that constitutes an unusual form of activism on the part of Navajo women.

Problem Drinking, Social Death, and Harmony

When a lot of people come out, they will say, "But you guys are not living the Beauty Way!" You know? Because they see something else, they see something totally inharmonious. I think that is how they would see it, but to me, I think we still live in harmony. I really do, because you have extremes. I think now it manifests itself in extremities, you know. You have an extremely well balanced person with someone that is dying of alcohol. To me, that is harmonious. I know that it is because we have to give something up, and you know, just that concept of giving and taking, is sort of there. And for us to be so plentiful, as Navajos, to be as plentiful as we are, we have to give something up. And it happens to be people with weak wills who succumb to alcohol. On the same instances, we also feel like those people who have given up on the Blessing Way philosophy and have become Christian, you know, that is giving something up. We are like losing, and at the same time we have to do that in order to be strong and to fulfill the prophecy of Changing Woman that says that if we adhere by these

*things, "You will become the strongest people." For strength
you have to give up something. Do you know what I
mean?*

SUNNY DOOLEY

First-time visitors to the Navajo reservation frequently
are struck by the seeming lack of beauty and harmony in the
contemporary Navajo world. Tourists and others come expect-
ing harmony because they have been steeped in popular images
of Navajo people—weaving in Monument Valley or herding
sheep on horseback in scenic canyons—and popular accounts
of Navajo culture that portray them as "noble savages" living in
"harmony" and "walking in beauty."

Misunderstandings of the essence of harmony and harmonious relations in the Navajo world as well as widespread misleading representations of American Indians generally contribute
to the generation and perpetuation of such images.[1] Visitors
indoctrinated by such imagery frequently are overwhelmed by
the mélange of reservation life—rundown tract housing, gang
symbols, revival tents, pickup trucks, litter, Christian churches, fast
food restaurants, and perhaps most disconcerting, 'adláanii,
"drunks."[2]

The toll alcohol use and abuse have taken in American Indian
communities is nothing short of catastrophic. American Indians
consume alcohol for diverse, complex, and frequently ambiva-
lent reasons.[3] By many accounts, the colonially induced "despair
experienced by American Indians of both genders has manifested itself in the most pronounced incidence of alcoholism
of any ethnic group in the United States."[4] Maladies suffered
by those who consume alcohol excessively include, but are not
limited to: cirrhosis, malnutrition, anemia, pancreatitis, intestinal
malabsorption, diabetes, alcoholic cardiomyopathy, delirium
tremens, cerebellar degeneration, dementia, and Korsakoff's

psychosis.[5] In addition, maternal consumption of alcohol contributes to increased incidence of fetal alcohol syndrome and other neonatal problems.[6]

Depending on the source consulted, deaths linked to alcohol use are three to six times higher for American Indians than for members of the general American population.[7] Alcohol is claimed as a factor in nearly 90 percent of all homicides involving American Indians and in most suicides and accidental-injury deaths. In fact, more than two-thirds of all treatments provided by physicians at Indian Health Service hospitals and clinics are for alcohol-related disease or trauma.[8]

Considering the degree to which alcohol has permeated American Indian experience, it is hard to imagine any anthropologist working in a North American Indian community who has not had encounters with Native problem drinkers while in the field.[9] I know that I certainly have. The experiences of such encounters may make it into fieldnotes, head notes, or scratch notes, but only rarely do they appear on the published page. While American Indian authors vividly portray American Indian characters who are problem drinkers, scholars whose research has not been directly focused on alcohol, alcoholism, or substance abuse, have been strangely silent on the subject.[10]

In addition to the reasons suggested by Robin Room for the tendency of anthropologists to "deflate" the problems associated with alcohol in societies worldwide, frank discussion of experiences with Native problem drinkers does not fit well with the advocacy stance of "ethnographic liberalism," which has tended to dominate scholarly studies of American Indian societies.[11] In many cases, anthropologists (myself included) seem hesitant to represent the less desirable aspects of Native life and tend instead to highlight the good things in Native culture, thereby presenting—to greater or lesser degrees—modern-day versions of "noble savages." Unfortunately, when topics such as problem drinking are avoided, Native perspectives on important topics are often overlooked.

Based on her personal experiences of contending with the loss of various family and community members to the seductive powers of alcohol, Sunny Dooley's commentary reveals profound reasons for the acceptance of such losses. Her reasoning offers insight into the relative constancy of Navajo personhood and the continued relevance of the compressed metaphorical narratives of emergence life-origins, which collectively form a viable philosophical system for Navajo people. Her statement demonstrates that the coping mechanisms employed by members of Navajo families like hers, grappling with the loss of a kinsman or woman to alcohol, are informed by the essential nature of complementarity within all aspects of life in the Navajo world. Ms. Dooley's commentary illustrates how Navajo ideologies of problem drinkers (and Christians) are analogized in Coyote's justification for the balance of life and death detailed in Navajo oral tradition.[12] Her assertion regarding the role of 'adláanii in this equation led me to consider how Navajo personhood, which is acquired gradually, may be attenuated under certain conditions, to such an extent that persons become socially equivalent to the dead. Her analysis caused me to rethink my own experiences with 'adláanii while on the reservation in order to gain an understanding of Navajo perspectives on problem drinkers, harmony, and mutability of Navajo personhood.

Recent anthropological insights into the changeable nature of personhood are based on the cultural constructionist point of view. Against this theoretical backdrop, information from diverse sources sheds light on Navajo views on the essence of harmony and on a state of being brought about by the "un-making" of Navajo personhood through involvement in the extreme forms of problem drinking currently found on the Navajo reservation, which rightfully falls under the anthropological rubric of "social death."

Fieldnote accounts demonstrating Navajo attitudes toward
'adláanii and interviews with Navajo consultants reevaluating
Navajo philosophical notions show that the loss of 'adláanii
comes to be accepted within families and communities because
parallels are drawn between problem drinkers and the deaths
that Navajo oral tradition dictates must occur in order for life
to continue, for the Navajo population to increase, and for harmony to exist.[13]

THE MAKING AND UN-MAKING OF PERSONS

D. W. told me that with her brother V. [a solitary man in
his mid-to-late forties] the family has tried everything to get
him to stop drinking. They have had traditional ceremonies
and Peyote meetings [Native American Church cere-
monies] performed for him.[14] They have put him through
detoxification programs a "couple of times." But, eventually, they had "given up." Now he just comes and goes as he
pleases without eliciting comment from family members.
When he is at his mother's [home], there is always a warm
place for him to sleep and he is welcome to eat at his sister's. She made a point of the fact that formerly he was
included whenever possible in various family activities by
being given responsibilities such as the gathering of firewood, the re-chinking of a hooghan [traditional home], or
the clearing of weeds from around the family residences.
Thus I see how 'adláanii such as V. are more than tolerated,
they are incorporated into the fabric of daily life, at least
marginally. She added that lately during his rare visits home
he usually prefers to sit in his cabin drinking by himself and
that she and other family members are convinced that they
have finally "lost him to the alcohol."[15]

Anthropological analyses in societies worldwide reveal that cross-cultural differences in conceptions of self and personhood abound.[16] On an abstract level, in many societies personhood consists of the relations—ties and obligations—that obtain among human beings and other entities.[17] In actual day-to-day existence, personhood in these societies consists of innumerable small thoughts and actions that simultaneously constitute and affirm these reciprocal obligations and relations.[18]

Furthermore, in many cultural contexts "[s]ocial life/death and physical life/death may not coincide at either end of the life course. Physical life may, and often does, start before social life."[19] This is so in the Navajo world where becoming a person is incremental. Attainment of full Navajo personhood is a gradual process accomplished through multiple social acts—thoughts, actions, rituals—including special treatment at critical points in the life cycle and continual repetition of reciprocal deeds.[20]

Notions of reciprocity influence both the Navajo sense of the self—perceptions of individuality and individual volition—and the Navajo person—the sum of socially sanctioned rules governing rights, prerogatives, obligations, and agency embodied in the corporeal body. The interpersonal reciprocity initiated at the First Laugh ceremony, when relatives gather to celebrate the child-of-a-few-months's first expression of emotion, continues through each developmental stage. Demonstrated through countless seemingly insignificant acts—the gathering of firewood, the grooming of hair, the chopping of kindling, the preparation of food, the re-chinking of a hooghan, ready assistance at a ceremonial, or the clearing of weeds—reciprocal relations simultaneously build and reaffirm Navajo personhood throughout life.

Beth Conklin and Lynn Morgan make a useful distinction between "structural-relational" and "processual-relational" notions of personhood, offering new insight into the relative permanence or impermanence of personhood. The first "situates the individual solidly in relation to other human beings in a social universe."[21] In the case of "processual-relational" personhood,

> social relatedness and personhood develop incrementally, so that personhood is more of an interactive process than a fixed location on a social grid. Rather than being bestowed automatically at a single point in time, personhood is acquired gradually during the lifecycle; it can exist in variant degrees, and different degrees of personhood reflect different social value. *The accrual of personhood is not necessarily a one-way process; under certain conditions, personhood may be lost, attenuated, withdrawn, or denied.*[22]

This insightful analysis says that there are cultural processes by which personhood can be deconstructed—lost, attenuated, withdrawn or denied—as well as those by which it can be constructed cross-culturally. Attenuation of personhood is readily apparent in the life histories of Navajo 'adláanii.

As they gradually lose touch with family and community, 'adláanii are decreasingly involved in reciprocal relations. Deterioration of the web of social relations results in the erosion of Navajo persons. Over time, Navajo who drink excessively move sequentially along a continuum, from beloved family members to problem drinkers, until they reach the point of being classified, in the words of Sunny Dooley, as *yóó'a'háás'kaah*, or "lost ones"—that is, impaired persons who are socially equivalent to the dead.[23]

In many societies, a distinction is made between the "physical body" and the "social persona." As David and Dorothy Counts aptly point out, "Not only are these different aspects of the individual thought of as separate, they may have different life spans: the social life and death of a person need not be coterminous with his or her physical life and death."[24] In the Navajo case, long term problem drinking frequently results in the attenuation of

personhood and the concomitant shift *toward* non-personhood
that constitute social death; but Navajo personhood is not fully
"lost" in such cases, for individuality and interpersonal relations
continue to some extent even after death, be it social or physical.

Although opinions vary among Navajo people regarding
exactly "what it is that is lost to the body when life ends," general consensus exists that a *ch' įįdii* or "ghost" separates from the
corpse and that it maintains "individuality" or a "personal identity" for a variable period of time.[25] Thus, Navajo people retain
personal volition even after physical death.[26]

The continuation of relations between Navajo who are living
and ch'įįdii exemplifies the perpetuation of some degree of
personhood after physical life has ended. The attenuation of
the personhood of Navajo 'adláanii to the point of social death
prior to physical death exemplifies the reverse process. The
social death of Navajo 'adláanii is evidenced by gradual familial
withdrawal—family members decreasingly encourage the participation of 'adláanii, such as V. (who was discussed in the excerpt
that opened this section), in reciprocal relations. Thus, like the
acquisition of the social relationships—ties and obligation—
fundamental to personhood, social death is also an incremental process in the Navajo world.[27] The need for deaths of one
form or another—social or physical—to maintain complementarity was clearly established in the vivid narratives of Navajo
oral tradition.

Although contemporary Navajo people feel protected within
the area inhabited by their Holy People, they do not expect life
to be static. They consider the songs, prayers, and ceremonies
given to them by Changing Woman to be the tools necessary to
restore their way of life whenever harmony is disrupted, so to
varying degrees, disruptions of one form or another are expected.
And indeed, disruptions such as those caused by the problematic behaviors of 'adláanii occur on such a regular basis that
they have come to constitute an integral component of the

fundamental process of "give and take" essential to maintenance of the Navajo way of life in the modern world.

ENCOUNTERS WITH 'ADLÁANII

An elderly woman, who seemed quite distressed, arrived
at the trading post while I was standing at a jewelry-counter
looking at earrings. She was surrounded by a group of concerned relatives. A young man, acting as spokesperson,
explained to the trader that the elder's home had been
robbed by an alcoholic relative and that they would like to
look through the pawn room for her jewelry so that she
could "rescue" her few prized possessions before they
became dead pawn. The trader quietly nodded, lifted the
counter-gate and then ushered them into the pawn vault.[28]

Initially, the incident with the elderly woman searching for her
stolen jewelry had little effect on me. The lesson was brought
closer a few weeks later, however, when my daughter and I
arrived at the home of Mrs. M., an elderly resident of a rural
portion of the southwestern quadrant of the reservation with
whom we had become acquainted. In the course of our visit,
she asked us for a ride into Gallup to search for her few prized
possessions. Her inebriated son had broken into her home
while she was in town and stolen her turquoise necklace and
bracelets.[29] When *she* needed a ride to Gallup to look for the
stolen items in pawn shops, the actions of 'adláanii were sud-
denly no longer the distanced, objectified behaviors of "other"
Navajo, rather they had become those of a member of one of
the extended families that I had come to know.

My personal experiences with 'adláanii on the Navajo reservation are vivid in my memory. I noticed the influences the
actions of 'adláanii had on the lives of Navajo people, such as

this elder, out of the "corners of my eyes," so to speak. That is, study of them was not a direct focus of my research, but 'adláanii and their actions collectively formed an undercurrent that was ever-present, although not always intrusive. Initial encounters such as mine with an elderly 'adláanii man who was attempting to sell a turquoise ring for $5.00 in the Bashas' grocery store parking lot in Chinle, Arizona, or with the shabbily dressed, filthy 'adláanii staggering along the streets of Gallup, New Mexico, are easily ignored or dismissed.

As my fieldwork progressed, 'adláanii continually imposed themselves on me and those with whom I consulted. For example, when I interviewed Mrs. E. at her home in a small reservation community near Chinle, Arizona, her son was present in an intoxicated state. P., who had accompanied me to her grandmother's home, was disturbed by her father's condition.

> She repeatedly asked him to excuse himself, but he stubbornly refused . . . and interrupted our discussion numerous times saying, "Hey, may I interject?" and then launching unbidden into some tangential story. Mrs. E. admonished him in Navajo not to talk into the "machine," saying, "Shhsh! You will get it in here (indicating my tape recorder with her chin). Don't talk!" She obviously did not want his inebriated words to go off the reservation. . . . [His presence was very disruptive throughout, but most offensive at the close of the interview.] After paying Mrs. E. for our interview, I turned my attention to loading . . . . the car.' . . . Hearing some commotion coming from the shade, I started back to see what was happening. I was shocked to see Mrs. E.'s son wrestling with her while P. was trying to get her father to release his hold on her grandmother. As they saw me coming around the corner of the house, Mrs. E. harshly chastised her son and he went into the house. . . . [During the ride back to Tsaile, Arizona,] P.

told me that she was very embarrassed. She explained that
her grandmother had placed the money down the front
of her blouse. After his mother refused his request for the
cash to buy more liquor, her father had reached down her
blouse and attempted to extract the money.[30]

In defense of her father, P. went on to tell me that although
his social drinking had contributed to the marital problems that
led to her parents separation and subsequent divorce, he had
sobered up and stayed sober for years. At fifty years of age, he
had been in the prime of his life—a respected member of the
chapter government—when his long term live-in girlfriend left
for an off-reservation job. He missed her terribly and began keeping company with an alcoholic sister to assuage his loneliness.
Gradually, he began spending more and more time by himself,
drowning his sorrows in the liquor.[31]

P.'s embarrassment is revealing. In their attempts to quiet
Mr. E., P. and her grandmother were striving to filter the elements of Navajo life I experienced. They did not want me to
see "that side" of their lives. This is demonstrative of the multiple levels of filtration that make up the ethnographic experience—consultants filter what anthropologists are exposed to in
the field and anthropologists filter their texts. In marked contrast, a family with whom I subsequently visited seemed wholly
unconcerned with what I might think of this side of Navajo life.
When I interviewed Mrs. N., I had encounters with two of her
problem-drinking sons.

While I was visiting a trading post in a small reservation community in New Mexico with a friend interested in purchasing
some Navajo textiles, the trader told me of Mrs. N., a local
herbalist. Since it was close to evening, he suggested that I return
the following day around noon to arrange a meeting with her.
He was confident that she would be visiting his post then, as it
would be the first of the month when social security and aid

checks are issued. I went to the post at the appointed time and patiently waited there for Mrs. N. to arrive. She did not come.

> When her son D. stopped by the post [a young man who looked to be in his mid-twenties], the trader inquired about his mother. . . . The son assured us that his mother was expected home soon. Toward late afternoon, the trader offered to accompany me to look for Mrs. N. in order to arrange an interview. To no avail, he took me to the homes of three of her relatives. On our way out to one homesite, we again encountered her son D., this time he was with a male companion. When we stopped to inquire whether Mrs. N. had returned, the son explained that he and his friend were on their way to the post. . . . Mrs. N.'s son offered to take me out to his mother's house after his companion made some purchases at the post. We gave them a ride back to the post to finalize the transactions. There, the two young men purchased two cans of Aqua Net hair spray. . . . When I asked him why they wanted the hair spray, the trader informed me that people sprayed the hair spray into two-liter pop bottles that had been filled with water and then drank the liquid [referred to regionally as "Ocean"] to get high. He continued, "That is what gives 'adláanii their distinctive semi-sweet odor."[32]

With their purchases complete, these two young men escorted me to Mrs. N.'s. After quickly introducing me to all relatives present, D. and his companion disappeared into the house. O., another of her sons, stayed for the duration of the interview, however, and he was mildly inebriated. This son, a good-looking young man in his late twenties who seemed confident in his cultural knowledge, interrupted his mother and older sister while they were trying to answer my questions and was generally disruptive. At the close of our interview, while Mrs. N's daughter and I discussed an appropriate time for another interview, he offered to serve as my translator on the following day. When I laughed his suggestion off, the older sister chuckled, "Oh, he will be alright in the morning!"[33] I did not give in. Instead I made my arrangements directly with the daughter, insisting that the interview be scheduled for a time when she was available to interpret.

> I paid Mrs. N. for the interview, explaining that I had added some cash for her daughter in exchange for her services as interpreter and would leave the division of the sum up to them. O. watched me attentively and then, looking puzzled, he asked me, "Where is mine?" I responded that I had not interviewed him, nor had I asked him to interpret. He became quite agitated and yelled at me. He followed me to my vehicle, pulling on my arm as he requested some cash. The hair on the back of my neck stood on end, [and] I was frightened by his behavior. Evening had fallen, and I had more than a mild degree of apprehension about getting into the "trooper" [our nickname for our Isuzu vehicle] and traversing those unfamiliar dirt roads in the dark. . . . On my way out of the community, I stopped at the trading post as P. B. [the trader] had asked me to do. He inquired how the interview had gone. I said "Fine," and that we had set up another for a future date. He asked if D. had caused any problems, I told him no but that Mrs. N.'s other son O. had been very obnoxious. He gasped, "O.? Are you sure that was his name?" I said yes and then he finished, "I didn't realize he was out of prison." He went on to explain that O. had been imprisoned for manslaughter. . . . I was unnerved upon realizing that I had been arguing with a convicted felon over an interpreter's fee![34]

In my presence, Mrs. N. and her family seemed unconcerned with the behavior of her inebriated son. According to the observations of Jerrold Levy and Stephen Kunitz in their influential study of Navajo problem drinking, his alcohol consumption would likely fall into the category of "male, peer group binge drinking."[35] Young men are generally not socially stigmatized for this pattern of drinking; however, grave concern may result from the social drinking of married men. Compensation generated by the employment of married men contributes to the welfare of many people beyond their own wives and children, so their problem drinking is taken very seriously.[36]

Family intervention in such cases is swift and relentless. For example, within a week of one married man's transgression, the family had arranged for a diagnostician to come to the house to determine why U. was drinking.[37] In this case, the practitioner determined that U. had been "witched" by a neighbor with whom the family was in the midst of a land dispute.[38] In another instance,

> A hand trembler was consulted the morning after T. E. [a husband and father in his early forties] got drunk and in a fistfight at E. C.'s Enemy Way.[39] She told the family that he needed an *Hóchxǫ́jí* [Evil Way].[40] He was sickened through contact with a dying relative. It turns out that, a few years back he administered mouth-to-mouth resuscitation to a clan sister to no avail—thus he was "contaminated by her ghost."[41]

I was not privy to the reasons these men chose to drink, but as my encounters with 'adláanii increased, my interest grew regarding how family and community members perceived such problem drinkers and how they fit them into the larger frame of Navajo notions of harmony.

HARMONY

> On whatever basis Navajos bound an entity, it is not in
> terms of homogeneity. Wholes seem to be composed of
> two parts which are in a sense complementary and in
> another sense opposed.[42]

Harmony is a fundamental aspect of the Navajo world. In the
Navajo view, harmony is based on holism that is in turn based
on the principle of duality, which permeates Navajo philosophy
and cosmology. Complementary pairs such as hunger and sati-
ation, male and female, as well as birth and death, exist on all
levels of the system of association formed by the network of relationships persons have to each other. An underlying aspect of
Navajo belief is that any whole is a combination of such dual
components.[43] In fact, "What Anglos call the pairing of opposites, Navajos conceptualize as the halves of a whole, with each
half necessary for completeness."[44]

  Nevertheless, John Farella asserts that several prior researchers
of Navajo culture have misrepresented Navajo wholeness, dualities, and harmony by projecting an underlying assumption from
their Euro-American philosophical backgrounds onto the Navajo
reality.[45] The evidence supporting this conclusion is indeed persuasive. Using highly charged language such as, "In the battle
between the forces of disorder and evil and those of order and
good," prior researchers have equated the Navajo notion of hózhǫ́
with the concept of "good," and they have equated the Navajo notion of hóchxǫ́ with the concept of "evil."[46] Using these concepts,
they have devised schemes to interpret Navajo views on duality,
harmony, and life that place hózhǫ́ and hóchxǫ́ in diametric
opposition to each other. In the view of Farella, "Their description of Navajo world views is almost pure Manicheism," wherein
the paradigm of "good versus evil" is the ultimate metanarrative.[47]
For example, Leland Wyman tells us that the term hózhǫ́

includes everything that a Navajo thinks is good—that is as opposed to evil, favorable to man as opposed to unfavorable or doubtful. It expresses for the Navajo such concepts as the words beauty, perfection, harmony, goodness, normality, success, well-being, blessedness, order, ideal, do for us.[48]

For Berard Haile, Sam Gill, Gary Witherspoon, and Wyman, hózhǫ́ embodies the primordial and ideal condition of the Navajo universe that stands in opposition to hóchxǫ́, the prior condition of the various colored subterranean worlds through which Navajo people believe their ancestors migrated.[49] Noting that upon completion this world was in a state of perfect order, Gill contends:

Indeed, this state of order, a state in which all living things are in their places and in proper relationship with all living things, constitutes the very definition of the concept of beauty (hózhǫ́), which is central to the Navajo world view. It stands in contrast with the preemergence condition of disorder, chaos, and ugliness (hóchxǫ́).[50]

Although he has modified his position more recently, in his highly influential early work, Witherspoon emphasizes this contrast as follows:[51]

[W]e can say that hózhǫ́ refers to the positive or ideal environment. It is beauty, harmony, good, happiness and everything that is positive, and it refers to an environment that is all-inclusive. . . . An opposite of hózhǫ́ is hóchxǫ́ which could be glossed as 'the ugly, unhappy, and disharmonious environment.' *It is not considered to be part of the natural cycle of the universe, and comes about only as a result of evil intentions and evil deeds.* When it does occur, the *normal*

condition of *hózhǫ́* can be restored through the curing
rites of the Navajo.[52]

These scholars are correct in identifying and noting the significance of dualities such as hózhǫ́ and hóchxǫ́ to Navajo philosophy and life. And contemporary English-speaking Navajo consultants often use the terms "good" and "evil" when talking about
these varying aspects of the world. Still, my experience on the
reservation demonstrates that there is more to Navajo life than
"beauty, harmony, good, happiness and everything that is positive," so I sought clarification through consultation with Navajo
experts, analysis of the origin stories, and observation of family
members interacting with 'adláanii who exemplify the antithe-
sis of hózhǫ́ in their behavior.

THE ROAD FROM LOVED ONE TO
LOST ONE

> We arrived at the "first night" of the E. C. Enemy Way
> about 11:45. . . . Some men were singing, but the bonfire
> had not yet been lit. As we sat in the car waiting, I observed
> that many men and some women were walking past our
> vehicle to a battered beige sedan to our right. As they
> walked away from this vehicle, they held small glass jars
> filled with what appeared to be a clear liquid. [No police
> were patrolling in the vicinity of the ceremony, hence the
> openness of these transactions.] Some went directly to
> their own vehicles, others wove their ways between vehi-
> cles and disappeared into the surrounding darkness. . . .
> The bon fire was lit about 12:15. We joined H. at E. C.'s
> fire to watch the singers. . . . When we returned to the
> trooper about 1:20 A.M. . . , there were several inebriated
> individuals visiting around vehicles in the area. I stood

outside to visit with H. While we chatted, a teenage boy in a red pickup began driving between the rows of vehicles. People moved out of the driver's way, as the truck repeatedly made its way around the circumference of the ceremonial ground. The truck sped up on its second trip around and it appeared to be almost completely out of control as it accelerated even more on its third [trip around]. I am sure my apprehension was clearly visible to those around me, yet no one else seemed to be looking directly at the truck. . . . As I puzzled over the nonchalance of those around me, a high pitched whine pierced our ears. While speeding around the dance area, the truck's driver had lost control of the vehicle and careened up onto a large stump. The front wheels were visibly off the ground, yet the driver persisted in attempting to "rev" the engine up enough to drive the vehicle off the stump. With gears grinding and the engine whining, the truck teetered precariously on the stump until the engine died. A man standing to my right audibly chuckled under his breath and commented, "Sounds to me like Tom wrecked his uncle's new truck!"[53]

By Navajo accounts, "drinking is not part of the life that 'was intended' for the Navajo. Instead, it is the product of evil intentions of beings like Coyote, who interfered with the plans of the creators."[54] In fact, the Navajo are not known to have used alcohol prior to its introduction by Spaniards after contact in the sixteenth century.[55] Distilled alcoholic beverages were only available on a limited basis until the 1820s when Mexican merchants began importing grain whiskey from the United States for trade to the Navajo and Ute for horses.[56] This whiskey supply was augmented by products from the first distillery in New Mexico, established in 1824.[57] "By the 1840s, whiskey had become an important and ubiquitous item in the Indian trade."[58] It remained a high priced luxury item until the early 1900s, its "usual cost being one yearling calf for a gallon of whiskey."[59]

As occurred amongst other American Indians, a short time after the introduction of alcohol to Navajo, a pattern of drinking emerged that was characterized by "drinking to stuporousness, boisterousness, aggressiveness, sexual promiscuity, and violence."[60] This drinking behavior is believed to have been modeled after that of non-Native trappers, troopers, and traders.[61] Models for milder forms of drinking were not prevalent until the 1940s, when Navajo men and women entered the armed forces and took off-reservation jobs in the defense industry. Non-Navajo living on the reservation have tended to present an "either-or model of behavior in regard to the use of intoxicants," thus it is not surprising that patterns of on-reservation drinking involve "either a considerable amount of heavy drinking or none at all."[62]

The patterns of Navajo alcohol use termed "traditional" by Levy and Kunitz in their study of Navajo drinking were predominated by male, peer-group binge drinking that took place either off reservation at bars, in back alleys, or on vacant tracts of land, or on reservation at rodeos, at the public portions of ceremonies, or at other favorite spots suitably removed from habitation.[63] The practice of binge drinking is fostered by laws prohibiting the possession, transport, or consumption of alcohol on reservation; the liquor supply simply must be consumed before returning to the reservation.[64] Alternately, on-reservation drinking took place in familial "party" contexts that typically involved men and women.[65] Importantly, each of these contexts was "defined and controlled by traditional Navajo values" such as "cooperation in all family activities and responsibility toward kin."[66]

Levy and Kunitz observed that solitary drinkers, be they male or, rarely, female, were "labeled as deviants by the community."[67] Martin Topper noted that drinking was most "heavily stigmatized" when "it took the individual away from the economic tasks that he or she was obligated to perform and it did not involve any sharing of 'drinks' among kinsmen. The sharing of alcoholic beverages symbolized other reciprocities and redistributions that were central themes in the Navajo economy and in Navajo culture in general."[68] Thus, in many respects "traditional" Navajo drinking patterns reinforce social and kinship relations.

Moreover, Farella argues that Navajo male drinking serves to reinforce the traditional system of social values and gender relationships while offering relief from generational and kinship constraints.[69] As he explains,

> [M]en are in something of a chronic anomalous position in Navajo society. They are virtually without status between adolescence and old age. Or to state this more correctly, their position in society is contingent on their relationship to women. They move from an idealized relationship of safety with their mother in their family of origin to a relationship of danger in their marriage. They often live in a community where they have no close relationships and where the people with whom they have the most contact are their in-laws.[70]

Men tend to drink with their sons, cousins, uncles, and sons-in-law. "When they are drinking, they are all of one generation; they are peers, that is they are brothers. . . . Drinking [therefore,] transforms a world where all but blood relatives are excluded to one where all are brothers."[71] Alcohol, and the irresponsible behavior frequently associated with its consumption, essentially transforms the relationship of risk (that of husband and wife) to one of safety (that of mother and son) because "[i]t both puts one's wife in a position of mother when one is behaving irresponsibly, and it maintains the son's loyalty to his family of origin. That is, because his marriage never quite works, he still maintains a primary focus on his family of origin."[72] Many of the chores assigned to 'adláanii—the gathering of firewood, the re-chinking of a hooghan, or the clearing of weeds from around family residences—are those routinely performed by children. This supports Farella's hypothesis insofar as the nature of these assignments places problem drinkers into the subordinate position of the "mother-child relationship."[73]

Over time, however, Navajo drinking patterns have shifted from predominately male social drinking to predominately solitary drinking, by men or women, or to communal drinking with strangers at community centers, fairs, or athletic events on reservation, or at bars, powwows, or isolated locations off reservation, or at various locations along the byways of border towns.[74] The process of solitary or communal alcohol consumption gradually dissolves the same reciprocal relationships essential to the cultural construction of Navajo personhood that are reinforced by social drinking, which takes place within the framework of clearly defined rules for personal interaction and economic relations.

As a result, tension exists between the destructive acts of drinkers and the often futile attempts of relatives to maintain the drinkers as persons. Problem drinkers are subjects with volition; it is they who determine to drink or not to drink. Family members who abhor any attempt to control the behavior of others, even 'adláanii, will say *T'áá bíbóholnííʼ*, "It is up to him or her to decide." But they can and do conduct damage control over the drinker's eroding personhood by countless attempts to maintain his or her connections to kin through small acts that fulfill reciprocal obligations—Or, as demonstrated in the following vignette, by supernatural means.

At the ceremony performed to relieve U. of the influence of the witch aggravated by the dispute over land, who was believed to have caused his brief drinking binge, family members took the opportunity to influence V., another member of the extended family who was struggling with problem drinking. V. had reportedly been picked up for "drunken and disorderly" behavior in a border town a few weeks prior and had not been home in nearly two months. After the ceremonial practitioner "worked on" U.,

> U. got up and let H. sit down in the patient's spot. After the ceremonial practitioner struck four blows with the feather fan onto H.'s limbs, each was accompanied by the shrill blast of the eagle bone whistle, he struck four additional blows with the fan and whistle in the air above H.'s head moving from north of H.'s head toward H. The last blow was struck onto the top of H.'s head. Noting the difference [between the ceremonial practitioner's treatment of U. and H.], I turned to T. E. for clarification. He explained that H. was a surrogate for V. [this was appropriate because H. and V. are brothers] and that this ceremonial act was an attempt to make V. want to return home.[75]

So although family members were not willing to confront V. directly about his drinking, unbeknownst to him, they were willing to pursue supernatural intervention.

Alternatively, in what sometimes seem to be desperate attempts, family members coping with problem drinkers often make concerted efforts to circumvent the erosion of persons by having 'adláanii complete routine chores such as collection of firewood, or as in the following situation, assistance at a ceremonial.

> H. had been on a drinking binge for over a week, so I was surprised to find him acting as the ceremonial practitioner's assistant when we arrived at T. E.'s Hóchxǫ́ji [Evil Way]. . . . Several times [during the ceremony] H. chewed various herbs, mixed them with water in his mouth and

then walked clockwise around the hooghan aspirating this mixture on all present and the room. When he aspirated some herbs onto me, his breath was overpowering. I am sure that on a Breathalyzer it would have rated well over the legal limit for intoxication! The odor was so overwhelming that I found myself holding my breath when next he stood before me ready to aspirate an herb. I was puzzled by the fact that the family incorporated him into the ceremony in this capacity in spite of his condition. I wonder whether they sought benefit for him through his participation? Or whether they were oblivious to his impaired condition?[76]

As role-related behaviors and prescribed reciprocal obligations, such simple acts serve to reaffirm the problem drinker's relations with kin and his or her status as a Navajo person.

Within the constellation of familial efforts to derail deterioration of their personhood, the drinking behaviors of the 'adláanii I encountered while in the field placed each of them on the continuum from "beloved family member" to "problem drinker" and finally, as in the case of Mrs. M.'s daughter, to "lost one." At the time of a subsequent visit to the home of Mrs. M., I found her quite distraught because her daughter, a young woman in her mid-thirties, had left her five children and gone to Gallup, New Mexico.

> She told us that no one has seen or heard from her daughter for 2 1/2 weeks. Mrs. M. confided to us that she suspected that K. [her daughter] was on a drinking binge because she had been struggling with problem drinking throughout her troubled second marriage. Mrs. M. has sent relatives into Gallup to search the bars and street corners for her daughter.[77]

•   •   •

> After eight weeks without contact, Mrs. M. seems to have
> resigned herself to the fact that her daughter has aban-
> doned her children. Realizing that Mrs. M. cannot con-
> tinue to care for all five children, family members stepped
> in last week and divided them amongst themselves. The
> paternal grandparents reportedly arrived on Wednesday
> morning to take the three youngest back to their place.
> A. [the eldest child from a previous marriage] was placed
> in a reservation boarding school, and a middle child went
> to live with an aunt.[78]

When I inquired about Mrs. M.'s grandchildren the following
summer, I was told that they were all fine, but that their mother
had never returned. Abandonment of her children, the most
unforgivable act for any Navajo woman, whose fundamental
social roles are mother and nurturer, was enough for the daughter's status to shift from a family member with a drinking problem to a "lost one" who is socially dead. Familial acceptance of
the social death of members such as her offers insight into
exactly what elements of life are requisite in order for harmony
to exist in the Navajo world.

REEVALUATION OF HARMONY

> MS: There are many anthropologists who have written
>   and said that the primordial condition of the Navajo
>   universe is hózhǫ́ which is translated as a condition of
>   beauty, harmony, balance. What is your opinion? Do
>   you think that is the primary condition of the Navajo
>   universe? Just hózhǫ́?
> HA: How would you, how could you have harmony and
>   balance without the two oppositions?
> MS: I don't know?

HA: There is no way to do it, you know, if you think about it. Really, how would you say, "It is 'a' harmony?" How would you say, "It is 'a' balance?" You have to have those two oppositions. So that is the way it is understood, so for that reason in Navajo you have Są'ah naagháí bik'eh hózhǫ.[79]

Navajo people like Hanson Ashley of Shonto, Arizona, from whom I sought clarification regarding the primordial condition of the Navajo universe and Navajo notions of harmony, were genuinely shocked at the seeming illogical nature of my questions. Detailed discussion with Navajo experts revealed a subtle but significant difference between how Navajo people perceive the relationship of the concepts of hózhǫ and hóchxǫ and how the concepts are related in the model promulgated by non-Navajo scholars. Harry Walters and I had the following discussion:

MS: Many people, when they write about the Navajo worldview and Navajo philosophy, they refer to the primordial condition of the Navajo world as hózhǫ. . . . And then they don't really talk about evil or negative things and umm, I have been a little bit puzzled by this. I am trying to sort out if that is an accurate representation of the Navajo worldview. Was the primordial condition of the Navajo universe hózhǫ? I mean, is that the way the world was when Changing Woman turned it over to the Earth Surface People? Or has evil always existed?

HW: The hózhǫ, harmony, peace, all of that. What it actually means is that there is negativeness in the world, there is evil in the world.

MS: What? Hózhǫ actually means that there are negative, evil things in the world?

HW: It means that there is a balance, there is a balance for the general good. The negative, evil can be used to

achieve good. [In response to my puzzled look] You
know, like ceremonies. The Naayéé'jí [Protection Way]
ceremonies can be used against people [to redirect
witchcraft powers and thus cure the individual afflicted
by them].[80]

Systematic review of the various accounts of Navajo origin
shows that although it is true that at the instant of its completion
the Navajo world was in a state of "natural order," the negative,
evil, and malevolent elements that would ultimately disrupt this
state were latent within it. As noted, witchcraft knowledge was
brought to the earth's surface by Coyote or First Man and First
Woman *prior* to the construction of the Navajo universe by the
Diyin Dine'é.[81] In addition, as a result of the sexual excesses of
the last world, some of the women who emerged into this world
were pregnant with beings who would prove to be child-eating
monsters, which represent disease and immoral behavior.[82] It
can therefore be argued that negative, evil, and malevolent
elements were just as primordial to the Navajo world as "beauty,
harmony, good, happiness, and everything that is positive." At
any rate, hóchxǫ is now firmly ensconced in the Navajo world,
and it is a fact of life that must be reckoned with on a regular
basis.

Moreover, whereas there is no question that hózhǫ is a fundamental aspect of Navajo philosophy and the ideal for relations in the Navajo universe, the Navajo notion of harmony is
based on the concept of balance and completion rather than
"goodness," as prior researchers have maintained.[83] As Hanson
Ashley explained it to me,

Among the Navajo people they believe that there is this,
the duality principle. . . . Out of that concept there is one
extreme to the other. And then there is the oppositions
that, the pair of opposition it is there. So, then out of that

people just make up to where there is, as it is now they say
there is "good" and there is "bad." There is "God" and his
"devil," there is, you know, all this opposition. But among
our people, [people] say that those types of understandings, the human, they are the ones that developed that.
They are the ones that established those. But really down,
if you go down to the essence of that, the pair of oppositions, it is good, they say, either way. And they talk about
the negative or the positive, both of them are good. They
need one another and they have to be balanced. So that is
the way it is for the human. . . . Those two have to be balanced, they have to be there equally.[84]

Ashley's statement clearly indicates that English terms such
as "opposed" or "opposition" must be used and interpreted with
care. In popular Euro-American usage, the term "opposition"
implies the existence of contesting parts. This is not wholly
representative of the Navajo view. English-speaking Navajo
consultants use these terms to denote the contrastive binary
forms established in the creation of the world—day/night,
male/female, as well as hózhǫ/hóchxǫ—standing in "opposition" to each other structurally; but as Ashley pointed out, these
contrastive domains are integrated by the principle of complementarity rather than contest. The emphasis placed on complementarity in all things by Navajo scholars indicates that as a
complement to hózhǫ, hóchxǫ is a fundamental aspect of the
Navajo way of life, a "structural necessity," if you will.[85]

DISCUSSION

"Some people have hurt themselves with the liquor. They
are pitiful, and we *mourn* for them."[86]

In extreme cases, 'adláanii become socially equivalent to the dead. Unlike the physically dead, with whom contact is avoided at all costs, the socially dead are not shunned, feared, or avoided; rather, such individuals are pitied and considered to be in need of mourning. This case study of Navajo 'adláanii contributes to current concerns within the discipline surrounding the permanence or impermanence of personhood by illustrating one type of cultural context in which personhood can be *de*constructed and by demonstrating that social death—erosion of Navajo personhood through breakdown of vital reciprocal relations with kin and community members—is a gradual process mirroring the incremental acquisition of personhood in the Navajo world.

The degree of disruption to social relations is a critical factor in determining culturally acceptable levels of drinking. For example, young men—such as Mrs. N's bothersome son—who only binge with peers on occasion, do not irreparably disrupt the web of social and reciprocal relations vital to the cultural construction of Navajo personhood. As a result, their drinking is not deemed terribly problematic except in cases in which an extreme injury is inflicted, a life is lost, valuable property is destroyed, or other financial losses are incurred—such as in the case of the teenager in the pickup truck at the Enemy Way.

In the nebulous sphere of life inhabited by problem drinkers, where personhood is ever on the brink of erosion, tension exists between the willfulness of the 'adláanii and the desires of family members. The actions of drinkers frequently threaten to sever the reciprocal ties to kin and community members that are essential to the social construction of Navajo personhood, even as the actions of family members are directed toward reaffirming and strengthening these same relationships. Drinking that disrupts these social ties and relations is considered *extremely* problematic, for it ultimately leads to a state of being best described as social death.

Within families and communities, the social deaths of 'adláanii come to be accepted by Navajo people because, as a complement to births, deaths of one form or another—social or physical—are deemed necessary to the continuation of Navajo life, fecundity, prosperity, and harmony. Intrinsic to this harmony is the concept of give and take, whereby Navajo people recognize the need for complementarity—for births to occur, deaths must occur—as an overarching theme of the Navajo philosophical system, which forms a charter or guide for life.

Although notions of give and take do not necessarily inform how family members cope with problem drinkers on a day-to-day basis, in the end they provide a foundation for rationalizing the loss of a problem drinker after he or she has reached a certain point of dysfunction due to involvement in the new forms of extreme drinking currently found on the Navajo reservation. If, despite the best efforts of family members, the erosion of a drinker's personhood cannot be circumvented, then the philosophical system outlining the need for complementarity provides a means for accepting the loss of a family or community member.

Thus, the mechanisms whereby Navajo personhood develops or attenuates and the philosophical precepts establishing the essential nature of complementarity become interwoven in the process of "giving up" problem drinkers who have become socially equivalent to the dead. For, as Sunny Dooley pointed out, the surrender of some individual Navajo to the seductive powers of alcohol fits into the scheme of giving and taking inherent to preservation of harmony in the Navajo world.

CHAPTER SEVEN

Final Thoughts

As she prepared to take her place as the inner form of the earth, Changing Woman admonished the Nihookáá Dine'é, "Do not forget those [songs, prayers, and ceremonies] that I have taught you. The day you forget them will be the last, there will be no other days."

PLINY GODDARD,
"Navajo Texts"

In their explanations of contemporary issues such as the hantavirus outbreak of 1993, the forced relocation of Navajo people off land partitioned to the Hopi tribe, a prophetic visit by Navajo supernaturals in 1996, inappropriate contact with snakes in 1994, the perils of uranium mining, and the loss of relatives to the seductive powers of alcohol, Navajo people make implicit or explicit reference to various elements and versions of Navajo oral tradition. This indicates that when faced with modern concerns, Navajo people seek insight in the stories that make up their oral history, the Navajo origin and emergence narratives.

The critical bodies of knowledge taught to the Nihookáá Dine'é just before the Holy People turned this world over to them were intended to sustain them in life and to restore proper relations whenever disruptions occurred. Collectively, the various forms of knowledge—songs, prayers, stories, and ceremonies— are understood to form a charter between the Navajo and the Diyin Dine'é, guaranteeing that if the Nihookáá Dine'é carefully follow the teachings of the Holy People, the natural order of the Navajo world will be preserved, and their special way of life will flourish.

Although Navajo people generally grant ontological status to their oral histories, they do not consistently foreground all events relayed in these vivid narratives. Rather, when faced with various life crises, Navajo medicine people, elders, and other tribal intellectuals selectively highlight specific episodes pertinent to the particular problem at hand. These allusions to key episodes in the origin story are efforts to conceptualize alternatives to established and traditionalized norms and are firmly located in the contemporary context of narration.

Such negotiations with the stories of how the world came to be are possible because the stories are compressed metaphoric accounts constituting teaching tools or parables, subject to different levels of analysis. They condense historical knowledge and human experience into vivid narratives with encoded insights, which can be discussed and debated to illuminate or resolve disparate personal and social issues, thus helping people cope.

The various ways these teachings are used to inform contemporary life are poignantly demonstrated in the cases of people coping with snakes in a public building, 'adláanii, relocation from ancestral homelands, or the untoward effects of the uranium mining industry. Contact with snakes in an uncontrolled setting, such as the ladies' restroom in Administration Building No. 2, is potentially dangerous because certain properties— including the naayéé'jí and hózhǫ́ǫ́jí powers of the snakes—can be transferred through contact between the snakes (or their bodily substances) and the people (or their bodily substances), and grave harm can result. Although notions of give and take do not necessarily inform how family members daily cope with problem drinkers, the principle of complementarity established in the origin stories (for births to occur, deaths must occur) provides a foundation for rationalizing the loss of a problem drinker after he or she has reached a certain point of dysfunction due to extreme forms of drinking. The testimonies of female spokespersons for tribal members who are facing the challenges of relocation or the loss of loved ones to illnesses directly attributable to work in the uranium mining industry show that understanding the philosophical system established by the Diyin Dine'é may help one to generate empathy and compassion on the part of outsiders.

A pervasive sentiment repeatedly echoed in Navajo exegeses about these diverse situations is that proper relations are breaking down, and people are not acting as they should. This failure to maintain relations is held to be responsible for the outbreak of hantavirus on the reservation in 1993. Elders hold that Navajo people brought the illness on themselves through wrongdoings such as the year-round performance of summer ceremonial dances in "Song and Dance" contests, the telling of stories out of season, the sale of artifacts, and the desecration of ceremonies. The breakdown of relations is further exemplified by the defilement of Mother Earth, in such irreverent acts as toxic waste dumping or mine pit digging on reservation lands and the removal from lands of the nurturers most especially connected to those locations. The dependency between Navajo and the earth is reciprocal; thus, the health and well-being of Mother Earth is dependent on the care of those people who have been given stewardship over particular locales, just as Navajo people are dependent on the continuing nurturance of the earth.

Elders see constancy in the messages brought to the Navajo
people over the last decade, regardless of whether they were
brought by illnesses, snakes, or the holy visitors to Rocky Ridge
in May of 1996. The messages are viewed as forewarnings that
many are not following the teachings of the Holy People and
that preservation of the Navajo way of life is jeopardized by this
lack of compliance. The apocalyptic nature of the warnings
brought by these diverse harbingers harks back to Changing
Woman's final admonition, before she became the inner form
of the earth: If Navajo people continue on the path they seem
to have chosen—abandonment of the traditions given to them
by Changing Woman and violation of the responsibilities established in the charter between the Nihookáá Dine'é and the
Holy People—then the world as they know it will cease to exist.
Elders repeatedly use these episodes to remind Navajo people
of their obligations and to demonstrate that everyone must
work together to stabilize the relationship between the Diyin
Dine'é and the Nihookáá Dine'é before it is too late.

Notes

INTRODUCTION

1. Sunny Dooley is a Navajo storyteller from Vanderwagen, New Mexico, who is committed to teaching traditional stories to Navajo children who have been raised without this important educational resource in their homes. A former Miss Navajo, she has retained the role of ambassador for Navajo culture to the non-Navajo world.

2. Sahlins, *Islands of History*, vii.

3. Lévi-Strauss, *The Savage Mind*, 257 58.

4. See Churchill, *Fantasies of the Master Race.*

5. It is beyond the scope of this work to summarize the voluminous literature extant on Navajo culture and society. Countless works have been published on the Navajo since their contact with Europeans and Euro-Americans; in fact, by some accounts, the Navajo are the most studied people in the world. Several bibliographies on the Navajo are readily available. See for example, Correll, Watson, and Brugge, *Navajo Bibliography*; Iverson, *The Navajos*; and Kluckhohn and Spencer, *A Bibliography of the Navaho Indians*. In addition, monographs on Navajo history and ethnography published prior to 1982, museum collections with substantial holdings of Navajo materials, and photographic records of Navajo life are summarized in David Brugge, "Navajo Prehistory and History to 1850," 498–501.

6. These linguistic studies give rise to the view that north was the center of dispersal for the Southern Athapaskan groups. Linguistic diversification, which is used as a measure of the proximity of language groups to each other over time, indicates that "the diversity within Athapaskan as a whole is no greater than that within the northern group of Athapaskan languages and that the internal diversity of the Southern Athapaskan group is considerably less" (Hale and Harris, "Historical Linguistics and Archeology," 172). Specialists agree that the Southern Athapaskan-speaking peoples came from the area of greatest population concentration in the Mackenzie Basin of Canada. Lexico-statistical data that provide clues as to the time of split suggest that the Southern and Northern groups split within the past thousand to thirteen hundred years (Greenberg, Turner, and Zegura, "The Settlement of the Americas," 479; Gunnerson, "Southern Athapaskan Archeology," 162; Hale and Harris, "Historical Linguistics and Archeology," 172).

7. An intermontane route through what is now Utah or Colorado and the Great Basin is supported by Julian Steward in "Ancient Caves of the Salt Lake Region" and "Native Cultures of the Intermontane (Great Basin) Area," Betty and Harold Huscher in "Athapaskan Migration via the Intermontane Region," and Morris Opler in "The Apachean Culture Pattern and Its Origin." James Gunnerson's "Plains-Promotory Relationships," James Hester's "Early Navajo Migrations and Acculturation in the Southwest," and David Wilcox's "The Entry of Athapaskans into the American Southwest" support a migration southwest through the northwestern and central plains, close to the eastern edge of the Rocky Mountains.

8. Forbes, *Apache, Navaho and Spaniard*, 57. See also Correll, *Through White Men's Eyes*; and Brugge, "Navajo Prehistory."

9. Brugge, "Navajo Prehistory," 489–501.

10. See Roessel, *Navajo Stories*; Correll, *Through White Men's Eyes*; and Bailey, *The Long Walk*.

11. See Correll, *Through White Men's Eyes*; and Roessel, *Pictorial History of the Navajo*.

12. See Bailey and Bailey, *A History of the Navajos*, for coverage of the reservation years.

13. On traders and trading posts, see Gillmor and Wetherill, *Traders to the Navajos*; McNitt, *The Indian Traders*; Adams, *Shonto*; Hegemann, *Navajo Trading Days*; and Moon, *Tall Sheep*.

14. Adair, Deuschle, and Barnett, *The People's Health*, 10.

15. On sustained droughts, see Frisbie, "Temporal Change in Navajo Religion: 1868–1990," 446. On loss of livestock, see Bailey and Bailey, *A History of the Navajos*, 210. On the Spanish influenza pandemic see Russell, "The Navajo and the 1918 Influenza Pandemic," 381.

16. On weaving, see Amsden, *Navaho Weaving*; Wheat, "Documentary Evidence for Material Changes and Designs," "Rio Grande, Pueblo and Navajo Weavers," and "Early Trade and Commerce"; and Kent, *Navajo Weaving*. On silver, see Lincoln, *Southwest Indian Silver*. Regarding sandpaintings on boards, see Parezo, *Navajo Sandpainting*.

17. On the development of the Navajo Nation, see Iverson, *The Navajo Nation*.

18. See Aberle, *The Peyote Religion*.

19. See Adair, Deuschle, and Barnett, *The People's Health*, 15–45; and Emerson, "Navajo Education."

20. See Kammer, *The Second Long Walk*; Benedek, *The Wind Won't Know Me*; and Brugge, *The Navajo-Hopi Land Dispute*.

21. On bilingual education and curricula centered on Native values, see Emerson "Navajo Education," 659–71.

22. The designs on baskets are a visual record of Navajo history. From center to rim are found the place of emergence, earth, sacred mountains, rainbow, and clouds integral to Navajo sacred space. For further information, see Fishler, "In the Beginning," 208–209; and Schwarz, *Molded in the Image of Changing Woman*, 39–40.

23. Pinxten and Farrer, "On Learning a Comparative View," 249.

24. Pinxten and Farrer, "On Learning," 249.

25. Witherspoon, *Navajo Kinship and Marriage*, 37.

26. O'Bryan, "The Diné," 112. The mountains demarcating Navajo sacred space are: Blanca Peak (east), Mount Taylor (south), San Francisco Peaks (west), and Hesperus Peak (north), with Gobernador Knob and Huerfano Mesa at the center.

27. Spencer, *Reflection of Social Life*, 12.

28. Zolbrod, *Diné Bahane'*, 25.

29. See Fishler "In the Beginning"; Goddard, "Navajo Texts"; Haile, *Upward Moving* and *Women versus Men*; O'Bryan, "The Diné"; Wyman, *Blessingway*; Yazzie, *Navajo History*; and Zolbrod, *Diné Bahane'*.

30. For a discussion of the type of heavy editing done to the accounts to conform them to Victorian sensibilities, see Zolbrod, *Diné Bahane'*, 7–29.

31. O'Bryan, "The Diné," 1.

32. O'Bryan, "The Diné," 1; see also Goddard, "Navajo Texts," 127; and Yazzie, *Navajo History*, 9.

33. O'Bryan, "The Diné," 2.

34. On Air-Spirit beings, see Zolbrod, *Diné Bahane'*, 35. On Mist Beings, see O'Bryan, "The Diné," 2; and Yazzie, *Navajo History*, 9.

35. O'Bryan, "The Diné," 2.

36. Yazzie, *Navajo History*, 9.

37. In *Diné Bahane'* (50–51) Zolbrod refers to this as the fourth underworld and to these beings as First Man and First Woman.

38. Zolbrod, *Diné Bahane'*, 53.

39. See Stephen, "Navajo Origin Legend," 99; O'Bryan, "The Diné," 8; Yazzie, *Navajo History*, 30; Haile, *Women versus Men*, 25; and Zolbrod, *Diné Bahane'*, 63.

40. Goddard, "Navajo Texts," 130–31; Fishler, "In the Beginning," 4; O'Bryan, "The Diné," 8–10.

41. Yazzie, *Navajo History*, 15.

42. Fishler, "In the Beginning," 31.

43. Fishler, "In the Beginning," 31.

44. Sylvia Manygoats, as quoted in Kelley and Francis, *Navajo Sacred Places*, 36–37 (bracketed commentary in the original).

45. Kelley and Francis, *Navajo Sacred Places*, 37.

46. Witherspoon, *Language and Art*, 16–17.

47. On the sun and the moon, see Goddard, "Navajo Texts," 134, 135–37; Fishler, "In the Beginning," 19–23; and Yazzie, *Navajo History*, 21. On the stars, see Goddard, "Navajo Texts," 137–38; and Yazzie, *Navajo History*, 21. On day and night, see Yazzie, *Navajo History*, 24–25. On the seasons, see Goddard, "Navajo Texts," 134–35; and Yazzie, *Navajo History*, 27. And, on the necessity for births and deaths, see Goddard, "Navajo Texts," 138; Fishler, "In the Beginning," 31–33; and Yazzie, *Navajo History*, 20.

48. Goddard, "Navajo Texts," 138; Fishler, "In the Beginning," 31–32; O'Bryan, "The Diné," 31–32; Yazzie, *Navajo History*, 20; and Zolbrod, *Diné Bahane'*, 82–83.

49. On the "black wood," see Goddard, "Navajo Texts," 138; and O'Bryan, "The Diné," 31–32. On the "hide scraper," see Zolbrod, *Diné Bahane'*, 82–83.

50. Zolbrod, *Diné Bahane'*, 82, both emphases in original.

51. Wyman, *Blessingway*, 573.

52. O'Bryan, "The Diné," 166.

53. Aberle, "The Navajo-Hopi Land Dispute," 161, 169; and Kelley and Francis, *Navajo Sacred Places*, 33–35.

54. Wood and Vannette, *A Preliminary Assessment*, 24.

55. Wyman, *The Red Antway*, 91.

CHAPTER ONE

1. I was on the reservation during July and August 1993. I never interviewed Navajo individuals about the "mystery illness" directly, as it would have been culturally inappropriate to bring up this topic. Navajo people were greatly concerned about the illness, and the people I knew were well aware of the cancellation of numerous conferences, research projects, and visits to the reservation by tourists. When I arrived on the reservation with my children, a member of the extended family who has sponsored my research told us, "We wondered if you would come down this year, or if you would be scared off by the illness like other Anglos." I told them that I was as concerned for our safety as they were for the safety of themselves and their families but that we would just be cautious and go right to the hospital if anyone became ill. While consulting with Navajo experts that summer, the illness frequently came up in conversation. After local newspapers published the discovery of the biomedical explanation—hantavirus—many Navajo people told me that they did not believe hantavirus to be the true cause. When I asked them what they felt the cause was, they told me that is was a breakdown of proper relations in the Navajo world as evidenced by "Song and Dance" contests, lack of knowledge on the part of Navajo young people, and the damage to Mother Earth caused by uranium mines. I connected these opinions about the illness with what I had already learned about the twelve levels of knowledge and Navajo theories of disease and disharmony.

2. Symptoms of early infection include fever, headache, abdominal and lower back pain, nausea and vomiting, and in some cases, facial flushing and redness of the eyes. Symptoms of advanced infection include decreased urine output, circulatory problems, shock, bleeding, and fluid buildup in the lungs.

3. *Discover*, December 1993.

4. *People Weekly*, 21 June 1993.

5. This one-hour special presentation of *The New Explorers* aired on 18 May 1994, at 8 P.M. For additional information on media coverage, see Bales, "Hantavirus and the Media."

6. The *Navajo Times* reported twenty-seven confirmed cases and twenty-seven suspected cases under investigation (2 September 1993). Twenty-five occurred in New Mexico, nineteen in Arizona, nine in Colorado, and one in Utah. Victims ranged in age from two to eighty-four with an average age of thirty-four; twenty-eight were male and twenty-six were female; 51 percent were American Indian, 39 percent were white, and 10 percent were Hispanic. To date seventy-four cases have been reported in eighteen states across the United States (*Navajo Times* 26 May 1994).

7. *Seattle Times*, 2 June 1993.

8. *Navajo Times*, 1 July 1993; and Jonah Nez, personal conversation with the author, Upper Greasewood, Ariz., 22 July 1993.

9. *Navajo Times*, 22 July 1993.

10. Harry Walters, interview by author, Tsaile, Ariz., 12 August 1993. Professor Walters is a husband, father, and grandfather from Cove, Arizona. Walters expresses his profound commitment to the preservation of Navajo culture on a daily basis in his dual role as Chairman of Diné Studies and Director of the Ned Hatathli Cultural Center Museum at Navajo Community College in Tsaile, Arizona.

11. Harry Walters, interview by author, Tsaile, Ariz., 20 March 1995.

12. Walters, interview, 12 August 1993.

13. Wilson Aronilth, interview by author, Tsaile, Ariz., 3 July 1991. Mr. Aronilth is a Navajo elder from Naschitti, New Mexico. Mr. Aronilth has taught a variety of courses at Navajo Community College in Tsaile, Arizona, since 1969, including Silversmithing and Navajo Philosophy and Culture.

14. Walters, interview, 12 August 1993.

15. Witherspoon, *Language and Art*, 91.

16. Walters, interview, 20 March 1995.

17. Witherspoon, *Navajo Weaving*, 15.

18. Walters, interview, 12 August 1993.

19. Walters, interview, 12 August 1993.

20. Walters, interview, 12 August 1993.

21. Walters, interview, 12 August 1993.

22. Sunny Dooley, interview by author, Gallup, N.Mex., 19 August 1992.

23. *Navajo Times*, 3 June 1993.

24. *Salt Lake Tribune*, 2 August 1993.

25. Ben Muneta, as quoted in *Navajo Times*, 24 November 1993.

26. Ben Muneta, as quoted in *Navajo Times*, 24 November 1993.

27. Earnest Becenti, as quoted in *Salt Lake Tribune*, 5 June 1993.

28. O'Bryan, "The Diné," 111.

29. Dooley, interview.

30. Mervyn Tilden, as quoted in *Navajo Times*, 12 May 1994.

31. *Navajo Times*, 10 June 1993.

32. Nelson Dempsey, as quoted in *Navajo Times*, 10 June 1993.

33. *Navajo Times*, 3 June 1993.

34. Lori Belone, as quoted in *Navajo Times*, 10 June 1993.

35. *Navajo Times*, 24 November 1993.

36. I wish to thank the anonymous reviewer who pointed out that the Navajo people with whom he/she is acquainted consider toxic waste dumping on the reservation to be the cause of the mystery illness. I personally had not heard of toxic waste dumping as an explanation.

37. Mae Bekis, interview by author, Tó'tsoh, Arizona, 28 July 1993. Mae Bekis is a practitioner of the Blessing Way, and as a mother and grandmother, she has a profound interest in preservation of Navajo traditional knowledge.

38. Lori Belone, as quoted in *Navajo Times*, 10 June 1993.

39. During the summer of 1993, members of the Navajo families I know in the Tsaile, Wheatfields, Lukachukai, and Pinon areas of Arizona told me about Blessing Way ceremonies they had had or were planning as prophylactics against the illness. Blessing Way singers with whom I am acquainted, such as Mae Bekis of Tó'tsoh, Arizona, and Archie Begay of Upper Greasewood, Arizona, noted the increase in requests for Blessing Way ceremonies in these areas during the summer of 1993 as a result of the mystery illness. Wesley Thomas of Mariano Lake, New Mexico, observed that many families in the eastern quadrant of the Navajo reservation had Blessing Way ceremonies in their immediate and extended families during the summer of 1993. Thomas, whose family had such a ceremony in June of 1993, told me that his family had to wait for a week to schedule their ceremony because all the Blessing Way singers in his area were exceptionally busy due to the illness.

40. Lori Belone, as quoted in *Navajo Times*, 10 June 1993.

41. Walters, interview, 12 August 1993.

42. *Navajo Times*, 26 May 1994.

CHAPTER TWO

1.   Katherine Smith, in Osawa, *In the Heart.*
2.   Kammer, *The Second Long Walk,* 197. See also Scudder, *No Place to Go,* 49–50; and Benedek, *The Wind Won't,* 311.
3.   Jack Hatathlie, as quoted in Benedek, *The Wind Won't,* 85.
4.   See for example Benedek, *The Wind Won't;* Florio and Mudd, *Broken Rainbow;* Kammer, *The Second Long Walk;* and Osawa, *In the Heart.*
5.   This is not to say that the attachment Navajo people feel toward the land has not been given sensitive treatment elsewhere. On Navajo views toward land and land "ownership," see David Aberle, "The Navajo-Hopi Land Dispute and Navajo Relocation," 169–70; Feher-Elston, *Children of Sacred Ground,* 102–104; Florio and Mudd, *Broken Rainbow;* Joe, "Breaking the Navajo Family"; Kammer, *The Second Long Walk,* 1–19, 209–12; and Scudder, *No Place to Go,* 33–40. On Navajo spiritual obligations to the land, see Aberle, "The Navajo-Hopi Land Dispute and Navajo Relocation," 161, 169, and 183. My point here is that prior works have not addressed Navajo beliefs about the cultural construction of the human body and personhood upon which these particular references are based.
6.   Navajo views on the cultural construction of the human body and personhood are explored at greater length in my book *Molded in the Image.* My study builds on a solid core of prior works on related topics, such as Austin, Begishe, Manygoats, Werner, and Werner, "The Anatomical Atlas of the Navajo with Illustrations"; Bailey, "Some Sex Beliefs and Practices in a Navajo Community"; Haile, *Soul Concepts of the Navaho* and *Navaho Sacrificial Figurines;* Kelly, Lang, and Walters, *Navaho Figurines Called Dolls;* McNeley, *Holy Wind;* Pinxten, Dooren, and Harvey, *Anthropology and Space;* and Wright, Bauer, Clark, Morgan, and Begishe, "Cultural Interpretations and Intracultural Variability in Navajo Beliefs about Breastfeeding."
7.   Roman Bitsuie, telephone conversation with author, 25 October 1999. Residents of these homesites faced eviction on 1 February 2000. In October of 1999, Mr. Bitsuie reported that a Navajo Nation Council work group was studying alternatives to eviction and would be reporting back to the full Navajo Nation Council.
8.   For further information on this complex issue, see Aberle, "The Navajo-Hopi Land Dispute and Navajo Relocation"; Benedek, *The Wind Won't;* David Brugge, *The Navajo-Hopi Land Dispute;* Clemmer,

Roads in the Sky; Feher-Elston, *Children of Sacred Ground*; Joe, "Breaking the Navajo Family"; Kammer, *The Second Long Walk*; Scudder, *No Place to Go*; and Topper "FJUA Relocation"; as well as the following film documentaries, Florio and Mudd, *Broken Rainbow*, and Osawa, *In the Heart.*

9. Bitsuie, telephone conversation, 25 October 1999.

10. Frazer, *The Golden Bough*; Mauss, *A General Theory of Magic*; and Tylor, *Primitive Culture.*

11. On the "law of opposition," see Frazer, *The Golden Bough*, 5; on the "law of similarity," see Mauss, *A General Theory*, 64, 71.

12. Frazer, *The Golden Bough*, 5.

13. Mauss, *A General Theory*, 64.

14. Mauss, *A General Theory*, 64.

15. Mauss, *A General Theory*, 65.

16. Since the Victorian scholars, every generation of anthropologists has investigated such effects in specific cultures, and interest continues today (see for example, Nemeroff and Rozin, "The Laws of Sympathetic Magic" and "The Contagion Concept in Adult Thinking in the United States"). Various terms have been used by anthropologists to refer to this type of influence including: *mana* (Mauss, *A General Theory of Magic*), pollution (Douglas, *Purity and Danger*), taboo (Leach, "Anthropological Aspects of Language"), taint (Jackson, *Paths Toward a Clearing*), and contagion (Nemeroff and Rozin "The Contagion Concept"). According to *Webster's Unabridged Dictionary*, to pollute is to make foul or unclean, or to defile. Taint refers to the action by which one thing physically infects, spoils, or injures another. Contagions contaminate and make impure or corrupt what they contact. Due to the predominantly negative connotations associated with these latter terms, I purposively use *effect* or *influence* in place of the words *pollutant*, *taint* or *contagion*. Since the influence one thing can have on another in the Navajo world is inherently positive and/or negative (that is, beneficial or harmful results can be manifest depending on the circumstances), it is crucial to use a neutral term.

17. For a focus on restrictions surrounding exposure to menstrual blood, see Douglas, *Purity and Danger*; Durkheim, "La prohibition de l'inceste et ses Origines"; Stephens, *The Oedipus Complex*; Weideger, *Menstruation and Menopause*; Young and Bacdayan, "Menstrual Taboos and Social Rigidity." For examples of focus on the use of parts of the body, bodily fluids, and offal in witchcraft, see Evans-Pritchard, *Witchcraft, Oracles, and Magic*; Fortune, *Sorcerers of Dobu*; and Middleton and Winter, *Witchcraft and Sorcery.*

18. Buckley and Gottlieb, "A Critical Appraisal," 3–50.

19. On the role these practices play in social control, see Walker, ed., *Witchcraft and Sorcery*. On the maintenance of social distance and economic distinctions, see Lindenbaum, *Kuru Sorcery*. On relief of psychological tensions, see Kluckhohn, *Navaho Witchcraft*. And, on the reasons for the existence of such "bizarre" behaviors among millions of contemporary people, see Walker, ed., *Witchcraft and Sorcery*, 6. On this last point, see also Luhrmann, *Persuasions of the Witch's Craft*.

20. See Bailey, "Some Sex Beliefs and Practices"; Dyk, *Son of Old Man Hat*; Keith, "The Navajo Girl's Puberty Ceremony"; Kluckhohn, *Navaho Witchcraft*; Morgan, "Human-Wolves Among the Navaho"; Reichard, *Navaho Religion*, 35; Wright, "Attitudes Toward Childbearing and Menstruation Among the Navajo"; and Wyman and Harris, "Navajo Indian Medical Ethnobotany," 59.

21. Farnell, "Introduction," 4–10.

22. See Douglas, *Purity and Danger* and *Natural Symbols*; and Turner, *The Forest of Symbols*.

23. Lamphere, "Symbolic Aspects in Navajo Ritual," 282.

24. Synnott, *The Body Social*, 37.

25. Farnell, "Introduction," 4.

26. Lock, "Cultivating the Body," 134.

27. See for example Gordon, "Tenacious Assumptions in Western Medicine Examined"; Lock, "The Anthropological Study of the American Medical System"; and Rhodes, "Studying Biomedicine as a Cultural System."

28. Foucault, *The Birth of the Clinic*, 124–47.

29. On images of female reproductive organs as inverted versions of male organs, see Laqueur, "Orgasm, Generation, and the Politics of Reproductive Biology" and *Making Sex*.

30. Lock, "Cultivating the Body," 146.

31. It is beyond the scope of this work to attempt to summarize the vast literature on the body that has developed over the last quarter century. I refer the reader to Blacking, *The Anthropology of the Body*; Farnell, "Introduction," 1–28; Lock, "Cultivating the Body"; Shilling, *The Body and Social Theory*; and Synnott, *The Body Social*, especially 228–64.

32. Battaglia, ed., and other contributors, *Rhetorics of Self-Making*; Ewing, "The Illusion of Wholeness"; Hollan, "Cross-Cultural Differences in the Self"; and Rosaldo, "Toward an Anthropology of Self and Feeling."

33.   On awareness of oneself as a "perceptible object," see Hallowell, *Culture and Experience*. On how notions of the person as a social construct have blurred, see Ewing, "The Illusion of Wholeness," 254–58.

34.   Theoretical insights gained from work in Melanesia emphasize the ongoing construction of the human body. In some Melanesian societies, the body is revealed as a collection of "substances and flows from a number of sources momentarily come together" (O'Hanlon, "Unstable Images and Second Skins," 603). Contrary to the complete body of biomedicine, these bodies are subject to fundamental alteration during the life-cycle. Alterations occur through physical manipulations, and ingestion, or expulsion of bodily substances. Studies from Melanesia, Southeast Asia, and Africa provide models for the complex ways in which sharing, ingestion, or expulsion of substances contributes to the building of the body and personhood (Battaglia, *On the Bones of the Serpent*; Gillison, "Images of Nature in Gimi Thought"; Herdt, *Guardians of the Flutes, Rituals of Manhood*, and "Sambia Nosebleeding"; Meigs, "Male Pregnancy and the Reduction of Sexual Opposition" and *Food, Sex, and Pollution*; Poole, "Transforming 'Natural' Woman"; and Strathern, *The Gender of the Gift*) as well as how attributes can be transferred through bodily and non-bodily substances (Daniel, *Fluid Signs*; and Riesman, *First Find Your Child a Good Mother*, 163).

Ingestion of bodily substances other than semen or blood has been found to affect personhood in Africa and elsewhere. For example, in his study of child development in Fulani society, Riesman learned that beyond its contribution to nutrition and development of the physical body, breast milk has lasting effect on the development of Fulani personhood. The moral qualities of the mother are passed to her children in breast milk (Riesman, *First Find Your Child*, 163). A parallel view about the transmission of personal characteristics through breast milk is found among the Navajo. In their study of Navajo beliefs about breastfeeding, Wright et al., learned that in the Navajo view, a nursing mother is feeding the child "a part of herself," which marks the child both as her own and as human. Breastfeeding passes on traditional values (making the child better behaved) as well as some of a mother's own attributes (Anne Wright et al., "Cultural Interpretations," 786–89). I have not personally investigated Navajo beliefs about breast milk. The findings of Wright et al., however, exemplify the Navajo beliefs about synecdoche and personhood discussed in this work.

35.   Deezbaa' June, in Osawa, *In the Heart*.

36.   Walters, interview, 10 August 1993.

37.   Hanson Ashley, interview by author, Shonto, Arizona, 27 July 1993. Mr. Ashley is a mental health professional employed by the Indian Health Service who works part-time as a translator of ceremonial language for Navajo educators.

38.   Walters, interview, 12 August 1993.

39.   Anonymous elder #1, interview by author, Ganado, Ariz., 10 July 1991.

40.   On animation by means of Changing Woman's voice, see Franciscan Fathers, *An Ethnological Dictionary*, 356; Goddard, "Navajo Texts," 168; Wyman, *Blessingway*, 448; and Nakai Tso, interview by author, Tsaile, Ariz., 8 August 1992. On animation by means of the combined song of Changing Woman and other Diyin Dine'é, see Fishler, "In the Beginning," 91. On animation by means of Holy Winds, see Goddard, "Navajo Texts," 147; Matthews, *Navaho Legends*, 137; and O'Bryan, "The Diné," 102–103.

41.   Schwarz, *Molded in the Image*, 67–112.

42.   Schwarz, *Molded in the Image*, 79.

43.   Nancy Walters, in Osawa, *In the Heart*.

44.   Sadie Billie, conversation with author, White Valley, Ariz., 28 July 1992. Mrs. Billie is a wife, mother, and grandmother who currently works as a court advocate for mothers and children.

45.   See Aberle, "The Navajo-Hopi Land Dispute," 183–85, on the Manybeads-Sacred Lands case in which Navajo plaintiffs contended that removal from HPL would violate their religious freedom.

46.   Ursula Knoki-Wilson, interview by author, Chinle, Ariz., 10 August 1992. Mrs. Knoki-Wilson (M.S.N., University of Utah, Salt Lake City, Utah) works for the Fort Defiance Indian Hospital in Fort Defiance, Arizona, as a supervisory nurse-midwife. She is a leading authority on traditional Navajo concepts of prenatal health and childbirth. Her publications focus on traditional American Indian childbearing practices (Wilson, "Traditional Child Bearing Practices among Indians") and the challenge of multicultural health care (Wilson, "Nursing Care of American Indian Patients").

47.   In interviews, Mae Bekis (5 August 1992) and Ursula Knoki-Wilson (10 August 1992) told me that placentas are buried in the ash pile. Harry Walters said that they are buried in a badger hole (18 August 1992).

48.   In an interview on 18 August 1992, Harry Walters told me that the placenta can be placed in a live bush. On 21 August 1992 Sunny Dooley reported burial of the placenta beneath a juniper or pinyon tree.

49. Knoki-Wilson, interview, 10 August 1992.
50. Newcomb, *Navajo Omens*, 29.
51. On burial of a boy's cord in a corral, see Newcomb, *Navajo Omens*, 29; Leighton and Kluckhohn, *Children of the People*, 17; Bailey, "Some Sex Beliefs and Practices," 74. On tying of it to the tail or mane of a horse, see Newcomb, *Navajo Omens*, 29. This was confirmed by Ursula Knoki-Wilson in an interview on 10 August 1992. In contrast, Mrs. Joe McCabe told me, during an interview on 19 August 1992, that it should be tied to a sheep. Cords that are attached to livestock gradually disintegrate within the customary use area of the child's matrilineal clan, thereby inducing a proclivity toward animal husbandry and an attachment to a specific locale.

52. Newcomb, *Navajo Omens*, 29; Bailey, "Some Sex Beliefs and Practices," 74; and Bekis, interview, 28 July 1993.

53. Newcomb, *Navajo Omens*, 29; Bailey, "Some Sex Beliefs and Practices," 74; Leighton and Kluckhohn, *Children of the People*, 17; confirmed in interviews with Louva Dahozy on 19 August 1992, Knoki Wilson on 10 August 1992, and Walters on 18 August 1992, respectively.

54. Bailey, "Some Sex Beliefs and Practices," 74; and Bekis, interview, 28 July 1993.

55. Newcomb, *Navajo Omens*, 29; and interviews with Mae Bekis on 28 July 1993 and Ursula Knoki-Wilson on 10 August 1992, respectively.

56. Bailey, "Some Sex Beliefs and Practices," 74.
57. Leighton and Kluckhohn, *Children of the People*, 17.
58. Knoki Wilson, interview, 10 August 1992.
59. Wyman, *Blessingway*, 135–36.
60. Dooley, interview, 19 August 1992.
61. Mervyn Tilden, *Navajo Times*, 12 May 1994.
62. Mervyn Tilden, *Navajo Times*, 10 April 1995.
63. Roger Attakai, as quoted in Kammer, *The Second Long Walk*, 208–209.
64. Unidentified woman, in Florio and Mudd, *Broken Rainbow*, emphasis added.
65. Mae Tso, as quoted in Feher-Elston, *Children of Sacred Ground*, 100.
66. Ruth Benally, as quoted in Kammer, *The Second Long Walk*, 12.
67. Deezbaa' June, in Osawa, *In the Heart*.
68. Kammer, *The Second Long Walk*, 204–205; Topper, "FJUA Relocation."

69. Benedek, *The Wind Won't*, 211. See also Feher-Elston, *Children of Sacred Ground*, 100–102; and Joe, "Breaking the Navajo Family," 6–20.

70. Sam Wilson, as quoted in Kammer, *The Second Long Walk*, 193.

71. Unidentified relocatee, as quoted in Aberle, "The Navajo-Hopi Land Dispute," 170.

72. Anonymous consultant, as quoted in Joe, "Breaking the Navajo Family," 16–17.

73. Joe, "Breaking the Navajo Family," 17; Osawa, *In the Heart*.

74. Mae Tso, as quoted in Kammer, *The Second Long Walk*, 197.

75. Mabel Begay, as quoted in Kammer, *The Second Long Walk*, 187, emphasis added.

76. Unidentified woman in Florio and Mudd, *Broken Rainbow*, emphasis added.

77. Marie, in Osawa, *In the Heart*.

78. See Aberle, "The Navajo-Hopi Land Dispute"; Benedek, *The Wind Won't*; Brugge, *The Navajo-Hopi Land Dispute*; Joe, "Breaking the Navajo Family"; Kammer, *The Second Long Walk*; Scudder, *No Place to Go*.

CHAPTER THREE

1. Unlike the messages of many contemporary American Indian prophets and visionaries, the message brought by the holy visitors has not been commercialized or marketed to the broader public. For information on prophecies that have been so treated, see Geertz, *The Invention of Prophecy*; and Eliot, "The Red Road," 92–93.

2. *Navajo Times*, 23 May 1996.

3. Anonymous elder #2, interview by Wesley Thomas, Mariano Lake, New Mexico, 22 May 1996.

4. Hand trembling is one of several diagnostic methods used by Navajo people. When asked for assistance, a hand trembler washes her or his hands and forearms. Then, using one of a variety of designs and methods, pollen is sprinkled on the right forearm from the elbow along the radial margin, around the hypothenar eminence of the hand and along the palmar surface of the thumb to its tip, along each finger, and on the center of the palm. The diagnostician says a prayer to Gila Monster asking for information concerning the problem Sitting with eyes closed, the diagnostician sings one or two songs. During

the song or songs, her hand begins to shake. She concentrates on the current problem—in this case the identity of the holy visitors—and her hand stops shaking when her mind focuses on the correct answer. For more information on this method of diagnosis, see Morgan, "Navajo Treatment of Sickness"; and Wyman, "Navajo Diagnosticians."

5. Anonymous elder #2, interview.

6. Knoki-Wilson, interview, 10 August 1992.

7. The best known example of a visionary in Navajo oral history is the Visionary who acquired the *Tł'éé'jí,* "Night Chant" (see Faris, *The Nightway,* 35–40; Matthews, *The Night Chant,* 159–71, 197–212; Sapir, *Navaho Texts;* Spencer, "Mythology and Values," 155–61; and Wheelwright, "Tleiji or Yehbechai Myth by Hasteen Klah"), but Reichard notes that the hero of the Feather Chant combines characteristics of the Gambler with those of the Visionary (*Navajo Religion,* 68).

8. Despite the fact that all representatives of non-Navajo media were banned from the site, this was a "media event." Navajo people with whom I am acquainted mentioned hearing Navajo–language radio broadcasts in which the visitation was described, and specific directives were given regarding the need for Blessing Way ceremonies to be performed and for offerings to be made on the sacred mountains and elsewhere. Although I am only aware of the articles on the subject published in the *Salt Lake Tribune,* the *High Country News,* the *Arizona Republic,* the *Hopi Tutuveni,* and the *Navajo Times,* which are cited throughout this chapter, an anonymous reviewer noted that "the newspaper coverage of the event was extensive, well beyond the sources cited by the author." Interestingly, *Navajo Times* personnel pledged not to publish specific details of the event until approval was acquired from the Begay/Yazzle family and the proper ceremonies had been conducted at their homesite (*Arizona Republic,* 28 May 1996). In spite of this alleged ban, several articles in the *Navajo Times* (23 May 1996; 20 June 1996; 27 June 1996; 25 July 1996; 31 December 1996; 6 February 1997) referenced various aspects of the visit. In addition to this coverage, numerous E-mail postings circulated on the Internet.

9. See Dubisch, *In a Different Place,* 35–38, on pilgrimage sites. Interestingly, the location of the Holy Visit—Rocky Ridge, an isolated area on HPL—conforms to Victor Turner's suggestion that pilgrimage sites tend to be "out there"—that is, spatially peripheral and located outside the direct sphere of governmental and religious administrative centers (*Dramas, Fields, and Metaphors,* 191–96).

10.   *Salt Lake Tribune,* 17 May 1996; and *Hopi Tutuveni,* 24 May 1996.

11.   *Arizona Republic,* 28 May 1996.

12.   It is beyond the scope of this essay to attempt to summarize the vast literature on prophecy and transformative movements that has developed since publication of Mooney's classic work, "The Ghost-Dance Religion and the Sioux Outbreak of 1890," in 1896. For comparative theoretical models, see for example, Aberle, "The Prophet Dance and Reactions to White Contact"; Linton "Nativistic Movements"; and Wallace, "Revitalization Movements." On the Ghost Dance specifically, see Barber, "Acculturation and Messianic Movements"; DeMallie, "The Lakota Ghost Dance"; Hill, "The Navaho Indians and the Ghost Dance of 1890"; Hittman, "The 1870 Ghost Dance at Walker Reservation"; Kehoe, "The Ghost Dance Religion in Saskatchewan, Canada" and *The Ghost Dance;* Kracht, "The Kiowa Ghost Dance, 1894–1916"; Kroeber, "A Ghost-Dance in California"; Mooney, "The Ghost-Dance"; Moses, "'The Father Tells Me So!' Wovoka"; Overholt, "The Ghost Dance of 1890 and the Nature of the Prophetic Process"; Spier, "The Ghost Dance of 1870 among the Klamath of Oregon"; Stewart, "Contemporary Document on Wovoka (Jack Wilson) Prophet of the Ghost Dance in 1890"; as well as Thornton, *We Shall Live Again: The 1870 and 1890 Ghost Dance Movements as Demographic Revitalization.* On the Prophet Dance specifically, see Spier, *The Prophet Dance of the Northwest and Its Derivatives;* Suttles, "The Plateau Prophet Dance among the Coast Salish"; Vibert, "'The Natives Were Strong to Live': Reinterpreting Early-Nineteenth-Century Prophetic Movements in the Columbia Plateau"; and Walker, "New Light on the Prophet Dance Controversy." See also Cruickshank, "Claiming Legitimacy," and the essays on prophetic and revitalization movements in a special issue of *American Indian Quarterly,* edited by Trafzer, 1985.

13.   On how the powerful role played by prophets in American Indian communities and in the course of American Indian history have been ignored, see Trafzer, "Introduction," 233–35.

14.   Wallace, "Revitalization Movements."

15.   On these specific stages, see Wallace, "Revitalization Movements." On how such movements can be linked to "relative deprivation," see Aberle, "The Prophet Dance and Reactions to White Contact" and "A Note on Relative Deprivation Theory as Applied to Millenarian and Other Cult Movements"; Barber, "Acculturation and Messianic Movements"; Wallace, "Revitalization Movements."

On how they can be linked to "oppression," see Lanternari, *The Religions of the Oppressed.*

As this tale unfolds, the astute reader will note numerous parallels that can be drawn between the events following the visitation at Rocky Ridge and the development of revitalization movements documented elsewhere in the world as they are discussed by Wallace. These parallels affirm its status as an incipient revitalization movement resulting from multidimensional stresses, the ultimate outcome of which remains to be seen. According to Wallace's model for the development of such movements, this incipient movement is in the revitalization stage. The period of revitalization, directly preceding the attainment of a new "steady state," is said to consist of six phases: 1) "mazeway" reformulation; 2) communication; 3) organization; 4) adaptation, which frequently included resistance of various forms; 5) cultural transformation; and 6) routinization. Although this movement amongst Navajo people has conformed to the stages outlined by Wallace thus far, it is not guaranteed to become a sustained transformative movement. For, ultimately, we are left with the same dilemma as that faced by Wallace. His model has no explanatory or predictive power—it is unable to account for the fact that "many movements are abortive; their progress arrested at some intermediate point" (Wallace, "Revitalization Movements," 278).

16. Cruickshank, "Claiming Legitimacy," 148; Kehoe, *The Ghost Dance*, 101–11, 121–27; Vibert, "The Natives Were Strong to Live," 197–99.

17. Despite exposure to its tenets by Paiute, who tried to proselytize amongst them, in 1889–90, Navajo people resisted involvement in the Ghost Dance movement (see Barber, "Acculturation and Messianic Movements," 666–67; and Hill, "The Navaho Indians," 525–27). This demonstrates that transformative movements must be culturally appropriate or they will not be adopted. In the Navajo case, cultural prohibitions against contact with "the dead and all connected with them" circumscribed Navajo involvement in the Ghost Dance movement (Hill, "The Navaho Indians," 525).

18. Cruickshank, "Claiming Legitimacy"; DeMallie, "The Lakota Ghost Dance"; Vibert, "The Natives Were Strong to Live," 199.

19. Bailey and Bailey, "Historic Navajo Occupation"; Brugge, "A History of the Chaco Navajos"; Haile, "A Note on the Navaho Visionary," 359; Hewett, *The Chaco Canyon*; Kluckhohn, "Myths and Rituals," 60–61; and Watson, "Navahos Pray."

20. Quote is from Aberle, "A Note on Relative Deprivation Theory," 211.

21. Sam Begay, as quoted in *Salt Lake Tribune*, 17 May 1996.

22. On how insights and omens are conveyed via dreams, see Reichard, *Navaho Religion*, 550–51.

23. O'Bryan, "The Diné," 111.

24. Harry Walters, telephone interview by author, 23 May 1996.

25. Anonymous woman #1, telephone interview with author, 2 November 1996.

26. On repeated droughts, see Frisbie, "Temporal Change," 446; on loss of livestock, see Bailey and Bailey, "Historic Navajo Occupation," 210; and on loss of kin to Spanish influenza, see Russell, "The Navajo and the 1918 Influenza Pandemic," 381.

27. To link this prophecy to the influenza epidemic of 1918–19 does not necessarily cast it as a reaction to the incursion of Euro-Americans into the Navajo world. For, when faced with a devastating illness such as the hantavirus outbreak of 1993, Navajo people look inward to their own history and actions for answers, rather than blaming outside contagion.

28. Superintendent at Shiprock Agency, as quoted in Bailey and Bailey, "Historic Navajo Occupation," 207.

29. The identity of the visionary in this case remains unclear. He has been alternately identified as Naakai Jaan, "Mexican John," from Black Mountain (Haile, "A Note on the Navaho Visionary," 359; Brugge, "A History," 313), as Naltass Bega, "Navajo Dick," from around Mexican Water (Bailey and Bailey, "Historic Navajo Occupation," 209–10), as "an Indian in the Black Mountains [who] was struck by lightning and while unconscious 'saw the flood coming'; . . . [an] Indian [who] dreamed it three nights in succession . . . [or] a white man from Gallup [who] told his Indian friend about it" (Superintendent from Shiprock, as quoted in Bailey and Bailey, "Historic Navajo Occupation," 208). In regard to the latter claim, in a novel based on her own experiences while living on the Navajo reservation, Louisa Wetherill claims that the flood prophecy occurred in 1922 and that the story came from an elderly Navajo man from near Oljeto who was attempting to retell the story of Noah's Ark as it had been told by a missionary in the area (Gillmor and Wetherill, *Traders to the Navajos*, 234–35). The story of the flood prophecy is also a central element of Frances Gillmor's novel *Windsinger*.

30. Brugge, "A History," 313–14.

31. For information about accounts that reached the Chaco Canyon area, see Hewett, *The Chaco Canyon and Its Monuments*, 139; for information about accounts that reached Winslow, Arizona, see Bailey and Bailey, "Historic Navajo Occupation," 208; and for information about accounts that reached the Ramah area, see Kluckhohn, "Myths and Rituals," 59.

32. Superintendent at Shiprock Agency, as quoted in Bailey and Bailey, "Historic Navajo Occupation," 207.

33. Fishler, "In the Beginning," 4; Goddard, "Navajo Texts," 130–31; O'Bryan, "The Diné," 8–10; Yazzie, *Navajo History*, 15.

34. On those who sought refuge in the Santa Fe National Forest, see Brugge, "A History," 314; on those who sought refuge in the Carrizo, the Lukachukai, or the Black mountains, see Aberle, *The Peyote Religion*, 347; on those who sought refuge in the Chuska, or the Jemez Mountains, see Bailey and Bailey, "Historic Navajo Occupation," 208.

35. Hewett, *The Chaco Canyon and Its Monuments*, 139.

36. Bailey and Bailey, "Historic Navajo Occupation," 209; Brugge, "A History," 313–14.

37. Brugge, "A History," 313–14.

38. Bailey and Bailey, "Historic Navajo Occupation," 209.

39. Kluckhohn, "Myths and Rituals," 59.

40. Anonymous elder #3, telephone interview by author, 14 November 1996. This elder's commentary clearly indicates that, at least in the view of some contemporary Navajo, a direct correlation exists between the imprudent actions taken by Navajo seeking refuge from the predicted flood in 1920—performing ceremonies to stop the "work" without knowing the procedures required to restore the proper rainfall—and the recurring drought conditions experienced henceforth in the four corners region.

41. Frisbie, "Temporal Change," 466.

42. Aberle, *The Peyote Religion*; Frisbie, "Temporal Change."

43. Bailey and Bailey, "Historic Navajo Occupation," 473; Brugge, "A History," 445; Kluckhohn, "Myths and Rituals," 59. Precedent exists in Navajo oral tradition for White Shell Woman to bring messages in dreams. For example, Gladys Reichard documents an incident in which White Shell Woman brought an important message to a young girl via a dream (*Navajo Religion*, 496).

44. Kluckhohn, "Myths and Rituals," 59–60.

45. Bailey and Bailey, "Historic Navajo Occupation," 473; Brugge, "A History," 446; Kluckhohn, "Myths and Rituals," 60; Watson, "Navahos

Pray for the Good of the World," 16. Based on extensive ethnographic research in this area, Garrick and Roberta Bailey conclude that this woman was Mary Charley, a member of the Tódích'íí'nii, "Bitter Water Clan," who lived from 1875 to 1956. After this visitation, she attracted a large following. With the aid of a "talking" feather, she diagnosed the problems of patients and directed the performance of special versions of the Blessing Way ceremonies (Bailey and Bailey, "Historic Navajo Occupation," 474–76). Furthermore, the Baileys consider the account of the visit of White Shell Woman in 1936 to be a "confused version" of the visit by Hadahoniye' 'Ashkii, rather than a separate visitation (Bailey and Bailey, "Historic Navajo Occupation," 474).

    46.   Watson, "Navahos Pray," 16.

    47.   Watson, "Navahos Pray," 16.

    48.   Watson, "Navahos Pray," 17.

    49.   Brugge, "A History," 446; Watson, "Navahos Pray," 17.

    50.   Watson, "Navahos Pray," 16–17. After Hadahoniye' 'Ashkii's first visit, many Navajo sought counsel on the matter from Hastiin Tł'aai of the Newcomb (formerly Nava), New Mexico, region. Hastiin Tł'aai refused to credit the account, claiming that the visitor was an evil spirit rather than Hadahoniye' 'Ashkii, and many Navajo attribute his death on 2 March 1937 to his disbelief (Watson, "Navahos Pray," 18; Kluckhohn, "Myths and Rituals," 60).

    51.   Watson, "Navahos Pray," 17–18.

    52.   Watson, "Navahos Pray," 18.

    53.   Haile, "A Note on the Navaho Visionary," 359.

    54.   Bailey and Bailey, "Historic Navajo Occupation," 473.

    55.   Aberle, quoting Solon T. Kimball, in *The Peyote Religion*, 74. Based on personal communication with Solon T. Kimball, David Aberle reports that these may actually have been two separate visitations that occurred during the same period. In the first instance, Jesus Christ appeared to a Navajo woman while she was out herding. In the second, a Navajo (perhaps a woman) saw a Caucasian boy dressed in velvet that she believed to be Jesus Christ. It was this visitor who claimed he would lead the Navajo out of their terrible troubles (Aberle, *The Peyote Religion*, 74).

    56.   Anonymous elder #3, telephone interview.

    57.   Bailey and Bailey, "Historic Navajo Occupation," 473; see also Aberle, *The Peyote Religion*, 74. According to the Baileys, the recipient of this vision was Mary Etcitty, a member of the Mą'ii deeshgiizhinii, "Coyote Pass or Jemez" clan, who lived from 1908 to 1979. She was a

ndilniihii, "a diagnostician using the hand-trembling method," who was acknowledged to have had visions at different times throughout her life (Bailey and Bailey, "Historic Navajo Occupation," 477).

58. Anonymous woman #1, telephone interview.

59. E-mail message posted on NATCHAT list by Leo Jones on 12 July 1996. I include information, such as the following account of a visitation that was contained in an E-mail message posted on the NATCHAT list, with a modicum of apprehension. Readers should note that, owing to the nature of this form of communication, I was unable to scrutinize the veracity of these individual sources.

60. Anonymous elder #3, telephone interview.

61. *Hopi Tutuveni*, 24 May 1996.

62. *Arizona Republic*, 28 May 1996.

63. *High Country News*, 5 August 1996.

64. *High Country News*, 5 August 1996. In addition, between the time of the visit in May and August of 1996, Alfred Yazzie led pilgrimages to make offerings at each of the four sacred mountains bounding Navajo sacred space (*High Country News*, 5 August 1996). Upon completing this sequence of pilgrimages, which began with the sacred mountain of the East and concluded with offerings at the sacred mountain of the North, Alfred Yazzie shared information about the events at Rocky Ridge with reporters for *High Country News* (5 August 1996).

65. Anonymous elder #2, interview.

66. *Hopi Tutuveni*, 24 May 1996.

67. *Salt Lake Tribune*, 17 May 1996.

68. Anonymous woman #1, telephone interview.

69. Despite this posting, Hopi people are documented to have visited the site on several occasions (*Hopi Tutuveni*, 24 May 1996; *Navajo Times*, 6 February 1997), and other non-Caucasians reportedly visited as well (E-mail message posted on NATCHAT list by Leo Jones on 12 July 1996). By some accounts, however, non-Navajo visitors were banned from making offerings at the site. For example, Leo Jones reports that "A Navajo woman said that her husband who is of Hispanic descent was not allowed to make offerings at the site of the Holy Visit" (E–mail message posted on NATCHAT list, 12 July 1996).

70. *Hopi Tutuveni*, 25 May 1996.

71. *Arizona Republic*, 28 May 1996; *Salt Lake Tribune*, 17 May 1996.

72. E-mail message posted by Leo Jones on NATCHAT list on 12 July 1996.

73. Anonymous elder #3, interview.
74. Anonymous elder #3, interview.
75. E-mail message posted by Leo Jones on NATCHAT list on 12 July 1996.
76. *Hopi Tutuveni*, 24 May 1996.
77. Anonymous woman #1, telephone interview.
78. *Hopi Tutuveni*, 24 May 1996.
79. A reviewer reported having heard rumors of other visitations at undisclosed locations elsewhere in Navajo country about the time of the Rocky Ridge visitation. According to his sources, in each case, members of the concerned family purposively did not publicize the visitation, in order to avoid being subjected to the type of "furor" experienced at Sarah Begay's home. Also, I heard rumors of a visitation in the Ramah area that allegedly took place shortly after the Rocky Ridge visitation.
80. Anonymous elder #2, interview.
81. *Hopi Tutuveni*, 24 May 1996.
82. As quoted in *Arizona Republic*, 28 May 1996.
83. *Navajo Times*, 23 May 1996.
84. *Navajo Times*, 23 May 1996.
85. E-mail message from George Joe, 13 June 1996. Following then-Speaker Begaye's request, the volume of pilgrims declined but Navajo people continued to make pilgrimages to the site of the Holy Visit. By July of 1997, pilgrims were reportedly still going to the Begay residence, although much less frequently (George Joe, E-mail correspondence with author, 29 May 1997; Ray Baldwin Louis, telephone conversation with author, 16 July 1997).
86. The Navajo Tribal Council declared June 18 as an official day of prayer with the intention that this would become an annual event. This date was chosen because it is the day Navajo people began their walk back from Fort Sumner in 1868. In the words of then-Speaker Begaye, "That's when we truly demonstrated what can be done through unity, songs, language, way of life, and mostly prayers" (*Navajo Times*, 27 June 1996). The 1997 Navajo Nation Unity Day of Prayer was held on June 18 at the Window Rock Veteran's Memorial Park. According to Ray Baldwin Louis, Press Officer for the Office of Speaker Kelsey Begaye, the 1997 event was composed of three types of prayer services. Beginning at 5:30 A.M., a traditional medicine man sang songs from the Beauty Way and offered a prayer. A dozen or more people were in attendance and KTNN personnel conducted a

narrated simulcast on-site. Mr. Louis estimates that upwards of 70 percent of all Navajo people tune in to the radio at that hour of the morning, so many Navajo people are believed to have participated by listening to the radio broadcast. At noon, a Native American Church Roadman performed a "prayer circle," which included the fifty people in attendance. A portion of this service was broadcast on KTNN. In the evening, a Christian service was attended by approximately 150 people. Dozens of people called or wrote letters to then-Speaker Begaye to let him know that they had participated in the morning blessing from their homes. Representatives from fifteen chapters contacted then-Speaker Begay to inform him that they had held prayer services on-site, which were timed to coincide with the noontime service. Five chapters offered meals with their services. Mr. Louis reported hearing of numerous church services held simultaneously with the evening service (Ray Baldwin Louis, telephone conversation). Although enthusiasm for the event has seemingly waned with each passing year, resulting in each subsequent event being less and less elaborate, the Navajo Nation Unity Day of Prayer was commemorated in 1998 and 1999.

87. *Navajo Times*, 20 June 1996.

88. As a byproduct of the religious conflict rampant amongst those who follow the traditional religion (or rival ceremonial practitioners), the Native American Church, and the various Christian sects currently present in Navajo country, some Navajo vehemently opposed the overall approach of organizers of this event. For example, an ad run in the *Navajo Times* by Concerned Navajo Christians for Christ took exception with one of the central themes of the Navajo Nation Unity Day of Prayer. Members of this organization disapproved of the statement that, "we are all Navajos, it doesn't matter whether we are Traditional Believers, Native American Church members or Christians we are all praying to the same God" and that "It doesn't matter which approach we take . . . just so long as we all pray in unity. . . ." (27 June 1996). This ad claimed that

> The Speaker and his cooperators have made various other statements which attempt to place all belief systems of mankind on the same level as God's Word. No where in the Bible does it state that other beliefs [*sic*] systems are acceptable to God. No where in the Bible does it state we are to participate in joint prayer with other non-Bible based religious systems; or to incorporate or collaborate other non-Bible based religious systems into God's Word or Christianity. . . . As a matter of fact, the Bible

calls Christians to remain separate from the other world belief systems.

Further, the Bible cautions the Christian community to be aware of "False Prophets" and "False Doctrine." If a man or woman presents himself as a person who proclaims new revelations from God, he or she is considered a Prophet. If such a person proclaims hew [*sic*] doctrine that is not in line with what the Bible teaches then he or she is a "False Prophet" and is promoting "False Doctrine. . . ." If what they say does not confirm [*sic*] to the teachings of the Bible, then we as Christians must avoid participation in such activities. We must test everything that is said against God's Word to protect ourselves from being mislead [*sic*] by "False Prophets" and "False Doctrine" (*Navajo Times*, 27 June 1996).

89.   *High Country News*, 5 August 1996; *Navajo Times*, 27 June 1996. Three radio stations—the Navajo Nation's KTNN, KGLX from Gallup, KNDN from Farmington—and two TV stations—local NNTV5 in Farmington and KOB in Albuquerque—broadcasted the event from Window Rock (*High Country News*, 5 August 1996; *Navajo Times*, 27 June 1996).

90.   *Navajo Times*, 27 June 1996.

91.   *High Country News*, 5 August 1996.

92.   Begaye, as quoted in *Navajo Times*, 25 July 1996.

93.   *Hopi Tutuveni*, 24 May 1996.

94.   Anonymous woman #1, telephone interview.

95.   *High Country News*, 5 August 1996.

96.   Anonymous elder #3, interview.

97.   This type of passive resistance came in the form of alternative accounts such as the following two gleaned from the Internet. In the "UFO" version, which sounds in many respects like it could be a promotional ad for an upcoming episode of the *X Files* television program, blue and white aliens allegedly abducted Navajo people.

Has anyone heard about the UFO that landed in the middle of the Navajo Nation? A friend told me who works with them. She said it happened about 4–5 days ago, where a UFO landed and took a few people with them. She said they saw 2 aliens, they described them [as being] smaller than humans and that one was blue and the other white. Now the land where the UFO

landed is considered holy land and [?] will not let anybody
enter. She also said that the FBI is demanding access to the sight
[*sic*], I don't know if they let them in yet or not. (Anonymous E-
mail posted on NETREZ, 30 May 1996)

In what I have coined the "Magician" version, the visitors disappeared
in a "puff" of smoke as if they were props in a David Copperfield trick.

End of May, near Big Mountain, just before the gathering [Sun
Dance gathering in support of Navajo resisting relocation off
HPL]. Dineh Holy person, grandmother, of the Bitter Water
clan, woke to tell her family "They are coming." A night or two
later, big wind blows around and through the hogan. Grandmother tells her family, "They are here." All go outside, where
two figures stand, which grandmother recognizes as the two
Talking Gods, the Hero Twins, one dressed in white, one in
turquoise. They say, (paraphrase) "All the trouble you are having, the droughts and so on, are because you stopped honoring
the traditions, and are not giving us enough (honor? prayer?).
You must return to the traditions and do the proper ceremonies. You must tell all the people we came and said this, and
we will leave a sign." The family could not look directly at them,
and had not [*sic*] control of their bodies. *The figures vanished in
a puff of smoke.* (Gilbert, E-mail message posted on NETREZ, 9
June 1996, emphasis added)

    98.   *Hopi Tutuveni*, 24 May 1996; and *High Country News*, 5 August
1996, respectively.
    99.   Jenkins, as quoted in *Hopi Tutuveni*, 24 May 1996, paren-
thetical comment in original.
    100.   As quoted in *Hopi Tutuveni*, 24 May 1996.
    101.   Begay, as quoted in *Navajo Times*, 6 February 1997.
    102.   Anonymous elder #3, interview.
    103.   Aberle, "The Future of Navajo Religion," 74, 346, 347, 350;
Bailey and Bailey, "Historic Navajo Occupation"; Brugge, "A History";
Haile, "A Note," 359; Hewett, *The Chaco Canyon*; Kluckhohn, "Myths
and Rituals," 60–61; Watson, "Navahos Pray."
    104.   Anonymous elder #3, interview.
    105.   E-mail message posted on NATCHAT list by Leo Jones on 12
July 1996.
    106.   Anonymous woman #1, telephone interview.

107. Anonymous elder #3, interview.
108. Anonymous woman #1, telephone interview.
109. Anonymous elder #3, interview.
110. Harry Walters, telephone interview.
111. For information on previous examples, see Aberle, "The Future of Navajo Religion," 74, 346, 347, 350; Bailey and Bailey, "Historic Navajo Occupation"; David Brugge, "A History," 359; Haile, "A Note," 359; Hewett, *The Chaco Canyon and Its Monuments*; Kluckhohn, "Myths and Rituals," 60–61; and Watson, "Navahos Pray."
112. See Peter Iverson, *The Navajo Nation*, on the evolution of the Navajo Nation.
113. I am grateful to the anonymous reviewer who cautioned me to consider the inherently political nature of then-President Hale's and then-Speaker Begaye's actions. As an outcome of the very divisive politics evident in Window Rock throughout this period, Kelsey Begaye was elected president of the Navajo Nation in the autumn of 1998.

CHAPTER FOUR

1. Shorty, as quoted in *Navajo Times*, 18 August 1994.
2. *Navajo Times*, 18 August 1994.
3. Yazza, as quoted in *Navajo Times*, 18 August 1994.
4. Writing for the *Gallup Independent*, Richard Sitts noted, "The bottom line is that most folks, no matter what nationality, either fear or dislike snakes, period. Snakes have a bad rap, mainly because of their physical appearance, which they can't help. But they are part of living in the Southwest, like them or not" (8 August 1994).
5. Consider, for example, the following observation made by Gladys Reichard, "Navajo are *afraid* of snakes and would never kill them because long ago the snake was a man" (*Social Life of the Navajo Indians*, 144, emphasis added).
6. Some of the numerous warnings Navajo are given regarding contact with snakes include: "Don't kill a snake when it is raining. Lightning will strike your home" (Bulow, *Navajo Taboos*, 89); "Dreams of snakes are not bad unless the snakes bite" (Reichard, *Social Life*, 145); and "Don't go to the bathroom in front of a snake. He will be jealous of your wife and turn her yellow" (Bulow, *Navajo Taboos*, 90).
7. On observing the construction of a sandpainting, see Kluckhohn and Wyman, "An Introduction to Navaho Chant Practice,"

61–62. On hearing certain songs, see Hill, "Navaho Warfare," 9; and Wyman, "The Agricultural and Hunting Methods of the Navaho Indians," 98. On being massaged at birth, see Bailey, "Some Sex Beliefs and Practices," 75; on massage at puberty, see Frisbie, *Kinaaldá*, 13. On contact with Anasazi ruins, see McPherson, *Sacred Land, Sacred View*, 119–21; on contact with menstrual blood, see Bailey, "Some Sex Beliefs and Practices," 10–11. On witnessing accidents, see Haile, "Origin Legends of the Navajo Enemyway," 25. On washing laundry, see Hill, "Navaho Warfare," 18; and Reichard, *Navaho Religion*, 35. On drinking breast milk, see Wright et al., "Cultural Interpretations," 788.

8. Anthropological interest in metaphoric structures such as homology and complementarity is not new. A substantial body of literature exists on homologous relationships that are commonly constructed among physical topography, domestic architecture, social arrangements, and parts of the human body (see, for example, Bastien, "Qullahuaya-Andean Body Concepts"; Griaule, *Conversations with Ogotemmeli*; Reichel-Dolmatoff, *Amazonian Cosmos*; and Turner, "The Social Skin"). Such homologies simultaneously create and reproduce the dominant social and moral order through time and space, constituting a culturally constructed landscape which is accepted as "natural" by the people living it (Lock, "Cultivating the Body," 135). Anthropologists have employed a wealth of theoretical approaches to understand the human predilection to organize the raw materials of experience and social life into binary contrastive domains or dualities. Claude Lévi-Strauss used such contrastive categories as a means for reducing the complexity of life to "hidden elementary structures," which he believed shed light on the universal aspects of the human mind. He concluded that it was a fundamental property of the human mind to think in opposites and posited that the most fundamental oppositions are self/other and nature/culture (Lévi-Strauss, *The Savage Mind*, 191–216). Dualism in social life and symbolic classification has been taken up by numerous anthropologists as the means for understanding a variety of social phenomena, from dietary restrictions to maintenance of social distinctions. These studies include the pioneering work of Robert Hertz into the preeminence of the right hand ("The Pre-eminence of the Right Hand"), the cross-cultural comparison of lateral contrasts—left and right—(Needham ed., *Right and Left*), an analysis of dual organizations as mechanisms for attainment of harmony and order (Maybury-Lewis and Almagor, *The Attraction of Opposites*), and more recently symbolic models of division (the world) and unity (the human

body) in African cosmology and experience (Jacobson-Widding, ed., *Body and Space*).

9.   Prior studies of Navajo worldview metaphors, such as Farella, *The Main Stalk*; Pinxten and Farrer, "On Learning a Comparative View"; and Witherspoon, *Language and Art*, are the foundation for application of new approaches focusing on the "predictive and performative" aspects of metaphor as a backdrop for understanding human experience, action, and interaction (Fernandez, ed., *Beyond Metaphor*, 7).

In contrast to structuralist approaches that saw metaphoric structures as static and elementary, an interactionist approach holds that metaphoric significance comes through the linking of domains of experience through action and interaction. Domains are reorganized as parts of a more powerfully integrated totality. This linking often results from ritual action in special circumstances such as healing or puberty ceremonies. See Terence Turner, "'We Are Parrots,' 'Twins Are Birds,'" 121–58, for an analysis of this point using Bororo, Kayapo, and Nuer data.

10.   As used here, the term "self" refers to the awareness people have of themselves as perceptible subjects and to the ways in which that awareness and that experience of themselves are culturally shaped. The term "person" refers to the social construct based on culturally sanctioned rules governing rights, prerogatives, obligations, and agency that are embodied in the corporeal body.

11.   As quoted in *Salt Lake Tribune*, 6 August 1994.

12.   As quoted in *Salt Lake Tribune*, 6 August 1994.

13.   Yazzie, *Navajo History*, 13.

14.   Raymond Jim, as quoted in *Salt Lake Tribune*, 6 August 1994.

15.   On guardians of the Sun's house, see Fishler, "In the Beginning," 47; Matthews, *Navaho Legends*, 111; Oakes, *Where the Two Came to Their Father*, 41; and Zolbrod, *Diné Bahane'*, 205.

16.   Harry Walters, interview.

17.   As quoted in *Navajo Times*, 18 August 1994.

18.   *Navajo Times*, 18 August 1994.

19.   Yazza, as quoted in *Navajo Times*, 18 August 1994.

20.   O'Bryan, "The Diné," 127–38; Wyman, *Blessingway*, 594–99.

21.   O'Bryan, "The Diné," 129.

22.   O'Bryan, "The Diné," 129.

23.   O'Bryan, "The Diné," 130.

24.   Yazza, as quoted in *Navajo Times*, 18 August 1994.

25. Although the names of the first clans are subject to debate, it is generally agreed that Changing Woman selected men and women from the first Nihookáá Dine'é to live as husband and wife and thus established the four original clans of the Navajo and the practice of clan exogamy (Aronilth, *Foundations of Navajo Culture*, 83; Matthews, *Navaho Legends*, 148; O'Bryan, "The Diné," 167; Reichard, *Navaho Religion*, 28; Wyman, *Blessingway*, 458, 634; Yazzie, *Navajo History*, 74).

26. Aronilth, *Foundations*, 83; Fishler, "In the Beginning," 94.

27. Fishler, "In the Beginning," 96. Many accounts detail the specific part of Changing Woman's body from which each clan was formed, but, as noted above, there is no consensus in the various accounts of this episode about exactly which clans originated from Changing Woman's flesh, or which clans originated from which part of her body. The clans most frequently mentioned as one of the four original clans are Honágháahnii, "One-Walks-Around Clan" (Austin and Lynch, *Saad Ahaah Sinil Dual Language*, 3; Matthews, *Navaho Legends*, 148; Yazzie, *Navajo History*, 74), Kinyaa'áanii, "The Towering House Clan" (Aronilth, "Foundations of Navajo Culture," 83; Austin and Lynch, *Saad Ahaah*, 3; Matthews, *Navaho Legends*, 148; Wyman, *Blessingway*, 458; Yazzie, *Navajo History*, 74), Tódích'íi'nii, "Bitter Water Clan" (Aronilth, "Foundations," 83; Austin and Lynch, *Saad Ahaah*, 3; Matthews, *Navaho Legends*, 148; Wyman, *Blessingway*, 458, 634; Yazzie, *Navajo History*, 74), Bit'ahnii, "Under His Cover Clan" (Matthews, *Navaho Legends*, 148; Wyman, *Blessingway*, 634), Tó'ahaní, "Near the Water Clan" (Aronilth, "Foundations," 83; Wyman, *Blessingway*, 458, 634), and Hashtł'ishnii, "Mud Clan" (Aronilth, "Foundations," 83; Austin and Lynch, *Saad Ahaah*, 3; Matthews, *Navaho Legends*, 148; Wyman, *Blessingway*, 458, 634; Yazzie, *Navajo History*, 74).

28. Fishler, "In the Beginning," 95.

29. Farella, *The Main Stalk*, 176; Griffin-Pierce, *Earth Is My Mother, Sky Is My Father*, 66; Witherspoon, *Language and Art*, 118–44, 159–60.

30. Walters, interview, 18 August 1992.

31. Dooley, interview, 19 August 1992. This holds true for male and female but not *nádleehé*. Nádleehé, which literally translates "one who changes repeatedly," is the term currently used to refer to male-bodied people of alternative gender in Navajo society. Nádleehé have a unique capacity for simultaneously filling male and female roles.

32. Aronilth, *Foundations*, 147.

33. Aronilth, *Foundations*, 147; Ashley, interview; Bekis, interview, 28 July 1993; Avery Denny, interview by author, Chinle, Ariz., 11 August

1993; Knoki-Wilson, interviews, 1992, 1993; McPherson, *Sacred Land, Sacred View,* 44; Nakai Tso, interview; Walters, interviews, 18 August 1992, 10 August 1993. In our discussions, English-speaking Navajo consultants consistently used the terms "male" and "female" to refer to the contrastive sides of the body. The English term "male" literally translates into Navajo as *biką,* which when applied to humans indicates "someone's male sexual partner," and "female" literally translates into Navajo as *ba'ááad,* which when applied to humans indicates "someone's female sexual partner." Due to this choice of terminology, I initially wondered if the Navajo people with whom I consulted were referring to a form of dual sexuality in the physical composition of the body. The characteristics and qualities associated with each side of the body make it clear, however, that this distinction does not refer to sexuality. These terms, biką and ba'ááad, are commonly used to make biological sexual distinctions among domestic or game animals such as sheep, goats, and deer, and they have been used by prior researchers to refer to male and female (Matthews, *The Night Chant,* 60; Reichard, *Navaho Religion,* 176). According to the Navajo with whom I conferred, these terms are considered impolite when used in reference to human companions (Knoki-Wilson, interview, 29 July 1993).

When I asked people what Navajo terms they would use to refer to the respective sides of the body, a variety of terms were mentioned. Walters used the term naayéé' k'ehjigo, "on the side of protection," for the male side and hózhǫ́ǫ́jígo, "on the side of peace, harmony, and order," for the female (interview on 18 August 1992). Ashley told me he preferred the terms *dinego,* "the man's side," and *asdzááángo,* "the lady's side," to connote the concepts of masculine and feminine respectively (interview on 27 July 1993). In his lectures at Navajo Community College, Avery Denny of Low Mountain, Arizona, uses są́ah naagháii to refer to the male side and bik'eh hózhǫ́ to refer to the female because at the most abstract level of knowledge, the level of songs and prayers, these terms embody all that is male and female (interview on 11 August 1993).

34.   Knoki-Wilson, interview, 10 August 1992.

35.   Walters, interview, 18 August 1992.

36.   Denny, interview; Knoki-Wilson, interview, 29 July 1993; and Walters, interview, 10 August 1993.

37.   Hanson Ashley, interview; Denny, interview; Knoki-Wilson, interview, 29 July 1993; and Walters, interview, 10 August 1993.

38.   Knoki-Wilson, interview, 10 August 1992.

39. Knoki-Wilson, interview, 10 August 1992.

40. Bekis, interview, 22 March 1995.

41. Aronilth, *Foundations*, 145–48, and interview; Jean Jones, interview by author, Rock Point, Ariz., 25 July 1991; Regina Lynch, interview by author, Tsaile, Ariz., 16 July 1991; Bekis, interview, 5 August 1992; see also Schwarz, *Molded in the Image*, 87–92.

42. Aronilth, interview.

43. Dooley, interview.

44. Ruth Roessel, interview by author, Round Rock, Ariz., 26 July 1991. Ruth Roessel is a wife, mother, grandmother, and educator from Round Rock, Arizona, who has taught at all grade levels, including at Navajo Community College in Tsaile, Arizona. She is best known for editing a collection of narratives entitled *Navajo Stories of the Long Walk Period* and for her book entitled *Women in Navajo Society*.

45. Quotes from interviews with Sunny Dooley on 19 August 1992, Flora Ashley on 29 July 1991, Mae Bekis on 28 July 1993, and Jean Jones on 25 July 1991, respectively. Flora Ashley of Shonto, Arizona, is a wife, mother and grandmother who teaches Navajo language and culture at the boarding school in her community. Jean Jones of Rock Point, Arizona, is a mother, and grandmother who teaches sash weaving at the Rock Point Community School in Rock Point, Arizona.

46. Anonymous woman #2, interview by author, Farmington, N.M., 17 March 1995.

47. Bekis, interview, 28 July 1993.

48. Zolbrod, "Secrets," 26.

49. Zolbrod, "Secrets," 29.

50. Hill, "The Agricultural and Hunting Methods," 176.

51. Luckert, *The Navajo Hunter Tradition*, 153.

52. By some accounts, a hunter can be changed into a snake if he does not obey prohibitions against the eating of snake meat (Wheelwright, *The Myth and Prayers of the Great Star Chant and the Myth of the Coyote Chant*, 20–23) or deer intestines (Luckert, *The Navajo*, 153). A close connection exists between snakes and deer intestines. According to hunting tradition, "the pinkish-reddish intestines" of the first deer to be butchered were removed near what is today Sanders, Arizona, and "these became pink snakes" (Luckert, *The Navajo*, 36).

53. Shorty, as quoted in *Navajo Times*, 18 August 1994.

54. Bulow, *Navajo Taboos*, 90.

55. On the connection to the intestines, see Luckert, *The Navajo*, 36; On the connection to the backbone, see Hill, "The Agricultural

and Hunting Methods," 176, and Mitchell, *Navajo Blessing Way Singer,* 290–91.

56. Bekis, interview, 22 March 1995.

57. Bekis, interview, 22 March 1995; Reichard, *Navaho Religion,* 12, 93; Wheelwright, *The Myth and Prayers,* 77–79.

58. Reichard, *Navaho Religion,* 93.

59. Reichard, *Navaho Religion,* 12.

60. Wheelwright, *The Myth and Prayers,* 77–79.

61. Hill, "Navaho Warfare," 11–14.

62. On Na'at'oyee, see Reichard, *Navaho Religion,* 645–48 and Interview with Bekis on 22 March 1995; On Diné binílch'ijí and Nílch'ihjí, see Interview with Bekis on 22 March 1995.

63. Bekis, interview, 22 March 1995.

64. Ewing, "The Illusion of Wholeness"; Hollan, "Cross-Cultural Differences in the Self." Many anthropologists maintain that the experience of "wholeness, continuity, and autonomy" associated with the "self" in many Euro-American societies is a culture-bound notion that is not applicable to most cultures where the self is experienced "contextually and relationally" (see Shweder and Bourne, "Does the Concept of the Person Vary Cross-Culturally?"). This type of self representation has been referred to as "interdependent or relational" (Ewing, "The Illusion of Wholeness") as opposed to "independent and autonomous" (Spiro, "Is the Western Conception of the Self 'Peculiar' within the Context of the World's Cultures?"). The former has generally been considered to be a non-Western construct and the latter a Western construct.

65. On the "critical anthropology of selfhood," see contributions to Battaglia, ed., *Rhetorics of Self-Making.*

66. The notion that the constructs of "self" and "person" can be conflated is not a new idea. See for example, Michelle Rosaldo's insightful critique of the conceptual opposition of self and person commonly found in anthropological discourse ("Toward an Anthropology of Self and Feeling," 145–50).

CHAPTER FIVE

1. Craig, "Someone Drew a Line."

2. Florio and Mudd.

3. In Florio and Mudd, *Broken Rainbow.*

4. In Florio and Mudd, *Broken Rainbow.*

5. For example, the *Navajo Times* reports that in February of 1997, while giving testimony before U.S. District Judge Earl Carroll on the efficacy of a proposed resolution to the land dispute, Betty Tso, "emphasized through tears, 'I'm losing my family by testifying and signing the accommodations agreement'" (20 February 1997).

6. Some scholars hold that the facial expressions displayed as happiness, surprise, fear, anger, disgust, or sadness are universal and thus cross-culturally recognizable (see for example, Ekman *The Face of Man* and "Expression and the Nature of Emotion").

7. Mary Louise Johnson, as quoted in Brugge, Benally, et al., *Memories Come to Us in the Rain and the Wind*, 50, translation by Timothy Benally.

8. Brugge, Benally, et al., *Memories Come to Us*; Eichstaedt, *If You Poison Us*, xv; Spieldoch, "Uranium Is in My Body," 176–77.

9. Eichstacdt, *If You*, xv, 166–67; Spieldoch, "Uranium," 174, 179.

10. Eichstacdt, *If You*, 98.

11. Eichstaedt, *If You*, xv; Spieldoch, "Uranium," 174.

12. Eichstaedt, *If You*, 47–65.

13. Eichstaedt, *If You*, 95–96.

14. Spieldoch, "Uranium," 174.

15. Spieldoch, "Uranium," 175.

16. Spieldoch, "Uranium," 174.

17. On the history of radioactive colonialism in Native North American more generally, see Churchill and LaDuke, "Native North America."

18. At the time of this writing, various bills aimed at making the law more culturally sensitive and extending coverage to millers (as with miners, this will be limited to specific diseases and based on level of exposure) have been passed and signed into law. Specific regulations for each change remain to be written.

19. Nancy Walters, in Osawa, *In the Heart.*

20. Lutz and White, "The Anthropology," 406.

21. Lutz and White, "The Anthropology," 405.

22. Lutz and White, "The Anthropology," 406–7.

23. Rosaldo, "Toward an Anthropology of Self and Feeling," 143.

24. Quotes from Irvine, "Registering Affect," 130, and Reddy, "Emotional Liberty," 258, respectively. See also, Beisner, *Literacy, Emotion, and Authority*; Brenneis, "Shared and Solitary Sentiments"; Briggs,

Never in Anger and *Inuit Morality Play;* Lutz, "The Domain of Emotion Words on Ifaluk"; as well as, Myers, "Emotions and the Self" and "The Logic and Meaning of Anger Among Pintupi Aborigines."

25. Lutz and White, "The Anthropology," 419.

26. Lutz and White, "The Anthropology," 405.

27. Irvine, "Registering Affect," 130.

28. While this statement remains true, it is worth noting that recently some scholars have pointed out the limitations of such collective approaches and have begun calling for renewed focus on the individual aspects of emotional experience, such as the realm of personal meaning (Chodorow, *The Power of Feelings*) and notions of liberty (Reddy, "Emotional Liberty").

29. Quote from Leavitt, "Meaning and Feeling in the Anthropology of Emotions," 523.

30. Hanson Ashley, interview.

31. For further information, see Schwarz, *Molded in the Image,* 141–146.

32. Bekis, interview, 5 August 1992.

33. Hanson Ashley, interview.

34. Dooley, interview.

35. Crying with no purpose is associated with needing or desiring something to happen. For example, if a child cries when he or she is injured, the tears that are shed are recognized as deriving directly from the physical pain. But if a child cries for no apparent reason, it is believed that his or her action will create another reason.

36. Wesley Thomas, personal communication with author on 6 March 1994. See also Franciscan Fathers, *An Ethnological Dictionary of the Navaho Language,* 510–11.

37. Personal conversation with Sadie Billie on 28 July 1992.

38. By other accounts, the first person to die was either a twin hermaphrodite (Matthews, *Navaho Legends,* 77–78) or a woman (Fishler, "In the Beginning," 31–32; Goddard, "Navajo Texts," 138).

39. O'Bryan, "The Diné," 31.

40. Frisbie, "Introduction," 303.

41. Contemporary Navajo funerals are syncretic events that meld Christian and Navajo beliefs about death and mourning. Mary Shepardson describes Christian funerals for Navajo people after 1970 at which the deceased lay "in state in the church" as relatives and friends of all ages filed past to view the body (Shepardson, "Changes in Navajo Mortuary Practices and Beliefs," 389–90). Funeral directors serving

Navajo clients told Joyce Griffen that they had observed bereaved Navajo attending funerals in funeral homes or in churches on the reservation having eye contact with or touching the body of the deceased ("Variations on a Rite of Passage," 370). For further information on how burial practices are changing, see Griffen, "Variations" and Shepardson, "Changes in Navajo Mortuary." On how traditional Navajo burials did not involve public ceremonies, see Frisbie, "Introduction," 303.

42.   On how interment was a private or "family" matter, see Franciscan Fathers, *An Ethnological Dictionary*, 453, and Frisbie, "Introduction," 303. On the potentially dangerous effects of death involved in the process, see Reichard, *Social Life*, 141.

43.   Franciscan Fathers, *An Ethnological Dictionary*, 453; Frisbie, "Introduction," 303; Reichard, *Social Life*, 142.

44.   Franciscan Fathers, *An Ethnological Dictionary*, 454; Frisbie, "Introduction," 303; Reichard, *Social Life*, 142–43.

45.   Franciscan Fathers, *An Ethnological Dictionary*, 454; Frisbie, "Introduction," 303; Reichard, *Social Life*, 142–43.

46.   Franciscan Fathers, *An Ethnological Dictionary*, 454–55; Frisbie, "Introduction," 303; Reichard, *Social Life*, 143.

47.   Franciscan Fathers, *An Ethnological Dictionary*, 454; Frisbie, "Introduction," 303; Reichard, *Social Life*, 143.

48.   Louise Lamphere reports having witnessed Navajo mourners openly shed tears at Christian-style funerals for relatives or friends (personal correspondence with author on 5 April 1999). I do not know if these people limit their expressions of emotion to the time between death and burial.

49.   Reichard, *Social Life*, 143; Shepardson, "Changes in Navajo Mortuary," 387–88.

50.   On the brief period of wailing see, Franciscan Fathers, *An Ethnological Dictionary*, 455; Frisbie, "Introduction," 303; and Reichard, *Social Life*, 143. On the significance of the communal meal, see Shepardson, "Changes in Navajo Mortuary," 387.

51.   Shepardson, "Changes in Navajo Mortuary," 387–88.

52.   Brugge, "A Comparative Study of Navajo Mortuary Practices," 323; Kluckhohn and Leighton, *The Navaho*, 202; Shufeldt, "Mortuary Customs of the Navajo Indians," 205.

53.   Helen Johnson, as quoted in Brugge, Benally, et al., *Memories Come to Us*, 36.

54.   Jessie Harrison, in Florio and Mudd, *Broken Rainbow*.

55.   Doug Brugge, personal correspondence with the author, 14 March 1998.

56.   This is clearly a women's issue because as Brugge noted, men do not tend to cry in these types of situations. Men do, however, cry in other situations such as while offering spontaneous prayers at Native American Church ceremonies (Aberle, *The Peyote Religion*, 153–54, 156).

57.   Flora Ashley, interview; Lynch, interview; Irene Kee, interview with author, Crystal, N.M., 3 August 1992; see Schwarz, *Molded in the Image*, 84, 88–89, 109.

58.   Kathlene Tsosie-Blackie, as quoted in Brugge, Benally, et al., *Memories Come to Us*, 40.

59.   Kathlene Tsosie-Blackie, as quoted in Brugge, Benally, et al., *Memories Come to Us*, 40.

60.   Quote from personal communication with Wesley Thomas, 18 June 1998. At the time of this writing, Wesley Thomas is an assistant professor of American Indian Studies at Idaho State University, whose doctoral research focused on Navajo views of gender.

CHAPTER SIX

1.   On representations of Native Americans, see Berkhofer, *The White Man's Indian*; Bird, *Dressing in Feathers*; Dorris, "'I' is not for Indian"; Duran, "Indigenous versus Colonial Discourse"; and Moffitt and Sebastian, *O Brave New People*.

2.   This is a generic term that is generally used to refer to all Navajo who drink (Young and Morgan, *The Navajo Language*, 873). Navajo people may use other terms when referring to specific categories of drinkers (see Topper, "Drinking as an Expression of Status," 113–19, and "Navajo 'Alcoholism,'" 231).

3.   See, Brod, "Alcoholism as a Mental Health Problem of Native Americans," 1387–90; Kunitz and Levy, *Drinking Careers*; Levy and Kunitz, *Indian Drinking*; May and Smith, "Some Navajo Indian Opinions about Alcohol Abuse and Prohibition," 327–28; O'Nell, "'Feeling Worthless'"; O'Nell and Mitchell, "Alcohol Use Among American Indian Adolescents"; Spicer, "Toward a (Dys)functional Anthropology of Drinking"; and, Waddell and Everett, *Drinking Behavior among Southwestern Indians*.

4.   Jaimes, "American Indian Women," 325; see also Duran and Duran, *Native American Postcolonial Psychology*, 93–156.

5. Barker et al., *Principles of Ambulatory Medicine*, 224–26; Mancall, *Deadly Medicine*, 5.

6. Mancall, *Deadly Medicine*, 6.

7. May, "Alcohol Policy Considerations for Indian Reservations and Bordertown Communities," 12–19; Mancall, *Deadly Medicine*, 6.

8. Mancall, *Deadly Medicine*, 6; see also, Barker et al., *Principles of Ambulatory Medicine*, 224–26.

9. Following Thomas Brod's ("Alcoholism as a Mental Health Problem of Native Americans") admonition that we avoid using the term alcoholism until we understand more about American Indian drinking and how it is rooted in particular world views, the phrases "problem drinker" and "problem drinking" are intentionally used herein in place of the terms "alcoholic" or "alcoholism." In support of the need for cultural rather than essentialist understandings of drinking patterns and behaviors, many scholars and biomedical practitioners have moved away from what has been termed the "disease concept of alcoholism" (Fingarette, *Heavy Drinking*; see also Kunitz and Levy, *Drinking Careers*, 238–39, and Duran and Duran, *Native American Postcolonial Psychology*, 112). "Clinicans now generally hold that alcoholism is a behavioral disorder rather than an illness in the biological sense" (Mancall, *Deadly Medicine*, 5).

10. Works by Indian authors that touch on this subject include: Alexie, *The Lone Ranger and Tonto Fistfight in Heaven*; Morris, *From the Glittering World*; Northrup, *Walking the Rez Road*; and Silko, *Ceremony*. Of related interest to the silence of scholars on this topic is Robin Room's contention that "there is a systematic tendency in the modern ethnographic literature on alcohol towards 'problem deflation'" ("Alcohol and Ethnography," 171). In his view, this deflation stems from: a disciplinary emphasis on "social functionalism" and everyday life; coupled with a tendency toward extreme relativism; and the fact that while many were members of the "wet generations" of Americans, the majority of these researchers were not trained in the study of alcohol use and abuse ("Alcohol and Ethnography," 171–77). For further information, see Dwight Heath's overview of developments in anthropological analyses of alcohol use worldwide during the "coming-of-age" of such studies ("A Decade of Development in the Anthropological Study of Alcohol Use").

11. See Room, "Alcohol and Ethnography." The phrase "ethnographic liberalism" was coined by James Clifford (*The Predicament of Culture*, 78–80) to connote the set of roles and discursive possibilities

through which ethnographers strive to cope with the inherent ambiguity of simultaneously being both advocates of particular groups and citizens of colonial nations.

12. The sentiment expressed by Sunny Dooley in the epigraph is not limited to those who are troubled by converts to Christianity. In fact, when the Native American Church first came to Navajo territory, opposition was strong from traditionalists who reportedly "felt deeply hurt" and "spoke of having 'lost' their kin" to Peyotism (Aberle, "The Future," 225). As acceptance of Peyotism increased and many other religions found converts among the Navajo population, perspectives shifted. While many mainline faiths maintain syncretistic stances with regard to Navajo traditional religion, other faiths do not. Certain religious organizations, especially the Church of Jesus Christ of Latter-day Saints and several evangelical Protestant denominations, prohibit Navajo converts from participation in traditional ceremonies or other "doings" and require them to discard all trappings of traditional life, including baskets, pollen bags, and even grinding stones. Peyotists and traditionalists often report feeling "hurt" when relatives convert to such sects and some claim that "they have 'lost' kin, and that their converted kin are throwing away their past and failing to honor their dead relatives who had ceremonial knowledge and who brought Peyote to the community. The converts are also seen as in some sense rejecting their Navajo-ness" (Aberle, "The Future," 226). Thus, such Navajo converts are perceived as being lost to perpetuation of Navajo language and culture as well as to the fulfillment of Changing Woman's prophecy. It is beyond the scope of this chapter to discuss this form of loss more fully. For further information regarding the contested history and practice of these various religions in Navajo country, I refer readers to David Aberle's "The Future" and Charlotte Frisbie's "Temporal Change," especially 483–93.

13. On this portion of the oral history, see Fishler, "In the Beginning," 31–32; Goddard, "Navajo Texts," 138; O'Bryan, "The Diné," 31–32; Yazzie, *Navajo History*, 20; Zolbrod, *Diné Bahane'*, 82–83. As noted, problem drinking was not a direct focus of my research while in the field. Thus, I never conducted formal interviews on this topic. Navajo individuals with whom I am acquainted, however, often discussed their concerns about 'adláanii relatives with me as a sympathetic listener; many of these narratives provided fodder for further thought on the subject and excerpts from them appear in the text of this chapter. After completing this analysis of Navajo views on 'adláanii,

I asked my Navajo colleagues Wesley Thomas and Sunny Dooley to read and evaluate it. Dr. Thomas told me that he found it to be an accurate representation of Navajo attitudes toward 'adláanii and went on to tell me about rites of social rebirth intended to reintegrate former 'adláanii who had become socially dead into reciprocal kin and community relations (personal communication with author, Seattle, Washington, 4 October 1997). I subsequently contacted Ms. Dooley by telephone to discuss my interpretation of her commentary and my analysis of Navajo views on 'adláanii. I explained to her that I understood her statement on the need to "give something up" in order for Navajo people to remain so "plentiful" as an allusion to the portion in the Navajo origin story wherein Coyote established the need for deaths as a complement to births and that I understood her to mean that in order for the Navajo population to continue to increase by means of "births," "deaths" of some form must occur. She affirmed this interpretation of her statement. I then explained how I saw the existence of 'adláanii who had succumbed to the extreme forms of drinking now in evidence on the Navajo reservation as a form of "social death" in anthropological terminology. Ms. Dooley concurred with this explication and confirmed my analysis (1998).

14.   A variety of traditional ceremonies are documented to have been used in attempts to curb problem drinking (Ferguson, "Participation in Traditional Ceremonies by Navajos with Drinking Problems"). In addition, Native American Church doctrine promotes abstinence (Aberle, *The Peyote Religion*, 180, 212), and meetings have been shown to have positive effects on those attempting to curb their problem drinking, regardless of the purpose of the ritual (Aberle, *The Peyote Religion*, 188–89, 212; Kunitz and Levy, *Drinking Careers*, 114–16, 120–21).

15.   Author's fieldnotes from 20 August 1992.

16.   Battaglia, *On the Bones of the Serpent*; Battaglia, Debbora, ed., *Rhetorics of Self-Making*; Ewing, "The Illusion of Wholeness"; Hollan, "Cross-Cultural Differences in the Self"; Rosaldo, "Toward an Anthropology of Self and Feeling"; Shweder and Bourne, "Does the Concept of the Person Vary Cross-Culturally?"; Spiro, "Is the Western Conception of the Self 'Peculiar' within the Context of the World's Cultures?"

17.   Conklin and Morgan, "Babies, Bodies, and the Production of Personhood in North America and a Native Amazonian Society"; Lamb, "The Making and Unmaking of Persons"; Lock, "Contesting the Natural in Japan"; Strathern, *The Gender of the Gift*.

18. Navajo social relations are based on "a diffuse moral obligation to give aid [to relatives] when requested or when it appears to be
needed" (Lamphere, *To Run After Them*, 36). Because no expectation for
immediate or direct reciprocity exists in this system (Lamphere, *To Run
After Them*, 36), this type of aid resembles the ethic of "generalized reciprocity" delineated by Marshall Sahlins (*Stone Age Economics*, 193–94).

19. Counts and Counts, "Conclusions," 281.

20. On special treatment at critical points in the life cycle, see
Schwarz, *Molded in the Image*, 113–229). On the continual repetition
of reciprocal deeds throughout life, see Lamphere, *To Run After Them*,
1977.

21. Conklin and Morgan, "Babies, Bodies," 667.

22. Conklin and Morgan, "Babies, Bodies," 667, emphasis added.

23. The phrase *yóó'a'háás'kaah* literally means "an unnumbered
amount of them are lost [plural third person]." When referring to a
single lost one, the phrase *yóó'iiyáá'*, "a lost one [singular third per-
son]" would be used.

24. Counts and Counts, "Conclusions," 280. Notions of social
death vary cross-culturally (Counts and Counts, "Conclusions," 281–84).
Social death may be evidenced by a variety of behaviors. For example,
among the Dugum Dani of western Papua, New Guinea, individuals
who are deemed to have lost their "vital essences" during critical illness
may suffer various forms of neglect (Heider, *The Dugum Dani*, 229–30);
sustenance may be reduced or withheld from young victims of "child
sickness" in northeastern Brazil (Scheper-Hughes, *Death Without Weeping*, 381–86); infirm members of the Marind-Anim cultural group in
southern Papua, New Guinea, may be buried prior to physical death
(Baal, *Dema*, 171–73); or mortuary rites may be performed prema-
turely over victims of sorcery among the Murngin of Arnhem Land
in northern Australia (Warner, *A Black Civilization*, 9, see also 194–97).
In each of these cases, attribution of social death and implementation
of accompanying practices hastens the individual's demise and speeds
the onset of physical death. In marked contrast to the previous examples, in societies worldwide the condition of slavery is often considered
to be a form of social death which is potentially reversible (Patterson,
Slavery and Social Death, 38–45). Should the individual be freed from
enslavement he or she can be reintegrated into his or her home community or integrated into another society. Direct linkages between
social death and imminent physical death are also not easily drawn in
the Navajo case, where the socially dead may continue to live for years.

25.   See Brugge, "A Comparative Study," 312, and Shepardson, "Changes in Navajo Mortuary Practices," 384, respectively.

26.   Ch'įįdii are believed capable of returning to the earth to avenge wrongs done to them during life (Brugge, "A Comparative Study," 324) or offenses such as improper burial, the holding back of any of their belongings, failure to kill a horse or sheep, or disturbance or removal of grave goods or their body parts after interment (Wyman, Hill, and Osanai, "Navajo Eschatology," 11). They are also deemed capable of causing "illness, misfortune, and premature or unnatural death" (Frisbie, "Introduction," 304). Owing to these possibilities, Navajo death rites are "oriented towards the prevention of such return rather than towards the loss situation" (Wyman, Hill, and Osanai, "Navajo Eschatology," 23).

27.   Moreover, since the Navajo problem drinker—no matter how distanced from his or her social relations—is not physically dead while he or she is classified as socially dead, this period of "social death" can be a liminal state as in the case of slaves. In the Navajo case, a socially dead individual who becomes abstinent can be gradually reintegrated into Navajo society by means of a series of ceremonies (personal communication with Wesley Thomas on 4 October 1997). This subject is currently under investigation by my colleague Wesley Thomas.

28.   Author's fieldnotes from 5 July 1991.

29.   Author's fieldnotes from 20 July 1991.

30.   Author's fieldnotes from 26 July 1991.

31.   Author's fieldnotes from 26 July 1991.

32.   Author's fieldnotes from 3 August 1992.

33.   Author's fieldnotes from 3 August 1992.

34.   Author's fieldnotes from 3 August 1992.

35.   *Indian Drinking,* 75–77.

36.   Reciprocity within families includes weekly or biweekly contributions by all employed members to a cash pool that is used to purchase items—school clothes, tires, boots, gasoline—needed by members of the extended family. The use of alcohol makes it more difficult to meet obligations to children, spouses, elders, nieces, nephews, and other relatives. And, an individual ceases to make such contributions if his or her excessive consumption of alcohol and the behaviors associated with it results in loss of a job.

37.   Crystal gazing is one of several diagnostic methods available to Navajo people. In preparation a fire is built. The practitioner makes

a dry painting that is approximately two feet in diameter. It features a four-pointed white star, each point aligned with one of the four cardinal directions. Heaps of sand representing the four sacred mountains may be placed between the points, and a line representing zigzag lightning with an opening in the east may surround the image (Wyman, "Navajo Diagnosticians," 244). The practitioner next dips his finger into the dried and powdered lenses from the eyes of night birds and paints this substance along his lower eyelids. The fire is extinguished and those who will wait indoors are told to concentrate on the problem at hand and seek personal insights. Accompanied by one person, who also has had the powdery substance painted onto his lower eyelids, the practitioner goes outside into the night. After praying to the "star-spirit" (Wyman, "Navajo Diagnosticians," 245) or Gila Monster (Morgan, "Navajo Treatment of Sickness," 394), he begins to sing while gazing directly at a star or at the light of a star reflected in a quartz crystal held upon the palm of his outstretched hand, which is aligned with a star (Morgan, "Navajo Treatment," 394). It is said that the star will soon begin to "throw out a string of light and at the end of this the star-gazer sees the cause of the sickness of the patient, like a motion picture" (Wyman, "Navajo Diagnosticians," 245). Once he has obtained enough information in this manner, the practitioner returns indoors. After the fire has been rekindled, he asks what if anything those who remained indoors saw, then he notifies the family of his findings (Morgan, "Navajo Treatment," 394–95; Wyman, "Navajo Diagnosticians," 244–45).

38. Author's fieldnotes for 29 July 1992.

39. The *Anaa'jí ndáá'*, Enemy Way, is a ceremony designed to cure sickness resulting from contact with a deceased non-Navajo. The need for this ceremony may arise due to a variety of exposures including, but not limited to, the following: events of war, a fatal automobile accident, sexual relations, contact with archeological burial sites, or hospital work. It is beyond the scope of this essay to fully describe this important summer ceremonial but numerous such accounts exist (see Haile, "Origin Legends of the Navajo Enemyway," "The Padres Present the Navaho War Dance"; Jacobson, "Navajo Enemy Way Exchanges").

40. In contrast to the Enemy Way ceremony, the purpose of this procedure is to cure sickness resulting from contact with a deceased Navajo. After the patient is ritually bathed, the influence of the ch'įįdii is exorcised from him or her by means of various infusions (Kluckhohn and Wyman, "An Introduction to Navaho Chant Practice," 52–53),

"brushing" with an eagle-feather fan (Kluckhohn and Wyman, "An Introduction," 72–73), and ash blowing (Kluckhohn and Wyman, "An Introduction," 73). Following these procedures, a layer of protection is applied to the patient's body by means of "blackening" with ashes or the application of grease paint—dry pigment, ochre and ashes that are each mixed with sheep fat (Kluckhohn and Wyman, "An Introduction," 96–97). The patient may also be "dressed" in ceremonial garments such as shoulder and wrist bands made of buckskin with claws and arrow points (Franciscan Fathers, *An Ethnological Dictionary*, 413–14; Kluckhohn and Wyman, "An Introduction," 103).

41. Author's fieldnotes for 8 August 1993.

42. Farella, *The Main Stalk*, 176.

43. Farella, *The Main Stalk*, 176.

44. Griffin-Pierce, *Earth Is My Mother*, 66.

45. *The Main Stalk*, 31–39.

46. Quote from Witherspoon, *Language and Art*, 39.

47. Quote from *The Main Stalk*, 31.

48. *Blessingway*, 7.

49. See for example, Gill, "Navajo Views of Their Origin"; Haile, *Soul Concepts of the Navaho*; Witherspoon, "The Central Concepts in Navajo World View (1)," *Language and Art*; and Wyman, *Blessingway*.

50. "Navajo Views of Their Origin," 504.

51. In chapter one of *Dynamic Symmetry and Holistic Asymmetry in Navajo and Western Art and Cosmology*, Witherspoon states that "Although the Navajo recognize the existence and even *the structural necessity* for disorder (hochǫ'[sic]), they cannot tolerate disorder for long periods of time. To them, it is sickness-illness in both the mind and in the body, fragmentation in the environment and in the universe, disharmony in customary relationships and holistic schemes. When it occurs, hózhǫ́—holism, health, and harmony—must be renewed, regenerated, or restored. That is the purpose of prayer, ritual, ceremony, myth, song and art" ("Holism in Navajo Language and Culture," 21, bold type in the original, emphasis added).

52. Witherspoon, *Language and Art*, 24–25, first two emphases added.

53. Author's fieldnotes for 6 August 1993. This is not to say that all present endorsed this type of risky behavior. Although prevalent, such drinking and behavior at the social portions of Enemy Way and other ceremonies remains a highly controversial subject among Navajo people (Aberle, *The Peyote Religion*, 212). In fact, such behavior

at Enemy Way ceremonials is frequently "attacked as being wholly inconsistent with sacred ritual and being the cause of adverse supernatural phenomena within the Navajo Nation" (Zion, "The Use of Navajo Custom in Dealing with Rape," 142).

54. Topper, "Navajo 'Alcoholism,'" 231.

55. Levy and Kunitz, *Indian Drinking*, 62.

56. Levy and Kunitz, *Indian Drinking*, 63.

57. Levy and Kunitz, *Indian Drinking*, 64.

58. Levy and Kunitz, *Indian Drinking*, 63.

59. Levy and Kunitz, *Indian Drinking*, 65–66.

60. Levy and Kunitz, *Indian Drinking*, 68.

61. Levy and Kunitz, *Indian Drinking*, 68–71; MacAndrew and Edgerton, *Drunken Comportment*, 146, 148–49.

62. Levy and Kunitz, *Indian Drinking*, 70–71.

63. *Indian Drinking*, 75–77. For alternative categorizations of Navajo drinking patterns, see Topper, "Drinking as an Expression of Status," 130–39 and Topper, "Navajo 'Alcoholism,'" 231–39.

64. Levy and Kunitz, *Indian Drinking*, 76. See also, May and Smith, "Some Navajo Indian Opinions about Alcohol Abuse and Prohibition," 325.

65. Levy and Kunitz, *Indian Drinking*, 77–78; Topper, "Navajo 'Alcoholism,'" 232, 233.

66. Levy and Kunitz, *Indian Drinking*, 129.

67. Levy and Kunitz, *Indian Drinking*, 78.

68. Topper, "Navajo 'Alcoholism,'" 235, see also 236.

69. Farella, "Culture as Intervention," 268–69.

70. Farella, "Culture as Intervention," 267.

71. Farella, "Culture as Intervention," 268–69.

72. Farella, "Culture as Intervention," 268.

73. Farella, "Culture as Intervention," 266–69.

74. On the shift from "social" to "solitary" drinking, see Levy and Kunitz, *Indian Drinking*, 66–67. On "communal" drinking on or off reservation, see Topper, "Navajo 'Alcoholism,'" 236.

75. Author's fieldnotes for 29 July 1992.

76. Author's fieldnotes for 8 August 1993.

77. Author's fieldnotes for 10 July 1992.

78. Author's fieldnotes for 22 August 1992.

79. Hanson Ashley, interview, 27 August 1993. Sạ'ah naagháí and bik'eh hózhǫ́ are ceremonial concepts that relate to the "essence of longevity (of the individual) and immortality (of the species)" and

the "essence of harmony, peace and order" (Young and Morgan, *Analytical Lexicon of Navajo*, 1081), respectively. In combination, these concepts form the ubiquitous phrase "sǫ'ah naagháí bik'eh hózhǫ," which can be glossed as the "essence of long life, harmony, and peace," that appears in nearly every Navajo song and prayer.

80. Walters, interview, 10 August 1993.

81. For an account of Coyote as the source of witchcraft, see Fishler, "In the Beginning," 31. For accounts that credit First Man and First Woman with bringing witchcraft to this world, see Haile, *Soul Concepts*, 75; Witherspoon, *Language and Art*, 39. Berard Haile credits First Man with origination of "invisible witchcraft" and First Woman with origination of "noisy medicine" and "gray witchcraft" (*Soul Concepts*, 75). For the most comprehensive study of Navajo witchcraft to date, I direct the reader to Clyde Kluckhohn's *Navaho Witchcraft*, wherein he credits First Man and First Woman with origination of "Witchery Way," and First Man with origination of "Sorcery," but neither with the origination of "Wizardry" (25, 31–32, 34).

82. Walters, interview, 12 August 1993.

83. On how the Navajo notion of harmony is based on the concept of balance and completion, see Farella, *The Main Stalk*, 176, and Griffin-Pierce, *Earth Is My Mother*, 66. The prior researchers to whom I am referring most specifically, are: Gill, "Navajo Views"; Haile, *Soul Concepts*; Wyman, *Blessingway*; as well as Witherspoon, "The Central Concepts" and *Language and Art*.

84. Hanson Ashley, interview, 27 July 1993.

85. Witherspoon, "Holism in Navajo Language and Culture," 21. Acknowledging the preliminary nature of the discussion contained herein, I only hope that my tentative sojourn into this area of concern will stimulate future researchers to further our understandings of Navajo views on these issues through consultations with Navajo philosophers.

86. Mae Tso, as quoted in Kammer, *The Second Long Walk*, 197, emphasis added. When I first selected this excerpt for inclusion, I took Mae Tso's comment at face value and assumed that she considered 'adláanii to be in need of mourning because they are socially dead. I am grateful to the anonymous reviewer who pointed out that Mae Tso is a monolingual speaker of Navajo and a Christian whose narratives were translated into English by her son Earl. A Navajo transcription of Mrs. Tso's narratives is not provided by the author of the work within which the quote appears (Kammer, *The Second Long Walk*, 197), therefore it is impossible to know exactly what she said in Navajo that was

interpreted as "mourn" by her son. Fearful that I might be guilty of
misconstruing Mrs. Tso's meaning by implying that as used here the
term "mourn" refers to "grieving for the dead," I sought clarification
from Wesley Thomas. In response to my inquiry about the phrase that
Mrs. Tso might have used and which her son would have felt com-
fortable translating into English as "we mourn for them," he generated the following list: *nihini' daaníłį*, "they occupy our minds"; *baa
chaał daaníłį*, "we are in the state of crying for them"; *baa nitsidííkees*,
"we think of them"; *bikee' yi'niił daaníłį*, "we long for them"; and *baa
daanihini'*, "we worry about them" (personal communication with
Wesley Thomas, 8 March 1998). Interestingly enough, Dr. Thomas
told me that each of the first three phrases are commonly used in reference to either physically or socially dead Navajo, while the latter
two phrases can only be used in reference to a socially dead Navajo
individual.

Glossary

'Adláanii:	drunk(s)
Alk'éí:	kin
Ałtsé Hastiin:	First Man
Ałtsé Asdzáán:	First Woman
Anaa'jí ndáá':	Enemy Way
Asdzą́ą́ Nádleehé:	Changing Woman
Ba'ááá:	someone's female sexual partner, when applied to humans
Béeshee:	Flint Way
Biil:	hand woven two-piece dress
Biką:	someone's male sexual partner, when applied to humans
Bił 'áhoot'į́į́d:	visionary
Bit'ahnii:	Under His Cover Clan
Ch'į́į́dii:	ghost
Ch'óol'į́'į́:	Gobernador Knob
Diné Bikéyah:	Navajoland
Diné binííłch'ijí:	Small Wind Way
Diné k'ehjí hane':	The second main level of knowledge in Navajo philosophy
Dinétah:	ancestral Navajo homeland
Diyin Dine'é:	Holy People

Haashch'ééti'í:	Talking God
Haashch'éé'ooghaan:	House Talking God
Hadahoniye' 'Ashkii:	Banded Rock or Mirage Stone Boy
Hajiinái:	place of emergence
Hashtł'ishnii:	Mud Clan
Hatáál k'ehjí hane':	The third main level of knowledge in Navajo philosophy
Hataałii:	singers or medicine men and women
Hóchxǫ́jí:	Evil Way
Honágháahnii:	One-Walks-Around Clan
Hooghan:	traditional Navajo home
Hózhǫ́ǫ́jí:	Blessing Way
Hózhǫ́ǫ́jigo:	on the side of peace, harmony, and order
Hózhǫ́ǫ́jí hane':	The first main level of Navajo philosophy
Hwéeldi:	Fort Sumner, New Mexico
Kénitsaaí:	moccasins with deerskin leggings
Kinaaldá:	puberty ceremony
Kinyaa'áanii:	The Towering House Clan
Mą'ii deeshgiizhinii:	Coyote Pass or Jemez Clan
Nádleehé:	a member of the third gender
Naayéé'jí:	Protection Way
Naayéé'jí hane':	The fourth main level of knowledge in Navajo philosophy
Naayéé' k'ehjigo:	on the side of protection
Na'at'oyee:	Shooting or Lightning Way Chant
Ndilniihii:	hand-trembler
N'dilniihjí:	Hand Trembling Way
Nihookáá Dine'é:	Earth Surface People
Níłch'ihjí:	Wind Way
Ntł'iz:	hard goods
Ntł'iz ni'nił:	ceremonial offering of ntł'iz to sacred sites
Sǫ'tsohjí:	Star Chant
Tábąąhá:	Water's Edge Clan
T'áá bíbóholníí':	it is up to him or her to decide
Táchii'nii:	Red Running into the Water People
Tádídíín:	pollen
Tééhoołtsódii:	Water Monster
Tó'áhaní:	Near the Water Clan
Tó'aheedlíinii:	Water Flow Together Clan
Tódích'íi'nii:	Bitter Water Clan

Ts'aa':	ceremonial basket(s)
Ts'its'ǫ́ǫ́s:	ceremonial bone whistle
Yeesélká':	food provisions for a journey
Yóó'a'háás'kaah:	lost ones
Yóó'iiyáá':	lost one

Bibliography

BOOKS AND ARTICLES

Aberle, David. "The Prophet Dance and Reactions to White Contact." *Southwestern Journal of Anthropology* 15 (1959): 74–83.

————. "A Note on Relative Deprivation Theory as Applied to Millenarian and Other Cult Movements." In *Millennial Dreams in Action: Essays in Comparative Study*, edited by Sylvia Thrupp. Comparative Studies in Society and History, Supplement II. The Hague, Netherlands: Mouton and Co., 1962. Pp. 209–214.

————. "The Future of Navajo Religion." In *Navajo Religion and Culture: Selected Views*, Papers in Honor of Leland C. Wyman. Edited by David Brugge and Charlotte Frisbie. Santa Fe: Museum of New Mexico Press. 1982. Pp. 219–31.

————. *The Peyote Religion among the Navaho*. 1966. 2d ed., Norman: University of Oklahoma Press, 1991.

————. "The Navajo-Hopi Land Dispute and Navajo Relocation." In *Anthropological Approaches to Resettlement: Policy, Practice, and Theory*, edited by Michael Cernea and Scott Guggenheim. Boulder, Colo.: Westview Press, 1993. Pp. 153–200.

Adair, John, Kurt Deuschle, and Clifford Barnett. *The People's Health: Anthropology and Medicine in a Navajo Community*. Albuquerque: The University of New Mexico Press, 1988.

Adams, William. *Shonto: A Study of the Role of the Trader in a Modern Navajo Community.* Bureau of American Ethnology 188. Washington, D.C.: Smithsonian Institution Press, 1963.

Alexie, Sherman. *The Lone Ranger and Tonto Fistfight in Heaven.* New York: HarperCollins, 1993.

Amsden, Charles. *Navaho Weaving: Its Technic and History.* 1934. Reprint, Glorieta, N.Mex.: The Rio Grande Press, Inc., 1974.

Aronilth, Wilson. "Foundations of Navajo Culture." Navajo Community College Library, Tsaile, Ariz. Mimeograph copy of an unpublished manuscript, 1985.

Austin, Martha, Kenneth Begishe, Betty Manygoats, Oswald Werner, and June Werner. "The Anatomical Atlas of the Navajo with Illustrations." Unpublished manuscript in the possession of Oswald Werner, Northwestern University, 1971.

Austin, Martha, and Regina Lynch. *Saad Ahaah Sinil Dual Language: A Navajo-English Dictionary.* Rough Rock, Ariz.: Rough Rock Demonstration School, 1983.

Baal, Jan van. *Dema: Description and Analysis of Marind-Anim Culture (South New Guinea).* The Hague: Martinus Nijhoff, 1966.

Bailey, Flora. "Some Sex Beliefs and Practices in a Navajo Community, with Comparative Material from other Navajo Areas." Reports of the Ramah Project. Papers of the Peabody Museum of American Archaeology and Ethnology, 40, no. 2. Cambridge, Mass., 1950.

Bailey, Garrick, and Roberta Bailey. "Historic Navajo Occupation of the Northern Chaco Plateau." Navajo Indian Irrigation Project, Contract #NOO C 1420 8136. Tulsa, Okla.: University of Tulsa Faculty of Anthropology, 1982.

———. *A History of the Navajos: The Reservation Years.* Santa Fe: The School of American Research Press, 1986.

Bailey, Lynn. *The Long Walk: A History of the Navajo Wars, 1846–68.* Tucson: Westernlore Press, 1988.

Bales, Fred. "Hantavirus and the Media: Double Jeopardy for Native Americans." *American Indian Culture and Research Journal* 18, no. 3 (1994): 251–63.

Barber, Bernard. "Acculturation and Messianic Movements." *American Sociological Review* 6 (1941): 663–69.

Barker, Randol, John Burton, and Phillip Zieve, eds. *Principles of Ambulatory Medicine.* Baltimore: Williams and Wilkins, 1995.

Bastien, Joseph. "Qullahuaya-Andean Body Concepts: A Topographical-Hydraulic Model of Physiology." *American Anthropologist* 87 (1985): 595–611.

Battaglia, Debbora. *On the Bones of the Serpent: Person, Memory, and Mortality in Sabarl Island Society.* Chicago: University of Chicago Press, 1990.

Battaglia, Debbora, ed. *Rhetorics of Self-Making.* Berkeley: University of California Press, 1995.

Beisner, Niko. *Literacy, Emotion, and Authority: Reading and Writing on a Polynesian Atoll.* Cambridge: Cambridge University Press, 1995.

Benedek, Emily. *The Wind Won't Know Me: A History of the Navajo-Hopi Land Dispute.* New York: Vintage Books, 1993.

Berkhofer, Robert. *The White Man's Indian.* New York: Alfred A. Knopf, 1978.

Bird, S. Elizabeth, ed. *Dressing in Feathers.* Boulder, Colo.: Westview Press, 1996.

Blacking, John. *The Anthropology of the Body.* London: Academic Press, 1977.

Brenneis, Donald. "Shared and Solitary Sentiments: The Discourse of Friendship, Play and Anger in Bhatgaon." In *Language and the Politics of Emotion,* edited by Catherine Lutz and Lila Abu-Lughod. Cambridge: Cambridge University Press, 1990. Pp. 113–25.

Briggs, Jean L. *Never in Anger: Portrait of an Eskimo Family.* Cambridge: Harvard University Press, 1970.

———. *Inuit Morality Play: The Emotional Education of a Three-Year-Old.* New Haven: Yale University Press, 1998.

Brod, Thomas M. "Alcoholism as a Mental Health Problem of Native Americans: A Review of the Literature." *Archives of General Psychiatry* 32 (1975): 1385–91.

Brugge, David. "A Comparative Study of Navajo Mortuary Practices." *American Indian Quarterly* 4, no. 4 (1978): 309–28.

———. "A History of the Chaco Navajos." Reports of the Chaco Center 4. Washington, D.C.: National Park Service, 1980.

———. "Navajo Prehistory and History to 1850." In *Handbook of North American Indians, vol. 10: Southwest,* edited by Alfonso Ortiz. Washington, D.C.: Smithsonian Institution Press, 1983. Pp. 489–501.

———. *The Navajo-Hopi Land Dispute: An American Tragedy.* Albuquerque: University of New Mexico Press, 1994.

Brugge, Doug, Timothy Benally, Phil Harrison, Martha Austin, and Lydia Fasthorse. *Memories Come to Us in the Rain and the Wind: Oral Histories and Photographs of Navajo Uranium Miners and Their Families.* Navajo Uranium Miners Oral History and Photography Project. Boston: Tufts University School of Medicine, 1997.

Buckley, Thomas, and Alma Gottlieb. "A Critical Appraisal of Theories of Menstrual Symbolism." In *Blood Magic: The Anthropology of Menstruation,* edited by Thomas Buckley and Alma Gottlieb. Berkeley: University of California Press, 1988. Pp. 3–50.

Bulow, Ernie. *Navajo Taboos.* Gallup, N.Mex.: Buffalo Medicine Books, 1991.

Chodorow, Nancy. *The Power of Feelings: Personal Meaning in Psychoanalysis, Gender and Culture.* New Haven: Yale University Press, 1999.

Churchill, Ward. *Fantasies of the Master Race: Literature, Cinema and Colonization of American Indians.* Monroe, Maine: Common Courage Press, 1992.

Churchill, Ward, and Winona LaDuke. "Native North America: The Political Economy of Radioactive Colonialism." In *The State of Native America,* edited by M. Annette Jaimes. Boston: South End Press, 1992. Pp. 241–66.

Clemmer, Richard. *Roads in the Sky: The Hopi Indians in a Century of Change.* Boulder, Colo.: Westview Press, 1995.

Clifford, James. *The Predicament of Culture: Twentieth-Century Ethnography, Literature, and Art.* Cambridge: Harvard University Press, 1988.

Conklin, Beth, and Lynn M. Morgan. "Babies, Bodies, and the Production of Personhood in North America and a Native Amazonian Society." *Ethos* 24, no.4 (1996): 657–94.

Correll, J. Lee. *Through White Men's Eyes: A Contribution to Navajo History,* 6 vols. Austin, Tex.: Dissemination and Asessment Center for Bilingual Education, 1979.

Correll, J. Lee, Editha Watson, and David Brugge. *Navajo Bibliography with Subject Index.* Research Report 2. Window Rock, Ariz.: The Navajo Tribe, Parks, and Recreation Research Section, 1969.

Counts, David, and Dorothy Counts. "Conclusions: Coping with the Final Tragedy." In *Coping with the Final Tragedy: Cultural Variation in Dying and Grieving.* Amityville, N.Y.: Baywood Publishing Company, Inc., 1991. Pp. 277–91.

Cruickshank, Julie. "Claiming Legitimacy: Prophecy Narratives from Northern Aboriginal Women." *American Indian Quarterly* 18, no. 2 (1994): 147–67.

Daniel, E. Valentine. *Fluid Signs: Being a Person the Tamil Way.* Berkeley: University of California Press, 1984.

DeMallie, Raymond. "The Lakota Ghost Dance: An Ethnohistorical Account." *Pacific Historical Review* 51 (1982): 385–405.

Dorris, Michael. "'I' is not for Indian." In *Through Indian Eyes,* edited by Beverly Slapin and Doris Seale. Philadelphia: New Society Publishers, 1992. Pp. 27–28.

Douglas, Mary. *Purity and Danger: An Analysis of Concepts of Pollution and Taboo.* London: Routledge and Kegan Paul, 1966.

————. *Natural Symbols.* New York: Vintage Books, 1970.

Dubisch, Jill. *In a Different Place: Pilgrimage, Gender, and Politics at a Greek Island Shrine.* Princeton: Princeton University Press, 1995.

Duran, Bonnie. "Indigenous Versus Colonial Discourse: Alcohol and American Indian Identity." In *Dressing in Feathers,* edited by S. Elizabeth Bird. Boulder, Colo.: WestviewPress, 1996. Pp. 111–28.

Duran, Eduardo, and Bonnie Duran. *Native American Postcolonial Psychology.* Albany: State University of New York Press, 1995.

Durkheim, Emile. "La Prohibition de l'Inceste et Ses Origines." *L'Année Sociologique* 1 (1897): 1–70.

Dyk, Walter. *Son of Old Man Hat.* 1938. Reprint, Lincoln: University of Nebraska Press, 1967.

Eichstaedt, Peter. *If You Poison Us: Uranium and Native Americans.* Santa Fe: Red Crane Books, 1994.

Ekman, Paul. *The Face of Man: Expressions of Universal Emotions in a New Guinea Village.* New York: Garland, 1980.

————. "Expression and the Nature of Emotion." In *Approaches to Emotion,* edited by Klaus Scherer and Paul Ekman. Hillsdale, N.J.: Erlbaum, 1984. Pp. 319–43.

Eliot, Alexander. "The Red Road: Native American Prophecy." *Parabola* 21, no. 1 (1996): 92–93.

Emerson, Gloria. "Navajo Education." In *Handbook of North American Indians, vol. 10: Southwest,* edited by Alfonso Ortiz. Washington, D.C.: Smithsonian Institution Press, 1983. Pp. 659–71.

Evans-Pritchard, Edward E. *Witchcraft, Oracles, and Magic Among the Azande.* Oxford: Clarendon Press, 1937.

Ewing, Katherine. "The Illusion of Wholeness: Culture, Self and the Experience of Inconsistency." *Ethos* 18, no. 3 (1990): 251–78.

Farella, John. *The Main Stalk: A Synthesis of Navajo Philosophy.* Tucson: The University of Arizona Press, 1984.

———. "Culture as Intervention." In *Families and Other Systems: The Macrosystemic Context of Family Therapy*, edited by J. Schwartzman. New York: Builford Press, 1985. Pp. 260–75.

Farnell, Brenda. "Introduction." In *Human Action Signs in Cultural Context: The Visible and the Invisible in Movement and Dance*, edited by Brenda Farnell. Metuchen, N.J.: The Scarecrow Press, 1995. Pp. 1–28.

Faris, James. *The Nightway: A History and a History of Documentation of a Navajo Ceremonial.* Albuquerque: University of New Mexico Press, 1990.

Feher-Elston, Catherine. *Children of Sacred Ground.* Flagstaff, Ariz.: Northland Publishing, 1988.

Ferguson, Frances. "Participation in Traditional Ceremonies by Navajos with Drinking Problems." In *Navajo Religion and Culture: Selected Views.* Papers in Honor of Leland C. Wyman. Edited by David Brugge and Charlotte Frisbie. Santa Fe: Museum of New Mexico Press, 1982. Pp. 157–63.

Fernandez, James, ed. *Beyond Metaphor: The Theory of Tropes in Anthropology.* Stanford: Stanford University Press, 1991.

Fingarette, Herbert. *Heavy Drinking: The Myth of Alcoholism as a Disease.* Berkeley: University of California Press, 1988.

Fishler, Stanley. "In the Beginning: A Navaho Creation Myth." Anthropological Papers, 13. Salt Lake City: University of Utah, 1953.

Forbes, Jack. *Apache, Navaho and Spaniard.* Norman: University of Oklahoma Press, 1960.

Fortune, Reo. *Sorcerers of Dobu.* New York: E. P. Dutton, 1932.

Foucault, Michel. *The Birth of the Clinic: An Archaeology of Medical Perception.* Translated by A. M. Sheridan Smith. New York: Vintage Books, 1973.

Franciscan Fathers. *An Ethnological Dictionary of the Navaho Language.* Saint Michaels, Ariz.: Saint Michaels Press, 1910.

Frazer, James. *The Golden Bough.* 1890. Reprint, edited by Theodor Gaster, Garden City, New York: Anchor Books, 1959.

Frisbie, Charlotte. "Introduction." *American Indian Quarterly* 4, no. 4 (1978): 303–308.

———. "Temporal Change in Navajo Religion: 1868–1990." *Journal of the Southwest* 34, no. 4 (1992): 457–514.

———. *Kinaaldá: A Study of the Navaho Girl's Puberty Ceremony*, 1967. Reprint, Salt Lake City: University of Utah Press, 1993.

Geertz, Armin. *The Invention of Prophecy: Continuity and Meaning in Hopi Indian Religion.* Berkeley: University of California Press, 1994.

Gill, Sam. "Navajo Views of Their Origin." In *Handbook of North American Indians, vol. 10: Southwest,* edited by Alfonso Ortiz. Washington, D.C.: Smithsonian Institution Press, 1983. Pp. 502–505.

Gillison, Gillian. "Images of Nature in Gimi Thought." In *Nature, Culture, and Gender,* edited by Carol MacCormack and Marilyn Strathern. New York: Cambridge University Press, 1980. Pp. 143–73.

Gillmor, Frances. *Windsinger.* Albuquerque: University of New Mexico Press, 1976.

Gillmor, Frances, and Louisa Wade Wetherill. *Traders to the Navajos: The Story of the Wetherills of Kayenta.* 1934. Reprint, Albuquerque: University of New Mexico Press, 1953.

Goddard, Pliny. "Navajo Texts." *Anthropological Papers of the American Museum of Natural History* 34, no. 1 (1933): 1–180. New York: American Museum of Natural History.

Gordon, Deborah. "Tenacious Assumptions in Western Medicine Examined." In *Biomedicine Examined,* edited by Margaret Lock and Deborah Gordon. Dordrecht, Netherlands: Kluwer, 1988. Pp.19–56.

Greenberg, Joseph, Christy Turner, and Stephen Zegura. "The Settlment of the Americas: A Comparison of the Linguistic, Dental and Genetic Evidence." *Current Anthropology* 27, no. 5 (1986): 477–97.

Griaule, Marcel. *Conversations with Ogotemmeli.* Oxford: Oxford University Press, 1965.

Griffen, Joyce. "Variations on a Rite of Passage: Some Recent Navajo Funerals." *American Indian Quarterly* 4, no. 4 (1978): 367–81.

Griffin-Pierce, Trudy. *Earth Is My Mother, Sky Is My Father: Space, Time, and Astronomy in Navajo Sandpainting.* Albuquerque: University of New Mexico Press, 1992.

Gunnerson, James. "Plains-Promotory Relationships." *American Antiquity* 22, no. 1 (1956): 69–72.

———. "Southern Athapaskan Archeology." In *Handbook of North American Indians, vol 9,* edited by Alfonso Ortiz. Washington, D.C: Smithsonian Institution Press, 1979. Pp. 162–69.

Haile, Father Berard. "Origin Legends of the Navajo Enemyway." *Yale University Publications in Anthropology* 17. New Haven: Yale University Press, 1938.

———. A Note on the Navaho Visionary. *American Anthropologist* 42, no. 2 (1940): 359.

———. *Soul Concepts of the Navaho.* Annali Lateranensi, vol. 7. Citta del Vaticano, 1943.

————. "The Padres Present the Navaho War Dance." St. Michaels, Ariz.: St. Michaels Press, 1946.

————. *Navaho Sacrificial Figurines.* Chicago: The University of Chicago Press, 1947.

————. *Upward Moving and Emergence Way.* American Tribal Religions, vol. 7. Lincoln: University of Nebraska Press, 1981a.

————. *Women versus Men: A Conflict of Navajo Emergence.* American Tribal Religions, vol. 6. Lincoln: University of Nebraska Press, 1981b.

Hale, Kenneth, and David Harris. "Historical Linguistics and Archeology." In *Handbook of North American Indians,* vol. 9, edited by Alfonso Ortiz. Washington, D.C.: Smithsonian Institution Press, 1979. Pp. 170–77.

Hallowell, A. Irving. *Culture and Experience.* Philadelphia: University of Pennsylvania Press, 1955.

Heath, Dwight. "A Decade of Development in the Anthropological Study of Alcohol Use: 1970–1980." In *Constructive Drinking: Perspectives on Drink in Anthropology,* edited by Mary Douglas. Cambridge: Cambridge University Press, 1987. Pp. 16–69.

Hegemann, Elizabeth. *Navajo Trading Days.* Albuquerque: University of New Mexico Press, 1963.

Heider, Karl. *The Dugum Dani: A Papuan Culture in the Highlands of West New Guinea.* Viking Fund Publications in Anthropology, no. 49. Chicago: Aldine Publishing Company, 1970.

Herdt, Gilbert. *Guardians of the Flutes.* New York: McGraw-Hill, 1981.

————. *Rituals of Manhood.* Berkeley: University of California Press, 1982a.

————. "Sambia Nosebleeding Rites and Male Proximity to Women." *Ethos* 10, no. 3 (1982b): 189–231.

Hertz, Robert. "The Pre-eminence of the Right Hand: A Study of Religious Polarity." 1909. In *Right and Left: Essays on Dual Symbolic Classifications,* edited and translated by Rodney Needham. Chicago: The University of Chicago Press, 1973. Pp.3–31.

Hester, James. "Early Navajo Migrations and Acculturation in the Southwest." *Museum of New Mexico Papers in Anthropology* 6, Navajo Project Studies 5. Santa Fe: Museum of New Mexico Press, 1962.

Hewett, Edgar. *The Chaco Canyon and Its Monuments.* Handbooks of Archaeological History. Albuquerque: University of New Mexico Press, 1936.

Hill, Willard W. "Navaho Warfare." *Yale University Publications in Anthropology,* no. 5. New Haven: Yale University Press, 1936.

————. "The Agricultural and Hunting Methods of the Navaho Indians." *Yale University Publications in Anthropology*, no. 18. London: Oxford University Press, 1938.

————. "The Navaho Indians and the Ghost Dance of 1890." *American Anthropologist* 46, no. 4 (1944): 523–27.

Hittman, Michael. "The 1870 Ghost Dance at Walker Reservation: A Reconstruction." *Ethnohistory* 20, no. 3 (1973): 247–78.

Hollan, Douglas. "Cross-Cultural Differences in the Self." *Journal of Anthropological Research* 48, no. 4 (1992): 283–300.

Huscher, Betty, and Harold Huscher. "Athapaskan Migration via the Intermontane Region." *American Antiquity* 8, no. 1 (1942): 80–88.

Irvine, Judith. "Registering Affect: Heteroglossia in the Linguistic Expression of Emotion." In *Language and the Politics of Emotion*, edited by Catherine Lutz and Lila Abu-Lughod. Cambridge: Cambridge University Press, 1990. Pp. 126–61.

Iverson, Peter. *The Navajos: A Critical Bibliography*. The Newberry Library Center for the History of the American Indian Bibliography Series. Bloomington: Indiana University Press, 1976.

————. *The Navajo Nation*. Albuquerque: University of New Mexico Press, 1981.

Jackson, Michael. *Paths Toward a Clearing*. Bloomington: Indiana University Press, 1989.

Jacobson, Doranne. "Navajo Enemy Way Exchanges." *El Palacio* 71 (1964): 7–19.

Jacobson-Widding, Anita, ed. *Body and Space: Symbolic Models of Unity and Division in African Cosmology and Experience*. Acta Universitatis Upsaliensis, Uppsala Studies in Cultural Anthropology 16, 1991.

Jaimes, M. Annette. "American Indian Women: At the Center of Indigenous Resistance in Contemporary North America." In *The State of Native America: Genocide, Colonization, and Resistance*, edited by M. Annette Jaimes. Boston: South End Press, 1992. Pp. 311–44.

Joe, Jennie. "Breaking the Navajo Family: Governmental Interference and Forced Relocation." *Diné Be'iina'* 1, no. 2 (1988): 1–21.

Kammer, Jerry. *The Second Long Walk: The Navajo-Hopi Land Dispute*. Albuquerque: University of New Mexico Press, 1980.

Kehoe, Alice. "The Ghost Dance Religion in Saskatchewan, Canada." *Plains Anthropologist* 13 (1968): 296–304.

————. *The Ghost Dance: Ethnohistory and Revitalization*. Edited by George and Louise Spindler. New York: Holt, Rinehart, and Winston, 1989.

Keith, Anne. "The Navajo Girl's Puberty Ceremony: Function and Meaning for the Adolescent." *El Palacio* 71, no. 1 (1964): 27–36.

Kelley, Klara, and Harris Francis. *Navajo Sacred Places*. Bloomington: Indiana University Press, 1994.

Kelly, Roger, R. W. Lang, and Harry Walters. *Navaho Figurines Called Dolls*. Santa Fe: Museum of Navaho Ceremonial Art, 1972.

Kent, Kate. *Navajo Weaving: Three Centuries of Change*. Santa Fe: School of American Research Press, 1985.

Kluckhohn, Clyde. "Myths and Rituals: A General Theory." *Harvard Theological Review* 35 (1942): 45–79.

———. *Navaho Witchcraft*. 1944. Reprint, Boston: Beacon Press, 1967.

Kluckhohn, Clyde, and Dorothea Leighton. *The Navaho*. 1946. Reprint, Cambridge: Harvard University Press, 1974.

Kluckhohn, Clyde, and Katherine Spencer. *A Bibliography of the Navaho Indians*. New York: J. J. Augustin, 1940.

Kluckhohn, Clyde, and Leland Wyman. "An Introduction to Navaho Chant Practice." *Memoirs of the American Anthropological Association* 53 (1940).

Kracht, Benjamin. "The Kiowa Ghost Dance, 1894–1916: An Unheralded Revitalization Movement." *Ethnohistory* 39, no. 4 (1992): 452–77.

Kroeber, Alfred. "A Ghost-Dance in California." *Journal of American Folklore* 17 (1904): 32–35.

Kunitz, Stephen, and Jerrold Levy. *Drinking Careers: A Twenty-Five-Year Study of Three Navajo Populations*. New Haven: Yale University Press, 1994.

Lamb, Sarah. "The Making and Unmaking of Persons: Notes on Aging and Gender in North India." *Ethos* 25, no. 3 (1997): 279–302.

Lamphere, Louise. "Symbolic Aspects in Navajo Ritual." *Southwestern Journal of Anthropology* 25 (1969): 279–305.

———. *To Run After Them: Cultural and Social Bases of Cooperation in a Navajo Community*. Tucson: University of Arizona Press, 1977.

Lanternari, Vittorio. *The Religions of the Oppressed: A Study of Modern Messianic Cults*. New York: Alfred Knopf, Inc., 1963.

Laqueur, Thomas. "Orgasm, Generation, and the Politics of Reproductive Biology." In *The Making of the Modern Body*, edited by Catherine Gallagher and Thomas Laqueur. Berkeley: University of California Press, 1987. Pp. 1–41.

———. *Making Sex: Body and Gender from the Greeks to Freud*. Cambridge: Harvard University Press, 1990.

Leach, Edmund. "Anthropological Aspects of Language: Animal Categories and Verbal Abuse." In *New Directions in the Study of Language*, edited by E. H. Lennebuerg. Cambridge: M. I. T. Press, 1964. Pp. 23–64.

Leavitt, John. "Meaning and Feeling in the Anthropology of Emotions." *American Ethnologist* 23, no. 3 (1996): 514–39.

Leighton, Dorothea, and Clyde Kluckhohn. *Children of the People: The Navaho Individual and His Development*. Cambridge: Harvard University Press, 1947.

Lévi-Strauss, Claude. *The Savage Mind*, 1966. Reprint, Chicago: The University of Chicago Press, 1962.

Levy, Jerrold, and Stephen Kunitz. *Indian Drinking: Navajo Practices and Anglo-American Theories*. New York: John Wiley & Sons, 1974.

Lincoln, Louise. *Southwest Indian Silver from the Doneghy Collection*. Austin: University of Texas Press, 1982.

Lindenbaum, Shirley. *Kuru Sorcery: Disease and Danger in the New Guinea Highlands*. Mountain View, Calif.: Mayfield Publishing Company, 1979.

Linton, Ralph. "Nativistic Movements." *American Anthropologist* 45 (1943): 230–40.

Lock, Margaret. "The Anthropological Study of the American Medical System: Center and Periphery." *Social Science and Medicine* 22, no. 9 (1986): 931–32.

———. "Cultivating the Body: Anthropology and Epistemologies of Bodily Practice and Knowledge." *Annual Review of Anthropology* 22 (1993): 133–55.

———. "Contesting the Natural in Japan: Moral Dilemmas and Technologies of Dying." *Culture, Medicine, and Psychiatry* 19, no. 1 (1995): 1–38.

Luckert, Karl. *The Navajo Hunter Tradition*. Tucson: The University of Arizona Press, 1975.

Luhrmann, Tanya. *Persuasions of the Witch's Craft*. Cambridge: Harvard University Press, 1989.

Lutz, Catherine. "The Domain of Emotion Words on Ifaluk." *American Ethnologist* 9 (1982): 113–28.

Lutz, Catherine, and Geoffrey White. "The Anthropology of Emotion." *Annual Review of Anthropology* 15 (1986): 405–436.

MacAndrew, Craig, and Robert Edgerton. *Drunken Comportment: A Social Explanation*. Chicago: Aldine Publishing Company, 1969.

Mancall, Peter C. *Deadly Medicine: Indians and Alcohol in Early America.* Ithaca: Cornell University Press, 1995.

Matthews, Washington. *The Night Chant, A Navaho Ceremonial.* Memoirs of the American Museum of Natural History Series, vol. 6. 1902.

————. *Navaho Legends.* 1897. Reprint, Salt Lake City: University of Utah Press, 1994.

Mauss, Marcel. *A General Theory of Magic.* 1902. Reprint translated by Robert Brain, New York: W. W. Norton, 1972.

May, Philip. "Alcohol Policy Considerations for Indian Reservations and Bordertown Communities." *Journal of the National Center for American Indian and Alaska Native Mental Health Research* 4 (1992): 5–59.

May, Philip, and Matthew Smith. "Some Navajo Indian Opinions about Alcohol Abuse and Prohibition: A Survey and Recommendations for Policy." *Journal of Studies on Alcohol* 49, no. 4 (1988): 324–34.

Maybury-Lewis, David, and Uri Almagor. *The Attraction of Opposites: Thought and Society in the Dualistic Mode.* Ann Arbor: The University of Michigan Press, 1989.

McNeley, James. *Holy Wind in Navajo Philosophy.* Tucson: University of Arizona Press, 1981.

McNitt, Frank. *The Indian Traders.* Norman: University of Oklahoma Press, 1962.

McPherson, Robert. *Sacred Land, Sacred View: Navajo Perceptions of the Four Corners Region.* Salt Lake City: Brigham Young University, 1992.

Meigs, Anna. "Male Pregnancy and the Reduction of Sexual Opposition in a New Guinea Highlands Society." *Ethnology* 15, no. 4 (1976): 393–407.

————. *Food, Sex, and Pollution.* New Brunswick, N.J.: Rutgers University Press, 1984.

Middleton, John, and Edward Winter. *Witchcraft and Sorcery in East Africa.* London: Routledge and Kegan Paul, 1963.

Mitchell, Frank. *Navajo Blessing Way Singer: The Autobiography of Frank Mitchell, 1881–1967.* Edited by Charlotte Frisbie and David McAllester. Tucson: The University of Arizona Press, 1978.

Moffitt, John, and Santiago Sebastian. *O Brave New People.* Albuquerque: University of New Mexico Press, 1996.

Moon, Samuel. *Tall Sheep: Harry Goulding, Monument Valley Trader.* Norman: University of Oklahoma Press, 1992.

Mooney, James. "The Ghost–Dance Religion and the Sioux Outbreak of 1890." *Fourteenth Annual Report of the Bureau of Ethnology.* Washington, D.C.: Government Printing Office, 1896.

Morgan, William. "Navajo Treatment of Sickness: Diagnosticians." *American Anthropologist,* n.s., 33 (1931): 390–402.

———. "Human-Wolves Among the Navaho." *Yale University Publications in Anthropology,* no. 11. New Haven: Yale University Press, 1936.

Morris, Irvin. *From the Glittering World: A Navajo Story.* Norman: University of Oklahoma Press, 1997.

Moses, L. G. "'The Father Tells Me So!' Wovoka: The Ghost Dance Prophet." *American Indian Quarterly* 9, no. 3 (1985): 335–51.

Myers, Fred. "Emotions and the Self: Theory of Personhood and Political Order among Pintupi Aborigines." *Ethos* 7 (1979): 343–70.

———. "The Logic and Meaning of Anger Among Pintupi Aborigines." *Man,* n.s. 23 (1988): 589–610.

Needham, Rodney, ed. *Right and Left: Essays on Dual Symbolic Classifications.* Chicago: The University of Chicago Press, 1973.

Nemeroff, Carol, and Paul Rozin. "The Laws of Sympathetic Magic: A Psychological Analysis of Similarity and Contagion." In *Cultural Psychology: Essays on Comparative Human Development,* edited by James Stigler, Richard Shweder, and Gilbert Herdt. Cambridge: Cambridge University Press, 1990. Pp. 205–32.

———. "The Contagion Concept in Adult Thinking in the United States: Transmission of Germs and of Interpersonal Influence." *Ethos* 22, no. 2 (1994): 158–86.

Newcomb, Franc Johnson. *Navajo Omens and Taboos.* Santa Fe: The Rydal Press, 1940.

Northrup, Jim. *Walking the Rez Road.* Stillwater, Minn.: Voyageur Press, 1993.

Oakes, Maud. *Where the Two Came to Their Father.* 1943. Reprint, Princeton: Princeton University Press, 1991.

O'Bryan, Aileen. "The Diné: Origin Myths of the Navaho Indians." *Bureau of American Ethnology Bulletin* 163. Washington, D.C.: U.S. Government Printing Office, 1956.

O'Hanlon, Michael. "Unstable Images and Second Skins: Artefacts, Exegesis and Assessments in the New Guinea Highlands." *Man,* n.s. 27, no. 3 (1992): 587–608.

O'Nell, Theresa. "'Feeling Worthless': An Ethnographic Investigation of Depression and Problem Drinking at the Flathead Reservation." *Culture, Medicine and Psychiatry* 16 (1993): 447–69.

O'Nell, Theresa, and Christina Mitchell. "Alcohol Use among American Indian Adolescents: The Role of Culture in Pathological Drinking." *Social Science and Medicine* 42, no. 4 (1996): 565–78.

Opler, Morris. "The Apachean Culture Pattern and Its Origin." In *Handbook of North American Indians*, vol. 10, edited by Alfonso Ortiz. Washington, D.C.: Smithsonian Insititution Press, 1983. Pp. 368–92.

Overholt, Thomas. "The Ghost Dance of 1890 and the Nature of the Prophetic Process." *Ethnohistory* 21, no. 1 (1974): 37–63.

Parezo, Nancy. *Navajo Sandpainting: From Religious Act to Commercial Art.* Albuquerque: University of New Mexico Press, 1983.

Patterson, Orlando. *Slavery and Social Death.* Cambridge: Harvard University Press, 1982.

Pinxten, Rik, Ingrid van Dooren, and Frank Harvey. *Anthropology and Space: Explorations into the Natural Philosophy and Semantics of the Navajo.* Philadelphia: University of Pennsylvania Press, 1983.

Pinxten, Rik, and Claire Farrer. "On Learning a Comparative View." *Cultural Dynamics* 3, no. 3 (1990): 233–51.

Poole, Fritz. "Transforming 'Natural' Woman: Female Ritual Leaders and Gender Ideology among Bimin-Kuskusmin." In *Sexual Meaning: The Cultural Construction of Gender and Sexuality*, edited by Sherry Ortner and Harriet Whitehead. Cambridge: Cambridge University Press, 1981. Pp. 116–65.

Reddy, William. "Emotional Liberty: Politics and History in the Anthropology of Emotions." *Cultural Anthropology* 14, no. 2 (1999): 256–88.

Reichard, Gladys. *Social Life of the Navajo Indians.* New York: Columbia University Press, 1928.

———. *Navaho Religion: A Study of Symbolism.* New York: Pantheon Books, 1950.

Reichel-Dolmatoff, Gerardo. *Amazonian Cosmos: The Sexual and Religious Symbolism of the Tukano Indians.* Chicago: The University of Chicago Press, 1971.

Rhodes, Lorna. "Studying Biomedicine as a Cultural System." In *Medical Anthropology: Contemporary Theory and Method*, edited by Thomas Johnson and Carolyn Sargent. New York: Praeger, 1990. Pp. 159–73.

Riesman, Paul. *First Find Your Child a Good Mother: The Construction of Self in Two African Communities.* New Brunswick, N.J.: Rutgers University Press, 192.

Roessel, Robert. *Pictorial History of the Navajo from 1860 to 1910.* Rough Rock, Ariz.: Navajo Curriculum Center, 1980.

Roessel, Ruth. *Women in Navajo Society*. Rough Rock: Navajo Resource Center, Rough Rock Demonstration School, 1981.
————, ed. *Navajo Stories of the Long Walk Period*. Tsaile, Ariz.: Navajo Community College Press, 1973.
Room, Robin. "Alcohol and Ethnography: A Case of Problem Deflation?" *Current Anthropology* 25 (1984): 169–78.
Rosaldo, Michelle. "Toward an Anthropology of Self and Feeling." In *Culture Theory: Essays on Mind, Self, and Emotion*, edited by Richard Shweder and Robert LeVine. Cambridge: Cambridge University Press, 1984. Pp. 137–57.
Russell, Scott. "The Navajo and the 1918 Influenza Pandemic." In *Health and Disease in the Prehistoric Southwest*, edited by Charles Merbs and Robert Miller. Arizona State University Anthropology Research Papers 34. Tempe: Arizona State University, 1985. Pp. 380–90.
Sahlins, Marshall. *Stone Age Economics*. Chicago: Aldine Publishing Company, 1972.
————. *Islands of History*. Chicago: The University of Chicago Press, 1985.
Sapir, Edward. *Navaho Texts*. Iowa City, Iowa: Linguistic Society of America, 1942.
Scheper-Hughes, Nancy. *Death without Weeping: The Violence of Everyday Life in Brazil*. Berkeley: University of California Press, 1992.
Schwarz, Maureen Trudelle. *Molded in the Image of Changing Woman: Navajo Views on the Human Body and Personhood*. Tucson: University of Arizona Press, 1997.
Scudder, Thayer. *No Place to Go: Effects of Compulsory Relocation on Navajos*. Philadelphia: Institute for the Study of Human Issues, 1982.
Shepardson, Mary. "Changes in Navajo Mortuary Practices and Beliefs." *American Indian Quarterly* vol. 4, no. 4 (1978): 383–95.
Shilling, Chris. *The Body and Social Theory*. Newbury Park, Calif.: Sage Publications, 1993.
Shufeldt, Robert W. "Mortuary Customs of the Navajo Indians." *The American Naturalist* 25 (1891): 303–306.
Shweder, Richard, and Edmund Bourne. "Does the Concept of the Person Vary Cross-Culturally?" In *Culture Theory: Essays on Mind, Self, and Emotion*, edited by Richard Shweder and Robert LeVine. Cambridge: Cambridge University Press, 1984. Pp. 158–99.
Silko, Leslie. *Ceremony*. New York: Penguin Books, 1977.
Spencer, Katherine. *Reflection of Social Life in the Navajo Origin Myth*. University of New Mexico Publications in Anthropology 3. Albuquerque: University of New Mexico Press, 1947. Pp. 1–140.

————. "Mythology and Values: An Analysis of Navaho Chantway Myths." *Memoirs of the American Folklore Society* (1957): 48. Philadelphia: American Folklore Society.

Spicer, Paul. "Toward a (Dys)functional Anthropology of Drinking: Ambivalence and the American Indian Experience with Alcohol." *Medical Anthropology Quarterly* 11, no. 3 (1997): 306–323.

Spieldoch, Rachel. "Uranium Is in My Body." *American Indian Culture and Research Journal* 20, no. 2 (1996): 173–85.

Spier, Leslie. "The Ghost Dance of 1870 among the Klamath of Oregon." *University of Washington Publications in Anthropology* 2 (1927): 34–56.

————. *The Prophet Dance of the Northwest and Its Derivatives: The Source of the Ghost Dance.* General Series in Anthropology, vol. 1. Menasha, Wis.: George Banta Publishing Company, 1935.

Spiro, Melford. "Is the Western Conception of the Self 'Peculiar' within the Context of the World's Cultures?" *Ethos* 21, no. 2 (1993): 107–153.

Stephen, Alexander. "Navajo Origin Legend." *Journal of American Folk-Lore* 43, no. 167 (1930): 88–104.

Stephens, William. *The Oedipus Complex: Cross-Cultural Evidence.* New York: Free Press, 1962.

Steward, Julian. "Ancient Caves of the Salt Lake Region." Bureau of American Ethnology Bulletin 116. Washington, D.C.: Government Printing Office, 1937.

————. "Native Cultures of the Intermontane (Great Basin) Area." In *Essays in Historical Anthropology of North America.* Smithsonian Miscellaneous Collections 100. Washington, D.C.: Smithsonian Institution Press, 1940.

Stewart, Omer. "Contemporary Document on Wovoka (Jack Wilson) Prophet of the Ghost Dance in 1890." *Ethnohistory* 24, no. 3 (1977): 219–22.

Strathern, Marilyn. *The Gender of the Gift.* Berkeley: University of California Press, 1988.

Suttles, Wayne. "The Plateau Prophet Dance among the Coast Salish." *Southwestern Journal of Anthropology* 13, no. 4 (1957): 352–96.

Synnott, Anthony. *The Body Social: Symbolism, Self, and Society.* New York: Routledge, 1993.

Thornton, Russell. *We Shall Live Again: The 1870 and 1890 Ghost Dance Movements as Demographic Revitalization.* New York: Cambridge University Press, 1986.

Topper, Martin D. "Drinking as an Expression of Status: Navajo Male Adolescents." In *Drinking Behavior among Southwestern Indians: An Anthropological Perspective*, edited by Jack Waddell and Michael Everett. Tucson: University of Arizona Press, 1980. Pp. 103–147.

———. "Navajo 'Alcoholism': Drinking, Alcohol Abuse, and Treatment in a Changing Cultural Environment." In *The American Experience with Alcohol: Contrasting Cultural Perspectives*, edited by L. Bennett and G. Ames. New York: Plenum, 1985. Pp. 227–51.

———. "FJUA Relocation: Applying Clinical Anthropology in a Troubled Situation." In *Anthropological Praxis: Translating Knowledge into Action*, edited by Robert Wulff and Shirley Fiske. Boulder, Colo.: Westview Press, 1987. Pp. 135–45.

Trafzer, Clifford. "Introduction." *American Indian Quarterly* 9, no. 3 (1985): 233–38.

Turner, Terence. "The Social Skin." In *Not Work Alone*, edited by J. Cherfas and R. Lewin. London: Temple Smith, 1980. Pp. 112–40.

———. "'We Are Parrots,' 'Twins Are Birds': Play on Tropes as Operational Structure." In *Beyond Metaphor*, edited by James Fernandez. Stanford: Stanford University Press, 1991. Pp. 121–58.

Turner, Victor. *The Forest of Symbols*. Ithaca: Cornell University Press, 1967.

———. *Dramas, Fields, and Metaphors: Symbolic Action in Human Society*. Ithaca: Cornell University Press, 1974.

Tylor, Edward. *Primitive Culture*. 1871. Reprint, New York: Gordon Press, 1974.

Vibert, Elizabeth. "'The Natives Were Strong to Live:' Reinterpreting Early-Nineteenth-Century Prophetic Movements in the Columbia Plateau." *Ethnohistory* 42, no. 2 (1995): 197–229.

Waddell, Jack, and Michael Everett, eds. *Drinking Behavior among Southwestern Indians: An Anthropological Perspective*. Tucson: University of Arizona Press, 1980.

Walker, Deward. "New Light on the Prophet Dance Controversy." *Ethnohistory* 16 (1969): 245–55.

Walker, Deward, ed. *Witchcraft and Sorcery of the American Native People*. Moscow: University of Idaho Press, 1989.

Wallace, Anthony F. C. "Revitalization Movements." *American Anthropologist* 58, no. 2 (1956): 264–81.

Warner, William Lloyd. *A Black Civilization: A Social Study of an Australian Tribe*. New York: Harper, 1958.

Watson, Don. "Navahos Pray for the Good of the World." *Mesa Verde Notes* 1 (1937): 16–18.

Weideger, Paula. *Menstruation and Menopause: The Physiology and Psychology, the Myth and the Reality.* New York: Delta, 1977.

Wheat, Joe. "Documentary Evidence for Material Changes and Designs in Navajo Blanket Weaving." In *Ethnographic Textiles of the Western Hemisphere,* edited by Irene Emery and Patricia Fiske. Irene Emery Roundtable on Museum Textiles, 1976 Proceedings. Washington, D.C.: The Textile Museum, 1976.

———. "Rio Grande, Pueblo and Navajo Weavers: Cross-Cultural Influence." In *Spanish Textile Tradition of New Mexico and Colorado.* Santa Fe: Museum of International Folk Art. Museum of New Mexico Press, 1979.

———. "Early Trade and Commerce in Southwestern Textiles Before the Curio Shop." In *Reflections: Papers on Southwestern Culture History in Honor of Charles H. Lange.* Edited by Anne Poore. Papers of the Archeological Society of New Mexico 14. Santa Fe: Ancient City Press, 1988. Pp. 57–72.

Wheelwright, Mary. "Tleiji or Yehbechai Myth by Hasteen Klah." *The House of Navaho Religion,* Bulletin 1. Santa Fe: Museum of Navajo Ceremonial Art, 1938.

———. *The Myth and Prayers of the Great Star Chant and the Myth of the Coyote Chant.* 1956. Reprint, Tsaile, Ariz.: Navajo Community College Press, 1988.

Wilcox, David R. "The Entry of Athapaskans into the American Southwest." In *The Protohistoric Period in the North American Southwest, AS 1450–1700,* edited by David R. Wilcox and W. Bruce Masse. Anthropological Research Papers No. 24. Tempe, Ariz.: Arizona State University, 1981. Pp. 213–56.

Wilson, Ursula. "Traditional Child Bearing Practices among Indians." In *Life Cycle of the American Indian Family,* edited by Jamice Kekahbah and Rosemary Wood. Norman, Okla.: American Indian and Alaska Native Nurses Association, 1980. Pp. 13–26.

———. "Nursing Care of American Indian Patients." In *Ethnic Nursing Care: A Multicultural Approach,* edited by Modesto Orque, et al. Saint Louis: C. V. Mosby, 1983. Pp. 272–95.

Witherspoon, Gary. "The Central Concepts in Navajo World View" (1). *Linguistics: An International Review* 119 (January) (1974): 41–59.

———. *Navajo Kinship and Marriage.* Chicago: The University of Chicago Press, 1975.

————. *Language and Art in the Navajo Universe*. Ann Arbor: The University of Michigan Press, 1977.

————. *Navajo Weaving: Art in Its Cultural Context*. Flagstaff: Museum of Northern Arizona, 1987.

————. "Holism in Navajo Language and Culture." In *Dynamic Symmetry and Holistic Asymmetry in Navajo and Western Art and Cosmology*, by Gary Witherspoon and Glen Peterson. New York: Peter Lang Publishing. 1995. Pp. 7–22.

Wood, John, and Walter Vannette. *A Preliminary Assessment of the Significance of Navajo Sacred Places in the Vicinity of Big Mountain, Arizona*. U.S. Department of the Interior, Bureau of Indian Affairs, Navajo Area Office, Window Rock, Ariz., 1979.

Wright, Anne. "Attitudes Toward Childbearing and Menstruation among the Navajo." In *Anthropology of Human Birth*, edited by Margarita Kay. Philadelphia: F. A. Davis Company, 1982. Pp. 377–94.

Wright, Anne, Mark Bauer, Clarina Clark, Frank Morgan, and Kenneth Begishe. "Cultural Interpretations and Intracultural Variability in Navajo Beliefs about Breastfeeding." *American Ethnologist* 20 (1993): 781–96.

Wyman, Leland. "Navajo Diagnosticians." *American Anthropologist* 38 (1936): 236–46.

————. "The Agricultural and Hunting Methods of the Navaho Indians." *Yale University Publications in Anthropology* 18 (1938).

————. *The Red Antway of the Navajo*. Navajo Religions Series 5. Santa Fe: Museum of Navajo Ceremonial Art (Wheelwright Museum of the American Indian), 1965.

————. *Blessingway*. Tucson: University of Arizona Press, 1970.

Wyman, Leland, and Stuart Harris. "Navajo Indian Medical Ethnobotany." *University of New Mexico Bulletin*, 3, no. 5 (1941): 1–76.

Wyman, Leland, W. W. Hill, and Iva Osanai. "Navajo Eschatology." *The University of New Mexico Bulletin* 377, Anthropological Series 4, no. 1 (1942): 5–48.

Yazzie, Ethelou. *Navajo History* vol. 1. Navajo Curriculum Center. Chinle, Ariz.: Rough Rock Demonstration School, 1971.

Young, Frank, and Albert Bacdayan. "Menstrual Taboos and Social Rigidity." *Ethnology* 4 (1965): 225–40.

Young, Robert, and William Morgan. *The Navajo Language: A Grammar and Colloquial Dictionary*. Albuquerque: University of New Mexico Press, 1987.

————. *Analytical Lexicon of Navajo*. Albuquerque: University of New Mexico Press, 1992.

Zion, James. "The Use of Navajo Custom in Dealing with Rape." *Law and Anthropology* 6 (1991): 131–67.

Zolbrod, Paul. *Diné Bahane': The Navajo Creation Story*. Albuquerque: University of New Mexico Press, 1984.

————. "Secrets of the Rugs." *El Palacio* 100, no. 3 (1995): 22–31.

VIDEO AND SOUND RECORDINGS

Brugge, Doug, Katherine Bomboy, Chenoa Stilwell, Mary Elsner, Timothy Benally, and Phil Harrison. *URANIUM: The Navajo Nuclear Legacy*. Videocassette. Boston: Tufts School of Medicine, 1997.

Craig, Vincent. "Someone Drew a Line." *Song Weaver*. Compact Disc. Muttonman Productions, 1995.

Florio, Maria, and Victoria Mudd. *Broken Rainbow*. Maria Florio and Victoria Mudd, writers and producers. Martin Sheen, narrator. Los Angeles: Direct Cinema, 1986.

Osawa, Sandra Sunrising. *In the Heart of Big Mountain*. Sandra Sunrising Osawa, writer, producer, narrator. Seattle, Wash.: Upstream Productions, 1988.

INTERVIEWS, ELECTRONIC MAIL, AND PERSONAL CORRESPONDENCE

Anonymous elder #1. Interview by author, Ganado, Ariz., 10 July 1991.

Anonymous elder #2. Interview by Wesley Thomas, Mariano Lake, N.Mex., 22 May 1996.

Anonymous elder #3. Telephone interview by author, 14 November 1996.

Anonymous e-mail. Posted on NETREZ, 30 May 1996.

Anonymous woman #1. Telephone interview by author, 2 November 1996.

Anonymous woman #2. Interview by author, Farmington, N.Mex., 17 March 1995.

Aronilth, Wilson. Interview by author, Tsaile, Ariz., 3 July 1991.

Ashley, Flora. Interview by author, Tsaile, Ariz., 29 July 1991.

Ashley, Hanson. Interview by author, Shonto, Ariz., 27 July 1993.

Bekis, Mae. Interview by author, Tó'tsoh, Ariz., 5 August 1992.
————. Interview by author, Tó'tsoh, Ariz., 28 July 1993.
————. Interview by author, Tó'tsoh, Ariz., 22 March 1995.
Billie, Sadie. Personal conversation with author, White Valley, Ariz., 28
    July 1992.
Bitsuie, Roman. Telephone conversation with author, 25 October
    1999.
Brugge, Doug. Personal correspondence with the author, 14 March
    1998.
Dahozy, Louva. Interview by author, Fort Defiance, Ariz., 19 August
    1992.
Denny, Avery. Interview by author, Chinle, Ariz., 11 August 1993 and
    8 October 1993.
Dooley, Sunny. Interviews with author, Gallup, N.Mex., 19 and 21
    August 1992.
————. Personal communication with author, 22 October 1998.
Gilbert, Linden. E-mail message posted on NETREZ, 9 June 1996.
Joe, George. E mail message to author, 13 June 1996.
————. E-mail correspondence with author, 29 May 1997.
Jones, Jean. Interview by author, Rock Point, Ariz., 25 July 1991.
Jones, Leo. E-mail message posted on NATCHAT list, 12 July 1996.
Kee, Irene. Interview by author, Crystal, N.Mex., 3 August 1992.
Knoki-Wilson, Ursula. Interview by author, Chinle, Ariz., 10 August
    1992.
————. Interview by author, Fort Defiance, Ariz., 29 July 1993.
Lamphere, Louise. Personal correspondence with the author, 5 April
    1999.
Louis, Ray Baldwin. Telephone conversation with author, 16 July 1997.
Lynch, Regina. Interview by author, Tsaile, Ariz., 16 July 1991.
McCabe, Asdzáán Joe. Interview by author, Fort Defiance, Ariz., 19
    August 1992.
Nez, Jonah. Personal conversation with author, Upper Greasewood,
    Ariz., 22 July 1993.
Roessel, Ruth. Interview by author, Round Rock, Ariz., 26 July 1991.
Thomas, Wesley. Personal communication with author, Tsaile, Ariz.,
    1 August 1993.
————. Personal communication with author, Seattle, Wash., 6 March
    1994.
————. Personal communication with author, Seattle, Wash., 4 Octo-
    ber 1997.

————. Personal communications with author, Seattle, Wash., 8 March
    and 18 June 1998.
Tso, Nakai. Interview by author, Tsaile, Ariz., 8 August 1992.
Walters, Harry. Interview by author, Tsaile, Ariz., 18 August 1992.
————. Interviews by author, Tsaile, Ariz., 10 and 12 August 1993.
————. Interview by author, Tsaile, Ariz., 20 March 1995.
————. Telephone interview by author, 23 May 1996.

Index